THE STORY OF EUGENE

The Story of
EUGENE

By

LUCIA W. MOORE

NINA W. McCORNACK

GLADYS W. McCREADY

LANE COUNTY HISTORICAL SOCIETY
Eugene, Oregon
1995

The Story of Eugene
by Lucia W. Moore, Nina W. McCornack,
and Gladys W. McCready

Unless otherwise credited, photographs are from
the Lane County Historical Museum

Cover design by Gwen Rhoads

First Printing: *June 1949*
Second Printing: *September 1995*

To order additional copies, contact the publisher:
Lane County Historical Society
PO Box 11532
Eugene, OR 97440

"None started but the brave;
None got through but the strong."

AUTHORS' PREFACE

It has been said that history is gossip; that if men had not gossiped in all ages, around the campfire and the fireside, much of our history would have been buried in oblivion.

The authors of *The Story of Eugene* have looked into the past with interest and warm sympathy, at the present with surprise, and a little into the future without superlatives. We have tried to put into these pages the men and women whose names are often heard and always honored, and who, we feel, would be happy because someone told the story of their town.

It is a proud story, with plenty of days when life was light and amusing, but with many when the going was rough; of times without money; times with nothing but mud. It is a tale of men and women whose resources of personal energy and endurance appear limitless.

Records have not always agreed; neither have memories. Dates available did not always check to the minute. Names written into old records with scratchy pen vary in spelling. But from courthouse and city hall, from attics and basements, from personal diaries, library and other files of early newspapers; from pictures and stories handed down, all of which were ours for the asking, we have drawn our picture. And we are grateful to all of those men and women who have kept such priceless things through the years.

If our story sketches Eugene's past for the people of its present, if it brings the builders of that past to life for those who will build for the future, we are glad. They must be present, those people out of the past, for no man builds through a hundred years and is completely gone.

FOREWORD TO THE FIRST PRINTING

A land without memories is a land without history.
                                        —ABRAM JOSEPH RYAN.

Through this first history of our town there runs something of the buoyancy and optimism of Eugene's founders, the courage and faith of its early builders. Here there is the straightforward truth and the sense of humor that I have long known in the pioneer family which produced these three authors.

To an inquiring young generation the book will be factually helpful, but at the same time amusingly revealing. To all of those readers who have known our town and valley it will show a great amount of research and a warm understanding. To those of us— and there are not many now—who knew Eugene as a village, the *Story* is nostalgic and gratifying.

CAL YOUNG

FOREWORD TO THE SECOND PRINTING

They were remarkable women, the three Wilkins sisters who wrote this book. They were daughters of Francis Marion and Emily Marie (Goltra) Wilkins. Their dad ran a drug store in Eugene and served as the city's mayor in 1905-07. The Wilkins sisters were granddaughters of Mitchell and Pamelia Ann Wilkins, who immigrated to Oregon in 1847, settling beneath the Coburg Hills northeast of the community of Coburg.

THE WILKINS SISTERS, AS THEY WERE OFTEN CALLED, TOGETHER WHEN THIS BOOK FIRST APPEARED IN 1949.
From left, Gladys McCready, Nina McCornack, and Lucia Moore.

The three sisters were writers, they were world travelers, they were historians, they were, indeed, living history themselves.

Nina Wilkins once recalled that she felt the urge to write about the time her baby teeth disappeared, and she subsequently wrote and published a one-page newspaper that sold for a penny, and sold well, she said, "because of a rumor column which I featured—news picked up by eavesdropping on every and all conversations." In 1905 she married Condon C. McCornack, the grandson of noted University of Oregon geologist Thomas Condon. They proceeded to tour the world through the ensuing years as an Army couple, her husband rising to the rank of brigadier general. She published books, musical compositions, magazine articles, and she also did painting and sculpture.

Lucia Wilkins worked in her father's drug store where she learned one important lesson in life: never marry a doctor. "From the vantage point of filling capsules in father's drug store, a doctor's life and troubles impressed me," she once remarked. That did not stop her from marrying Dr. Harold Clayton Moore, fresh out of medical school in 1913, who "promptly enlisted in the Army Medical Corps and dragged me around for more than thirty years, to my utter delight." She wrote verse and historical novels, one of them about the Oregon Trail, *The Wheel and the Hearth*, that won her a Silver Spur Award from the Western Writers of America.

Gladys Wilkins, the youngest of a family of five children, graduated in journalism from the University of Oregon. In 1918 she married Lynn McCready, destined to become a prominent banker in Eugene. Gladys accepted a temporary job with the *Eugene Morning Register* to replace an ailing society editor. "There I stayed for six or eight years," she recalled, "thoroughly underpaid but highly amused, intrigued, entertained or infuriated, depending on the day's assignments." The assignments included interviews with such celebrities as Aimee Semple McPherson and John Philip Sousa—"and what that newspaper got out of me for ten cents an inch was sheer robbery."

Together the three Wilkins sisters, Nina McCornack, Lucia Moore, and Gladys McCready, pulled together documentary research, interviews with aging pioneers, and their own recollections into this book, first published in 1949 by a New York publisher, Stratford House. It was hailed as a remarkable achievement, praised for its storytelling motif and its meticulous research.

"The book is history and it is something more," said the *Eugene Register-Guard* on its publication in June 1949. "It is an affectionate account of the growth of the city and of the men and women who made it. Marriage to Army husbands took Mrs. McCornack and Mrs. Moore all over the world. They saw all of the famous cities but the memories of Eugene lingered. They returned and with their sister, Mrs. McCready, they decided to tell the story of Eugene from the beginning. The authors have not pulled any punches. . . . the book is packed with facts and anecdotes but its greatest charm is in the understanding of the people who have made Eugene."

After publication the authors issued a new Foreword to the book adding some details of their three-year effort. It was to be inserted in copies yet unsold:

The challenge of co-authoring an historical volume proved to be most rewarding, for we were met with welcome help at every turn.

Old timers who could remember vividly the stories of the Skinners and of those few other men and women who truly founded Eugene, were happy to fill in the picture. In addition, they opened their personal memoirs to us that we might glimpse their lives, activities and customs firsthand, and we shared vividly many of their joys and problems. We can remember rainy afternoons around cheery fireplaces with open boxes of keepsakes and letters, clothing and old books, while we talked of home-keeping, children, and olden-day log school houses, of food and its care, and learning what "second-day dresses" meant.

We remember, too, with a very special gratitude, that we worked to a deadline. Because within three short years after those afternoons, most of the sturdy, lively friends who had given so freely of their time had disappeared from the scene, their memories gone forever.

Gone, too, as *The Story of Eugene* is being readied for this second printing, are the Wilkins sisters. Nina died in 1968, Lucia in 1982, and Gladys in 1990. Six months before her death, Gladys, then ninety-five, gave what turned out to be her last interview. "I love this town," she told *Register-Guard* writer Ann Van Camp, "I always have and I always will."

By then the book was long out of print. Copies that sold originally for $2.25 became collectors' items selling for as much as $65 whenever they reached used book stores. Gladys assigned the copyright to the Lane County Historical Museum and discussions ensued about reprinting of the book and about bringing it up to date to include the flow of history in the years since its 1949 publication. In 1995 the Lane County Historical Society and the Lane County Historical Museum entered into an agreement to publish this second printing.

The text of this second printing has not been changed. The updating will simply have to wait. Even the one factual error that Gladys McCready admitted to—they called Eugene pioneer T. G. Hendricks a Republican when he really was a Democrat—remains unchanged.

Most of the old pictures selected by the sisters also remain—at least the ones that could be located through the Museum and the University of Oregon Archives.

But something new has been added. When the Wilkins sisters undertook this project, there was no Lane County Historical Museum. The Museum was founded in 1951, two years after the book's publication. It has since amassed no fewer than 40,000 photos of Eugene and Lane County, a treasure to which the sisters had no access at the time of their efforts. The newly added twenty-four-page section in the back of the book presents an array of photographic views of Eugene in the early years—pictures the Wilkins sisters surely would have been happy to add to *The Story of Eugene* had they been available at the time.

CONTENTS

PART ONE

PART TWO

CONTENTS

PART THREE

THE STORY OF EUGENE

PART ONE

Chapter I

THE OLD SETTLER

June lay across the valley. The Old Settler shaded his eyes and looked far off toward the circle of blue mountains that bound the green of the valley on every side, like a crushed, wide blue girdle. The buckle of the girdle of mountains was a sharp-pointed butte to the South. The sheen of a river twisted out of the East to wind past the hill upon which the Old Settler stood. Trees fringed the river, willows and alders and maples: the valley was hip-high in lush grass that bent with the light wind, and was patterned with the blue and purple of lupin, wild flags and camas, the yellow of dandelions, the pink of wild roses, and the white of wild forget-me-nots that lay like shag rugs against the green where the land was low.

The Old Settler drew in a great, satisfied breath, and took up his musket. And he thought, how quiet it is! And how alone. There was no house in sight, and no man. Only trails that crossed and criss-crossed at the hill's base warned that here, unseen, were Indians who had made their silent way to the river. Nothing moved but the waving grass, and the branches of the tall firs, the leaves of young oaks and alders, and the light and shadows across the grass. To the east and to the west the river wound in a shimmering glass band among the trees.

That river would one day take farm products to markets at the mouth of the valley: the grassed land would be wheat, and orchards, and homes. One day the sky would be filled with the sound of business upon the earth below, and would see smoke from many chimneys. Because here the Old Settler would build a first cabin, and here—but he could not be sure of it now—others might come.

He turned to go down the hillside. At a bench of land along the west slope he stopped to look again at the chain of hills. The pointed one to the south seemed less high from here, and the coast mountains more remote; but the green floor of the land was close, and smelled sweet with the early summer.

Toward afternoon two Indians came, bringing trout from the river. "Build high up," they said, "Ya-po-ah." They pointed to the hillside.

He knew their jargon, and he asked, "Why?"

1

"Big waters come some day," they told him.

So the Old Settler chose the bench of land by the west slope of the hill called Ya-po-ah, and marked it, and cut his logs from the firs at the river's edge, and built one room, to claim the place for himself and for the young wife who waited in the lower valley of the Willamette for his return.

He was not an old settler at all. He only seemed old because his beard had grown long, and he had come a long way, and he had great distances in his eyes. He was Eugene Skinner, and not yet thirty-seven years of age. The land upon which he built would one day look out across the city of Eugene; the butte that rose above his cabin would be called Skinner's Butte. But these things, too, he could not know at the time. Young Mary Skinner, waiting, could have told him so, for she would give his names to the town and the hill.

IT IS an exciting experience to stand today where Eugene Skinner stood a hundred years ago and recapture the picture that he saw. Imagination can sweep away the town at one's feet, leaving the Valley of the Willamette spread eastward toward the Cascade Mountains and westward toward the Coast Range, with spurs of foothills hemming it close. Like crooked ribs of a great umbrella three rivers come down from the Cascade Range—the Mohawk and the McKenzie, the Middle Fork of the Willamette—to converge below Eugene at the umbrella's handle, the true Willamette River. The Coast Fork out of the Calapooia mountains, and the Long Tom, emerging from the Coast Range to water the west side of the valley, are other ribs that soon join the main stream. These are not the only rivers that swell the Willamette, but they are the ones which have been important to Eugene.

The men who first saw the valley said that it was filled with beauty; that it would surely grow anything. They said after awhile that the summers were gentle, with no excess of heat and dryness; that thunder storms rarely tore the sky. They said that winters might well be a bit less rainy to be sure, but that, after all, snows seldom fell to ankle depth, and almost never to knee depth; that there were no killing frosts to mention. A man couldn't have everything, but he could have nigh everything, they said, in the Willamette Valley.

He could have the rivers for vital ways to markets of flour and grain in the young Oregon City. He would have meadow lands for cattle to graze upon, lands for growing wheat, corn, potatoes—everything a man could ever need. There were the surrounding low, rolling hills for orchards, and beyond them, the timbered mountains standing tall. What more, they wanted to know, could a body want?

The rivers that water the valley are shining rivers. The McKenzie, out of the snows of the Three Sisters, pounds its eighty-mile length through mountain country, for some of that distance over rocks bright with color. Its white water was plentifully filled, for the old timer, with rainbow trout and Dolly Varden. The Willamette, less glamorous and turbulent than the McKenzie which flows into it, has the same deep glitter in the sun. Both can be muddied in winter and spring by the high waters that bring down silt, and in actual flood periods, settlers soon learned, both can be badly behaved.

There was the time in the winter of 1861-2 that Eugene's people traveled about in boats, and much of the valley lay under water; the time twenty years later when melting snows and a three day rain washed out the approach to the almost new covered bridge across the Willamette at Ferry street, floating a number of the town's board sidewalks and drowning livestock in areas between the two rivers. That flood carried out logs from the Springfield mill dam, washed away a farm house and barn, and did damage to the spanking new railroad between Eugene and Junction City.

Naturally, the old timers said, rivers flood when conditions are just right. The Missouri had covered their corn and tobacco fields, hadn't it? Why, a Willamette flood couldn't hold a trickle to Old Muddy on a rampage! And for awhile they remembered, and built high, as the Indians had advised, planted crops away from the river's banks. Then, down the years, with population growing and spreading, the river bottom lands have been occupied, have given freely of the wealth of their rich soil, sometimes collected their toll in floods.

The thought of the rivers as roads to market was a logical one, the result of complete lack of any other road fit to travel. The nearest flour mill was at Oregon City, ten days away down the valley or, as the Indians put it, "ten sleeps", with broad stretches of prairie intervening, often exceedingly wet. When, in 1848, a flouring mill opened at the new town of Salem and, in the following year, the Finley mill stood as near by as the Brownsville of our time, life was markedly simplified for the families in the upper valley.

Two other important things happened in 1848. A territorial

government for the Oregon country was set up at Oregon City, with General Joseph Lane of Indiana, and Mexican War fame, named first territorial governor. He, along with Joseph Meek, a buckskin-clad mountain man already great in the new country because he had led its voice vote away from Britain to the side of America, started westward to the land which Lane would govern. It took from August to March to cover the Santa Fe trail through the southlands, so that upon arrival at Oregon City Governor Lane found Governor Abernethy of Provisional government still at Oregon's reins. On March third Lane declared the laws of the United States to be in force in the territory. In the following year Lane County was formed by an act of the territorial legislature and named for Governor Lane.

The other event took place early in the spring of 1848 when a newcomer, Jacob Spores, who had taken up land the year before along the McKenzie River, five miles north of the cabin of the Skinners, began ferrying foot passengers across the river by canoe. Of the two happenings, the latter could have loomed greater in the minds of the few families whose small cabins dotted the prairies.

In the high valley the few Indians made very little serious trouble for the first of the white men. Up on his own "pleasant hill", Elijah Bristow, that plucky and indomitable chap who stepped off the first land claim in what was to be Lane County, and hewed logs for the first of the country homes, fought and won two small wars of his own, both over stolen stock. He accomplished this by the simple and direct expedient of brandishing anything at hand, from linchpin to rifle. Before the days of the Hudson's Bay Company ended in the upper valley one of their hunters, an Englishman, lost his scalp to Indians upon that butte to the south of Eugene which bears his name, Spencer. Tyee Tom, it is said, bragged happily of having scalped and otherwise mutilated Mr. Spencer.

"He come Champ-a-te," Chief Tom shrugged in explanation. Champ-a-te meant Rattlesnake Mountain, and from the spot where it rises fifteen hundred feet high the distance to Ya-po-ah is five miles. Across the valley between these hills the Calapooia Indians roamed, most of the time harmlessly.

There came a day, however, when Chief Tom was filled with resentment at the thought of the three palefaces in the cabin by Ya-po-ah. The Skinners spoke enough jargon to know their danger, and the Old Settler shouldered his musket. Through the night he walked around his cabin, while Mary Skinner bent above her fire to mold bullets and the small Mary Elizabeth whimpered from the depths of her cradle. The sun was high before Chief Tom and the Old Settler smoked the pipe of peace.

One wonders what Mary Skinner, watching signal smoke from the hills, felt about the nearness of the redmen. Perhaps they were two things to her—friendly neighbors, better than none; or, on days when she saw her husband drive away to the far Oregon City for supplies that it would take more than ten days to carry back, they may have been one with the coyotes and bears, the wildcats and cougars that roamed the hills where forests came so close to the lone, small cabin.

It might be interesting to follow the Old Settler again to the top of the butte late on a winter afternoon in 1848. That was the time when cabins dotted the valley and excited men had not left them to hurry to the gold that California had unearthed. Perhaps it is Christmas Eve, and Mary Skinner back in their own cabin by a log fire with her two babies, one of them the tiny Leonora, lately born the first white child in the county. Eugene Skinner is thirty-nine years old now, with a family and a wilderness on his hands. He watches the down drift of smoke from his cabin chimney and he knows that means rain. And anyway, the wind is in the south and the sky is red to the west where the sun is almost down. It lights in grey silhouette the cabins of Davis, Akin, Noble, not close by, but not so far away as the others.

He can see for miles, that Old Settler. Off to the south and east, too far for our own eyes, but easy for his imagination stands, on that Pleasant Hill, the log house he had helped to build for Elijah Bristow, two years and more ago. It was fine, he thought, that Elijah was not alone any more, but had his wife with him, and his family. Jim Hendricks had come along on horseback shortly ago, with his son, Tom, on a pony alongside, to say that there was a parcel of new folks on the Hill: besides the Briggs and Prior Blair and Charlie Martin, Charnel Mulligan and Wickliff Gouley, who had settled near Elijah earlier, there were now Jim and Caswell Hendricks, and Bob Callison, two Shelleys, William Bowman, Calvin Hale; and three Bristows, Abel, William and E. L. He'd put down the names as Jim Hendricks spoke them, so that he wouldn't forget the long list. Young Thomas Grundy, set to hurry on to Oregon City, had said, "Pa, let's go!" But Jim had tarried awhile to visit. Mulligan and Prior Blair, he said, talked coming down near the Skinners' to take land. Dodson had stayed near Elijah, but Captain Felix Scott who had come along north from California with those two and Skinner, had left for a place over by Jack Spores' claim. After Jim and his boy rode away the valley had seemed more silent than ever, and the Old Settler had learned the names so that he could talk about them to Mary.

There on the middle fork of the Willamette, across from Bristow, was the cabin of Cornelius Hills, put up last year. And half way to that spot, the two Cargell bachelors, alone. Yonder along the river, due east, was not the sign of a house! Likely some day a smart man would build where the river turned, which would be a godsend.

Off to the north was the cabin of Jacob Spores on the bank of the McKenzie. You could see it if you looked with care. Johnny Diamond had been with Spores for a time, but now he'd built a bit further north. There was the cabin of Peter Herb, the German. And quite a house on William Stevens' claim on the river. Stevens, by cracky, knew how to farm; and he had sons to help him, which was a fine thing in a new country. They'd arrived the first of December just a year ago, and already they'd been able to break forty acres of land for wheat with wooden plough and iron share and six yoke of oxen. It had been a sight to see. He had an idea, the Old Settler, that next year Stevens would have a real farm, with corn and vegetables, and still have room for pasturing his sixteen yoke of oxen and seventy-five head of cattle. Getting those across from the States must have been a deal in itself.

On beyond, and near to the line of hills ten miles away, was the cabin of Mitchell Wilkins. He'd brought his wife, Permelia Allen, and their new baby, Marion, from down in Clackamas County in October, and Cady had helped him build on the land Wilkins had taken for his claim the year before. Thomas Cady's place was just over at the point of hills called West Point; Dave Chamberlain's, too. And west of the Point Charlie Roth had a cabin. "Uncle Billy" Vaughn's family was out there too.

Somewhere, in the last fading twilight to the west and north, meandered the Long Tom river, and on its banks lay the claim of Lester Hulin. To a New York stater from Skinner's home town, the Long Tom might seem pretty far away, but in this country it was good to have neighbors as near as the Hulin place—or it would be if Hulin ever stayed around. He'd been away most of the year after Cayuse Indians or California gold. Like as not he'd find them both, too.

A man named Fergueson had put up the first cabin on the Long Tom, seeming to prefer that lazy river; and it was a good thing every man had six hundred and forty acres if he wanted six hundred and forty acres, or the Ferguesons would be feeling crowded, because Thomas Hinton and John Brown had stopped by the Long Tom, too, and Ben Richardson had a big family close by.

"It beats me," the Old Settler might have told you, "what a place this valley is getting to be!" And then he would remember about the loneliness of the women, and hurry down the hill to Mary, thinking that he ought to take her to see a neighbor real soon; she'd been alone too much.

Chapter II

THE STAGE SETTING

What started these men to Oregon? Depressed markets for crops? Steamboats on the Missouri and Mississippi burning side meat and corn for fuel? Flooded lands along Old Muddy? The sweating, teeth-chattering fever of the ague-ridden low Missouri Valley? All of these things bore their weight. But mostly, we like to think, it was a May day at Champoeg.

The "hard times" were the late thirties and early forties from the Missouri eastward. The "chills and fever" would be a curse along the river as long as mosquitoes swarmed (but no man knew that at the time). The day in May, in far off Champoeg where the Willamette River shone clean in the sun, was the day upon which the new country turned its back toward Britain, hung its allegiance and its future upon America. That was a story, when it reached the Missouri, to make a man look at the old Conestoga, and to start him thinking about his pappy or his grandpappy who had come to the Missouri frontier from Virginia and New York, from Kentucky and Tennessee, from North Carolina and Ohio. A Conestoga wagon that had made it that far could make it farther, to the wide, free land where a man could push out his elbows and plow his furrows into the sun: to where the hills were said to be remindful of Virginia, and the grass waved deep in the wind. The thought of it made blood boil up with the urge to push west!

Frightened women, hearing the talk of their men, shook with ague while they molded the tallow candles and bullets, readied the food barrels, and sewed canvas tops for Oregon.

It's a fine country, those with dreams in their eyes told the ones who only wanted adventure and lands. If enough of us go we can hold it forever for America. And they said, let's go when the prairie grass is green!

IT WAS in 1834 that the first missionaries ventured into the Oregon Country. They came with the wish to convert the Indians to the ways of the protestant church; to teach them, as well, how to study, how to be clean and fed and happy (by white man's standards) as practically and completely through the seasons of cold or drouth as during times of plenty and of sunshine. It is almost beside the point that Jason Lee and those who followed him failed in the matter of the Indians, through no fault of their own; it is important that, as they built their small missions in the valley of the Willamette, they grasped at once the need for settlement of the land and the fact that the British Hudson's Bay Company hoped to keep it, even far into the upper valley, for purposes of hunting and trapping; and they told each other that this wealth and this territory ought to belong to America.

In 1844 Jason Lee of the Methodist mission made a second journey back to the States to tell the exciting truth about Oregon Country to a disinterested Congress. Even the wisest of the senators listened unenthusiastically. Tipping knowingly from toes to heels and twisting heavy gold watch chains upon elaborate vests, they said that the far away and inaccessible West was hardly worth a thought. They would push it, they decided, into the Pacific ocean and wash their hands of the whole business. It was a senator from New Hampshire who stood up to declare, "If I had a son whose conduct made him a fit subject for Botany Bay, I would say, in the name of God, go." A fellow Senator from the same state said that "the wealth of the Indies would not be sufficient to build a railroad to the Columbia," and he thanked God "for His mercy in placing the Rocky Mountains across the way as an eternal barrier."

But the Methodist, Jason Lee, said simply, "Here is the germ of a great state."

They listened lightly to Jason Lee, these men filled with distaste for Oregon. Daniel Webster orated that the Pacific Coast was "a region of savages and wild beasts, of deserts of shifting sands and whirlpools of dust, of cactus and prairie dogs; a western coast of three thousand miles, rock-bound, cheerless and uninviting, and not a harbor on it." John Calhoun agreed that it was "a God-forsaken Asiatic region," and wanted none of it. A number of newspapers took the same stance. "Russia has her Siberia, and England her Botany Bay," was the opinion of the Louisville Journal in 1844, "and if the United States could ever use a country to which to banish rogues and scoundrels the utility of such a region as Oregon will be demonstrated."

All of this must have seemed little short of blasphemy to the enthusiastic Jason Lee.

The men like Senator Linn and Senator Thomas Benton of Missouri answered these men. "America," they said, "will one day need Oregon as much as Oregon needs America." To which the others said "Absurd!" and sat down, hoping that the matter had been finished.

As early as 1841 there had been talk out in Oregon of the need for some kind of provisional government. On a day in May of 1843 a hundred and two men gathered at a place called Champoeg, in Clackamas County, by the Willamette river, to take the problem in hand. They were in buckskins, in frock coats, in homespun, these men of the mountains, statesmen, farmers; they were from Canada, from Scotland, from Ireland. They were from many of the States. They were of many religions—Protestant and Catholic. They were young and they were old. They were, all of them, eager.

Those still active in the Hudson's Bay Company were eager to see Oregon in British hands; the men who had left the fur company to settle in the valley were divided in loyalty. The settlers from the States wanted American government. There were two— the old Canadian Lucier and the young Canadian Matthieu—who would decide the issue. With fifty by the side of the Hudson's Bay and Britain, and fifty answering the shout of the mountain man Joe Meek "All for America, follow me!" it was Matthieu and Lucier who waited, and talked low between the rows, while the river shimmered in the sun and the smell of dust on grass, and of wild roses, hung between two nations and two men. Lucier was questioning, his wise head bent, and his eyes on the eager young Matthieu. The responsibility that had rested heavily upon one hundred and two men now lay upon the shoulders of two, both Canadians!—Etienne Lucier, Hudson's Bay trapper, and Francis X. Matthieu, born in Canada of French parents. When these two turned to follow Joe Meek, the Oregon Country attached itself to America, whether or not America wanted it at the time. From this meeting grew the first Oregon Legislative Committee.

The Hudson's Bay men slipped away; the Americans slapped each other upon the back and said "Joe Meek always was a lucky son-of-a-gun!" And then they settled to the business of a provisional government.

And in Vancouver, at his Hudson's Bay desk, Dr. McLoughlin heard, looked at the blank wall before him, seeing handwriting there that other British eyes had missed.

While Britain and the United States jointly occupied the new country they had allowed its settlers their own brand of land laws. These laws allowed to every male arrival over a certain age six hundred and forty acres of land, which was quite a parcel—at least enough to keep a neighbor at arm's length. The valley's first men, so rich in ground, stepped off their acres, set stakes or blazed trees to mark a claim's corners, put up fences. Then, if they felt lonely, they walked the half mile to the edge of the claim and a neighbor's voice.

When Oregon was admitted to the Union of States as a Territory, 1848, she was not the Oregon we know now, but the broad Oregon Country which included the present states of Idaho, Washington and Oregon, and the part of Wyoming and Montana lying west of the summit of the Rocky Mountains. With the making of the Territory the Congress of the United States voided the old land law, and two years later replaced it with donation laws which granted to settlers in the territory prior to September first, 1850, a claim of three hundred and twenty acres to a single man, and six hundred and forty to a married man and his wife, one half to the wife in her own right. Those coming after December the first, 1850, and before December first, 1853 (later extended to 1855) could take up, in the case of a single man, one hundred and sixty acres; if married, three hundred and twenty, half assigned to the wife in her own right.

At this point Oregon saw a wife-rush comparable to the gold rush days of California. Every girl could have married at least twice. The pretty ones were swung off their feet, and bachelor-minded men changed to husbands at the drop of a beaver hat. The law gave an immediate stimulus to immigration, for in 1850 the number of white settlers in the whole of the Oregon Country was but thirteen thousand. By 1852 it had jumped upward by ten thousand more. And why not? The land law was a just law, the pioneers said. If a man uprooted himself and his family to move into a strange, awesome, empty land, reaching it by terrific measures and unforgettable hardship, he had earned the right, at least, to elbow room.

And he seems to have had it.

Chapter III

THE LITTLE SETTLEMENT

And so cabins stood alone where the earth and sky loomed large. Men who would build a new empire waded through the winter mud to plant small gardens and fields of grain, and in the spring wetness saw them come to ripening. And land's sakes, they said, how things do shoot up out of the ground. Why, in Ioway a man's wheat was likely to be stomped down by the wind and rain, or his house picked up in the spiral of a tornado. Some places, they reminded each other, if corn hadn't "fired" by the first of July, most likely it would before the fifteenth. Even in California, those told who had journeyed by that route to Oregon, the land dried up until river beds couldn't water a thirsty mosquito, and then, just when a mite of rain would have helped, along would come a roar of water down a river bed to drown a man's cattle and his hogs, and even his chickens and sometimes, his family. We're real sinful, they said, to growl about the weather in Oregon.

CABINS built for actual living followed close upon those one room log enclosures hurriedly put up to hold the land, or in some cases were made by the addition of another room. These for the women who would be coming!

The construction of such a house was fairly simple when once enough logs had been cut and smoothed; but the readying of the logs took time, and there was no time on anyone's hands what with winter coming on, or spring gardens to be planted. Just the same, one room or two, the cabin went up first. The logs were smoothed, if a man had time and patience, cut to fit and interlaced at the building's corners so that they could be chinked with moss and mud to shut out the cold. A cut out log or two made windows; more cutouts were the door. Roofs were of riven (split) boards held on by poles tied down by means of willow or other pliable twigs; or at best, pegs were used as a wooden kind of nails driven into augur-bored holes. This really took patience and time, and was well within the luxury class of roof, as were puncheon floors above the grade of the dirt floor. "Puncheon floors" were made by splitting logs and smoothing them with a broadaxe, then fitting them together board side up, and very good floors they must have been.

12

Fireplaces were for warmth, yes, but mostly for cooking. Chimneys were of mud and sticks. If a builder were very wise he allowed an extra foot of logs at corners of his house to act as ladders in case the roof caught fire or threatened to blow away. Beds were made by the device of boring holes in log walls, inserting poles for frames, placing boards over the frames and wild grasses atop for softness, or sweet smelling ferns out of the sunshine, or fir boughs for good sleeping when a day's work was done. One wonders whether the day's work was ever finished, with the children needing shoes for the winter, with mothers carding and spinning wool and sewing it into breeches, shirts and dresses. A man could use his evenings to cut and shape leather into shoes, tacking the soles over wooden forms. A woman had to spend her evenings at spinning. The dye pot always stood by the hearth.

The earliest cabin of the Skinners had not been built for beauty; hardly even for real use, further than to hold the land as required until Mr. Skinner could bring his family there for permanent occupancy. It had a door with skins hung across the opening; and it served as a shelter during the winter of 1846 for a boy of fourteen and a cattle man named Turnage. The two, here from the Applegate trail, were somehow joined by a sailor, Stillwell by name, and these three, the first white men to live on the slope that would one day look down upon Eugene, herded their cattle below the hill, hunted bear and killed wolves in the wooded area to the south and east.

Then the Skinners arrived, papa and mama, and the small Mary, born in Clackamas County the year before. And now the cabin grew, with two doors, and a window looking out across the prairie. It is easy to imagine Mary Skinner, her baby in her arms, contemplating its simplicity and saying, her heart swelling a little with the dream of it, "Mr. Skinner, we must have another room here, and that room must have a door to the sunset. And do let's have a small porch! Just a shelter where you can clean the mud from your boots and I can rock a little in my new rockingchair." She may have said "Gene", but more probably she said "Mr. Skinner."

If a cabin had no spring close at hand there must, of course, be a well. Even with a clean river running past a well and a bucket made life easier for a busy woman; and the means by which Eugene Skinner located a satisfactory well-site was quite simple. A clump of rushes, green on the slope of the hill, meant water close to the top of the ground. At once the Old Settler knew that here was no deep well problem; that a spring, cleared, widened and deepened, was his well for the taking. The easy answer to his need is, oddly enough, the easy answer to our question of where this first cabin stood. Or at least it is the answer within a few feet, and a satisfactory one to Eugene F. Skinner, grandson of the town's founder who lives within a short distance of the original home.

"There are lots of things that I don't know about my grandfather," he said, when sought out at his place of business. "But there is one about which I have no doubt. That's the location of the cabin. I can prove it to you the way I proved it to Cal Young. He and your father, Marion Wilkins, came to me wanting to find the exact place. They said there'd been some disagreement about it, which isn't surprising. So I took them up, and I showed them the patch of rushes that still grows above the well. My father, St. John Skinner, told me that his father had felt certain that water could be found just underneath those rushes. And sure enough, he only had to go down four feet before he struck it. There is no use to believe differently. My father told me that if we ever wanted absolute proof, all we need do is dig down, because when they left the first cabin for the new one—it was where the John Kelley home stands, on sixth and Lincoln—they filled the well with all the old crockery and things they could find so that cattle wouldn't get into it. 'Just dig down,' he said, but I never felt the need. I know that's where the well was." Mr. Skinner waited upon a customer, then turned again to us.

"The marker is not in just the right place," he went on. "I could have told them where it ought to go. But then I've been away from here until fourteen years ago." (The marker was placed by the Daughters of the American Revolution.) "I told my children I wanted to come back home to die, and here I am, not going to die for awhile. And I think Eugene has the greatest future of any town in the country!"

That is carrying on the spirit of the family.

"Do you know where my grandfather died?"

We admitted that we did not.

"Go back on Sixth street until you come to the house in the middle of the block between Lincoln and Charnelton. In the yard you'll see an enormous ivy tree. Number is 260 on Sixth. My grandmother, Mary Skinner, brought four little firs from back of the butte and planted them in a group together. They grew. Later she planted some ivy. It grew over those firs so thick they had to cut them. Some day when you have time, just stop your car and go over there and part that ivy. You'll find one of those firs with its big trunk all mixed up with the ivy trunk. The house that stands there is the house where Eugene Skinner died. His cabin was on the corner west, but he later bought that house from Jim McClaren. My grandfather was not old when he died. During the big flood of 1861 he took a heavy cold from exposure, and he was never well again. He was in his early fifties when he died."

The thought of Mary Skinner, left alone, intrudes here. One is glad that there were other cabins close by before that happened!

When the Skinner log house had been finished, there must have been a small garden—a square inside a rail fence where turnips and cabbages, and all those seeds carried from the home far away in New York could be planted. Beets, too, and radishes, with tender tops to cook along with the turnip greens in the spring. And what were greens without sidemeat? So then there were pigs squealing in the dust or wallowing in delightful mud when the rains had fallen.

When there were those other cabins, of the same kind as the Skinners', this was, of a certainty, going to be a town. There were more gardens, tended by women in long calico dresses, with babies in their arms. There were trundle beds underneath the shelf beds, and a man of family worried a little about his flour and his wool and clothes.

There was flour to be had; there were other provisions, machinery, wool, finished lumber from Oregon City or the new little Portland village. But that always present lack of roads fit to travel and the great distance involved made obtaining these necessities difficult. The hundred miles to Oregon City, or even the sixty to Salem, held men back.

It is difficult now to imagine the wide, empty country in 1847 and '48. The Oregonian tells us that there were "but fourteen rude houses" in Portland, and even San Francisco was "a village of sixty tenements, including houses, barns and tents."

Then Oregon Country heard about California's gold. Men forgot how far a mile could seem. Cabins, farms and fields, shops, offices, and wives were left alone. Not mud, nor dust, nor bad roads, nor Indians, nor the miles to be covered by pack horses between the Willamette Valley and the rivers of gold, stopped the going.

The father of these writers, who lived his boyhood at the foot of the Coburg hills, said in a later diary:

"The discovery of gold in California drove every able-bodied man the land around on a frenzied hunt for gold, leaving women and children and cripples at home, and often alone. My father was one who took the trail south to the mines. He left my mother with two babies, and a neighbor boy of fourteen to get along as best they could with the jobs on the farm. . . . Indians on the trail were plentiful, and not too friendly, but the men in my father's party were all familiar with Indian traits and habits, and by dealing kindly with them (but standing guard at night) they got through safely . . . and made a hasty retreat just as the snows were covering Mt. Shasta with winter white."

To pioneer women that was a vivid, bitter summer. Their men—farmers, doctors, lawyers, merchants, millers, blacksmiths, were away after gold. Some of them found it. Some only learned that Oregon crops were their real gold, and settled down to plant orchards and potatoes and fields of wheat; to build herds of good cattle; to plan for schools that would serve also as places of worship, and when these schools had outlived their usefulness as religious meeting places, to build churches; to look the future of Eugene in the face, and to roll up sleeves toward the end that that future might be good.

Chapter IV

THE NEW TOWN

"I, Eugene Skinner, proprietor of the town of Eugene City, in the county of Lane, territory of Oregon, do hereby certify that this is a true and correct plat of same."

"Be it remembered that September the sixth, A.D. 1852, the first term of commissioner's court of the county of Lane . . . was held at Eugene City . . ."

OREGON'S Territorial Legislature, in session in January of 1851, had created a new county within Oregon and named it Lane, for the Territory's first Governor.

Three months later Eugene Skinner and the newly arrived D. M. Risdon talked platting of a city, and established a meridian, carrying forward a survey for their townsite in August of that same year. So Eugene was Eugene City almost before there was a county of Lane.

In fact the first county election was not held until June, and the first meeting of the County Commissioner's Court took place more than a year later, in September of 1852. Records show that there were but fifty-one votes cast in the first county election. These made D. M. Risdon the Representative to serve in the legislature, John T. Gilfrey, County Judge, M. H. Harlow, County Clerk, Fielding McMurry, County Treasurer, G. R. Caton, Auditor, and Robert Robe, School Superintendent. There were four Justices of the Peace, Wm. Breeding, H. G. Hadley, W. C. Spencer and John Rowe. The county tax was .4 of a mill.

For a city with no citizens, Eugene had a busy 1851. Mr. Risdon built its first house, at a spot where Pearl street now runs through between Ninth, or Broadway, and Tenth. That puts it just south and west of the Eugene Hotel. Hilyard Shaw, whose cabin was far away from the new townsite on land now University of Oregon campus, came in to put up the Risdon house. He built it with a puncheon floor, a roof and sides of split boards, at a cost to Mr. Risdon of seventy-six dollars! Its size was twenty by fourteen feet.

There was other excitement in that year. "Jim" Huddleston, whose land claim lay to the south and west of Skinner's, moved his

17

trading post from beside the Skinner cabin to a spot on the river bank east of the butte where the Skinner ferry landing promised business. Mr. A. P. Ankeny, a river man from Pennsylvania and newly interested in Portland, cast his river-wise eye along the upper Willamette and, liking what he saw, went into business with Mr. Huddleston. The "slough" cutting through the townsite from south to north was deepened to make power for a sawmill, and Mr. Skinner deeded a half block of land north of Sixth street and along the slough to Hilyard Shaw for the mill site. William Smith, whose land lay east in what is Fairmount, helped Shaw build, own and operate the mill. The presence of this small mill explains the fact no doubt that within the town there were only a few log houses.

The Huddleston store on the river bank must have been warmed by a stove, and here men could gather from their isolated cabins to discuss the new town-to-be. Charnel Mulligan, down from Pleasant Hill and located on his land that lay south of the Skinner claim, joined these men; and Prior Blair, also from the Hill, came with Ben and Lemuel Davis from homes to the west. Hilyard Shaw and William Smith stopped their new power-saw to talk building. There was Sam Culver, from what was to be the Chichester place, now the Donald Erb memorial building site, and Mr. Breeding from toward the later College Hill. Abraham and Henry Peek ferried across the river from their land that would soon belong to Jacob Gillespie and the Walker Youngs.

And, of course, there sat the Old Settler, and across the cracker barrel, the newly-made Judge Risdon.

It is a lonesome kind of picture, but with a certain pleasantness about it. One suspects that there was a pickle barrel, and a spittoon, and sawdust on the floor from the new mill. There were good, shining boots for the men who had brought gold out of California. The river shimmered in the thin sunlight of early spring, running muddy with drift; then grew shallow with the summer so that the ferry scraped a sandbar and could scarcely make her landing. The bright colors of the poison oak dimmed, and the maples showed yellow against the firs. The hills turned more blue, and one morning were topped with a peppering of snow. The Old Settler and the others drew nearer to the stove, and said that it would soon be a new year.

"There's land", they said, "for all who want to build."

"We'll b-b-build your houses," Hilyard Shaw promised, stuttering a little. "There's p-p-p-plenty of lumber." THAT was 1851.

The town as first platted lay east of Skinner's butte. Its most northerly street was Water street, along the river, its most southerly was Seventh. It had High, Mill and Ferry streets. Besides the land deeded to Hilyard Shaw for a mill and to James Huddleston for the store site, Mr. Skinner filed deeds of land in April, 1852, to M. P. Deady, R. P. Boise and L. A. Rice, and gave land for a school.

On the sixth of September of 1852 the first meeting of the County Commissioner's Court was held, the story goes, under an oak tree "in the town of Eugene City." That court named as commissioners for three and two year terms respectively, Joseph Davis and Aden Powell. Mr. Skinner presented a petition signed by twelve householders for a road "from Jacob Spores via Skinner's ferry to intersect a road on the Long Tom . . . from Marysville to Winchester . . ." The petition was examined, the prayer granted, the road ordered. Supervisors were named for several newly fixed road districts, but the first of those appointed were to build the road "Spores via Skinner's." When James Huddleston had procured a grocery license for one year at a cost of fifty dollars the court adjourned. County machinery had begun to function.

In no time at all it developed a squeak. Charnel Mulligan, Prior Blair, Eugene Skinner, and a fourth settler (near the site of Springfield) offered land for county buildings. All but Skinner's were outside the platted town. In June, 1853, an election was held to decide the choice, but when the County Commissioners met to count the votes they found that no spot had received a majority. In spite of a loud dissent from Davis the other two settled upon the offer of Mulligan, but somehow, when it came to the matter of bonds the Old Settler looked them in the eye and paid half of the $5000 to bond the "said commissioners for said county", the other half was paid by Mulligan and forty acres of each was accepted as county lands. This explains why, two years later, the new courthouse was built upon a line that divided the two donation claims— a line that was the center of Eighth street, making it necessary one day to move the building to one side or other of that street. A newspaper account of 1869 says: "The county commissioners have passed an order to move the courthouse and the contract has been let to Mr. Harlow for $1000. It is not understood by a great many what necessity there is for this proceeding unless it is a dearth of business and a consequent decrease in the issue of script to deputies and 'courthouse people'. No doubt there will be much unpleasantness . . ." Had the Old Settler been alive then he might have been allowed a smile behind his beard at sight of the courthouse perched upon *his* side of the dividing line.

In recognition of the Mulligan and Skinner gifts, the County Commissioners meeting in April of 1856, gave to Martha Spores Mulligan (and belatedly in July, same year, to Mary Cook Skinner) "any lot in Eugene City not on the public square and belonging to the county, as a donation . . ." Let's hope that Mrs. Mulligan, two leaps ahead of Mrs. Skinner, did not choose land the latter had her eye upon. In further recognition, stained glass windows were placed in Eugene's "new courthouse" (our present one) to do honor to Charnel Mulligan and Eugene Skinner, but someone later objected to their weird light and had them removed.

Soon after the public square gift Mulligan platted additions to the east and west of his original donation. In 1853 Daniel Christian had come with his family from the Tualatin plains and taken a land claim extending from our present Eleventh street to about Twentieth, and eastward from near Willamette street to High. This, with the Huddleston, Hilyard Shaw, Skinner and Mulligan lands may be called Eugene's basic donation land claims, and are so mapped.

The Court of July, 1853 (Davis, McDowell and Ramsey present, with W. Bristow, sheriff's deputy) ordered a survey of the donation lands of Mulligan and Skinner, and the execution "as soon as possible of a correct and plain town plot . . ." wherein lots should be eighty feet front by 160 feet deep, blocks to contain eight lots, two lots to the quarter, and alleys fourteen feet wide. The survey must be presented at the next term of the court; the clerk was ordered to post notices throughout the county of sale of lots "for cash in hand at Eugene City, the name given for said seat of justice from and after this day July 5 A.D. 1853," and "ordered furthermore to proceed as soon as possible and employ a workman to build a clerk's office fronting on the public square . . . the size to be sixteen by twenty feet, one story high." Dr. A. W. Patterson made the survey. Prior Blair built the clerk's office, a building between Willamette, Oak, Ninth and Tenth that turned out to be almost a miniature of the courthouse that followed. Upon the building of the courthouse this office was moved to its present site on Seventh street between Pearl and High, where it continues to feel its rank as the fourth building raised in Eugene. Four small columns, like service stripes, give it the dignity it merits.

It was thus that Eugene, renamed by Mary Skinner, had crawled out of the mud and settled down to be a town.

The County Court paid in that year of 1853, twenty-nine dollars and a half to M. H. Harlow for "the expense of going to Marysville for the laws and books for the county." It paid four dollars to A. G. Hovey for issuing sixteen tickets of election of county officers. It appointed a grand jury for a "term of Court holden in March"; it sold licenses to peddle groceries to A. Marks, Dozenberry and Co., to Isaac Beerman at one dollar for one month, and to Harris & Co. at twenty-five cents for one week. The Skinner ferry license fee was five dollars, and Jacob Spores paid a fee of ten dollars per quarter on the McKenzie river ferry. The court fixed carrying fees for the Spores ferry at:

```
For each wagon and one yoke ox or
      one span horses............one dollar
Man  and  horse...............twenty-five  cents
Packhorse  and  mule...........twenty-five  cents
Loose horse...................twelve and a half cents
Footman ....................twelve and a half cents
Each yoke oxen................twenty cents
Each  sheep, hog..............four cents
```

In December of '53 Prior Blair was paid twelve dollars for stakes used to lay out the City of Eugene, and Z. Sweet and S. Calhoun each received eighteen dollars "for carrying chain and driving stakes."

We first know of Z. Sweet back in the days of the beginnings of the District Court, Second Judicial District of the Territory of Oregon "begun and holden at Eugene City . . . on the fifteenth day of March A.D. 1852." Present were the Honorable O. C. Pratt, presiding judge, E. F. Skinner, clerk, and R. P. Boise "Prosicuting atty." One of a newly appointed list of grand jurors, Mr. Z. Sweet, it seems, used "insolent language toward the Court . . . calculated and intending to disturb its proceedings." It was thereupon ordered that the said Z. Sweet be fined the sum of ten dollars . . . whereupon the said Z. Sweet, having repeated the use of contemptuous language, was fined ten dollars more . . . whereupon the offense being repeated, the said Mr. Z. Sweet was fined twenty-five dollars and placed in the custody of the Marshal until such time as the fines were paid. Two days later, which would make it Saint Patrick's Day, A.D. 1852, Mr. Sweet emerged from the custody of the Marshal and from the doghouse, apparently, by pleading guilty to contemptuous and disorderly conduct, to the satisfaction of everybody and the remission of his fine.

County business and city history merge as the July, 1853, County Court named the terms of sale of Eugene City lots to be one third down in cash, one third in six months, and one third in twelve months; and paid Prior Blair one hundred dollars for construction of the clerk's office building. The September Court ordered a stove to heat that building, the stove to cost thirty dollars, and following at once there is a duplicate order, which means that the clerk may have made a mistake or that the winter threatened to be a cold one. The County was a bit in debt, and from several directions claims came in, notably from Wm. Stevens and Jacob Gillespie, of "rongful assessments" of property by the County, and the clerk was ordered to make changes as proved on the assessment roll. By this date, then, Jacob Gillespie had taken up what had been the Peek lands across the river, and what is now that of Cal Young.

In October of 1853, Elias Briggs gave bond and received a license for a ferry across the Middle Fork of the Willamette opposite his house—in other words, to Springfield; such men as William McCabe, Dodson, Wm. Smith, Hilyard Shaw, John Gilfrey, R. Robe and Holland were issued orders on the treasury of various sums to be paid "out of any monies not otherwise appropriated", which makes one wonder whether they were ever paid the sums due. Fielding McMurry did receive $18.85 for services as County Treasurer for the year and E. Skinner was paid $25.00 by the District Court as its clerk for the quarter. And Z. Sweet was letting his house to the use of the County grand jury in the sum of $7.50. Benjamin Davis, having misplaced his order on the court for $9.00, was given another order but not the nine dollars, as he and Mr. Armitage, J. Gillespie and Marion Scott were to be paid sums owing them "out of monies not otherwise appropriated." The County debt in July, 1854, was $355.94.

September records, that year, read like this: "Value of taxable property is——. Number of poles is——. Amount of monies necessary is——. Therefore ordered that four mills to the dollar be accepted on the total valuation of personal property, and one dollar on each poll for County purposes." There were now nine voting precincts in the county, and an order for a tenth was rescinded. The county was ordered to elect two representatives, two County Commissioners, one County Superintendent, one County Treasurer, one Coroner, one Auditor, and one Assessor, with a Constable for each precinct except the sixth (in Willamette Forks).

The blank spaces in the records for the year 1854 would look as if the county threatened to give up; to end its business obligations. Not those men! They ordered bonds prepared by which E. Skinner and C. Mulligan, with their wives "respectively joined", would deed to the county that land they'd promised for the building site of the courthouse. Such bonds were sent to the families to be signed, and a special term was set for Monday, January 15, A.D. 1855, to consider plans for courthouse and jail.

The plan of A. A. Smith was adopted. The ground plot would be forty by sixty feet, the building two stories high, one floor to be the courtroom with fourteen foot high ceiling, the other to house offices and the jury room. There was much maneuvering now to have certain lots turned back for reasons not clear, since Skinner and Mulligan donations had been to the county for the court.

Hammitt and Harlow were allowed $1054.60 "on contract for building the courthouse, and $35.00 for building the backhouse." Both orders were actually drawn, this in the July term; and Asahel Bush was paid $30.00 for handling the advertising of sale of city lots. At the same term it was ordered that a space of 100 feet in width extend the entire distance around the public square, the same forever set apart . . . as a street or public highway except for eight feet reserved for sidewalks. Plans were changed to make the courthouse face south instead of west as at first designated.

And James Huddleston, County Treasurer, reported a balance on hand as of July 6th, 1855, $2038.96!

The county was well out of the red, so taxes went up from four mills to eight. Richard Parsons replaced R. Robe as "Supt. of common schools" in the county, and Z. Sweet was allowed three dollars for "crying the sale of lots" in Eugene City. Paul Brattain was authorized to sell county lots in Eugene, and Prior Blair was permitted to sell groceries at his house "near the Jockey Race Track." Skinner's ferry license went up to $8.00.

Now came liquor troubles. C. C. Croner asked a license "to sell less than one quart of liquors", his petition signed by 89 supposedly legal voters, and the petition against signed by 85. Upon investigation it was found that the numbers of legal names were, rather, 77 for and 80 against, and the petition was disallowed.

Lots were sold for five dollars to two churches; one and a fraction of a lot was offered for a school upon promise to build within two years. The Mulligan and Skinner donations of land were delivered and recorded, and with no notice that the courthouse had been completed, we next read that M. Harlow was engaged to build a fence 274 feet square and four boards high, to be painted with two coats of white lead, around the court square. Each fence was to have a gate at its center, raised two steps, with a platform four feet square at the top. This, it was urged and ordered, should be completed before the fall rains set in. There must be ladders to the roof of the building, and more ladders upon the roof, flanked by eight painted cans for water. Mr. Harlow was paid $460 for necessary materials. The window glass allowance was four dollars for twenty panes, also to M. Harlow. This on May 1st, 1857. Fall rains came early!

In August of '58, Mr. Harlow's bid on a jail, for work aside from iron work, was $2600.00 and the Bromley ironworks agreed to furnish their part for $3575.00, materials to be shipped from San Francisco. The order, changed to read stone instead of brick construction, was allowed by Philip Mulkey, Jacob Gillespie and A. B. Florence, and signed by Paul Brattain, clerk.

And so Eugene was almost a city. Her hard pioneering beginning was slipping into the past. She had a main street with all the essential kinds of stores; she had cabinet shops where skilled workmen made furniture for new frame houses. Eugene Skinner had moved down to Sixth street and Judge Risdon up to Seventh—by which one merely means to say that the town was spreading, stretching, coming alive. With ships shuttling between San Francisco and Portland, carrying household goods and wearables, it was no longer necessary for women to card and weave and sew every garment that was worn. Pianos and eastern furniture were "coming 'round the Horn" to the little Portland settlement, and some of them found their way up the valley; but it was possible, in Eugene's own cabinet shops, to find beds and chairs and cabinets beautifully worked out in native oak and maple. And over the counter of a store called Brumley's Eugene women could buy dress patterns of silk and satin brocades, or yards of sprigged muslin and delaine. There were bonnets with flowers and shoes with buttons, and dolmans of velvet to put the heart into any woman. The dolmans are gone, but pieces of the early furniture can still be found in the homes of those wise enough to appreciate and keep it.

There were close to six hundred people in the place, of whom three were doctors, four were lawyers, four preachers of the gospel. Four clergymen, but only one church!

For our pictured history of the time we depend upon lithographs. We must be forever grateful to men like Kuchel and Dresel with their "drawings from nature and on stone," and to such lithog-

EUGENE SKINNER, FOUNDER OF EUGENE
Photograph ca. 1860

MARY COOK SKINNER
Photograph ca. 1860

The roof of the Cabin was covered with split boards. — The chimney was built from the ground, and made of cobble stones.

(This sketch was made from memory.)

Dimensions of Cabin 25X30

North

This is a counterpart of the outlines of the cabin.

West

East

Front Porch Floor

(Flowers) Steps steps (were planted here)

Path   South   Path

The two hinges, and knob on front door, the glass, and sash for the windows, and the hardware for the Cabin were brought by Eugene Franklin Skinner from Dalles Oregon in 1846. There was a porch, and steps on the North side same as on the south, one window and a door. The floors of the Cabin, and porches were split logs made smooth with a plane. (Mr Skinner brought from Illinois) his kit of tools and he had a Carpenter to help him build the Cabin, The man came with him from Dalles Oregon It was he who felled the trees and hewed them in shape for the logs that were used in building the Cabin which had two rooms, the partition was on the west side of the door (running North, and south.)

SKETCH OF EUGENE AND MARY'S CABIN
Located on the west slope of Skinner Butte.
Drawn by Phoebe Skinner Kinsey, daughter of Mary and Eugene.

"EUGENE CITY, OREGON TERRITORY 1856-59," LITHOGRAPH

raphers as Britton and Rey, for their exactitude of detail as they drew upon paper the things they saw. Modern successors, Carlisle and Company, have saved these pictures of the past. In a lithograph done in 1856-9 by Kuchel and Dresel it is possible to pick out Eugene's first flour mill, a real church, the angled front of a livery stable, and many houses among the trees. There are barns low and rambling, as large as the houses or larger; and off to the east, past the high-roofed flour mill is quite plainly discernible, the low hill slope that later became the site of the State University. The foreground area just below Skinner's butte is railroad trackless and bare, and in the center of the picture, for justice, stands the proud new domed courthouse, like a small shadow of the high Spencer that looms beyond. Rail and picket fences mark off plentiful areas around homes, and Eugene must have been a quiet, pleasant, town. In an imagined close-up, one makes a picture of cabinet shops in the shade of trees, a paint shop under a man's barn roof, blacksmith shops where almost no road ran past.

And the picture has sounds, inevitably; the clink of anvils, the near jangle of a cowbell, the frightening clang of a firebell, and, on Sunday morning the first church bell. It has the smell of sun on tarweed and of the rain on fir needles. And then the picture has motion, for small figures come from their houses in dolman and bustle and boots, to move down the rows of new trees toward church and hymn singing, and the "Amen!" from the corner pew. That amen is the hallelujah echo from the three ministers who have as yet no churches of their own.

Chapter V

CHURCH BELLS WERE RINGING

God was here in the valley long before the circuit rider came from across the mountains. But some people didn't know it, so from the beginning they had to be told. Along with their New England conscience, their southern blood and their Scotch-English ancestry they had a background of religion. They believed in their Bible and those who didn't were labeled infidels and were lost. So the ancient circuit rider came into their lives. He lived off his disciples, and he earned his living. He rode up and down the valley and he finally died in the strenuous life. In their homes these pioneers held family prayers. They gave thanks for life and for food. The organizations of churches appeared and held meetings in school houses or the courthouse. Men chose their own form of worship. They were baptized in rivers, and by sprinkling, and by pouring, and they were saved by fear of damnation . . . then one day the sound of church bells in the quiet air of early spring brought to the hearts of the people a satisfying peace and hope. And the churches grew and were an important part in the life of the town. Fine city churches, with vested choirs and splendid ministers. And the call to worship was heard throughout the valley as the shadow of the lonely circuit rider disappeared over the western horizon.

VALLEY folks liked to go to church. It was a part of their background and had been a part of their everyday life before they'd moved west. But many of them, in those years of travel away from the settled part of the country, had come to Oregon ahead of the Churches and had to get along without them as best they could. It was no wonder then that dwellers in the valley had welcomed the Circuit Rider when he came riding in from North or South or East, following trails through forests, over mountain passes, fording rivers, from cabin to cabin, never leaving a call unanswered.

He came on horseback and he came quietly, looking severe and almost depressing in his black suit with his long cape swinging from around drooping shoulders, his Bible held in one hand as he handled the slack reins of his horse with the other. From under his wide brimmed hat narrow eyes peered ahead of him, down the road into the future, into people's hearts, their sins, and on into the promised land. All the possessions necessary for his preaching he carried in his saddlebags as he forded the rivers and followed roads or trails. He was a strong and healthy man and fitted well the conditions of the early existence of the pioneers.

As they saw him first ride into town people were awed by him and by his air of assurance of his own personal nearness to God. But in their own lives now they missed that assurance, missed the Church left behind them, and so they welcomed the traveling minister when he came among them at more or less frequent intervals, to talk and preach, to read his Bible and to remind them of church ties broken and left behind.

Mrs. Belknap, writing in her diary of the Circuit Rider said: "It is like a ray of bright sunshine on a dark cloudy day to meet him. Whole families go miles by ox-cart and on horseback. We have a Sunday school and prayer meeting and then hand shaking and visiting for an hour, and we go to our distant homes greatly refreshed. We have little space in our one-room cabin, but there is always a cosy corner for the minister and his books."

Since there were no Churches and so no parsonages there was no place for the Circuit Rider to live, so he "put up" with the people he'd come to serve, and, it may be assumed that some of them "put up" with him, for families were large and houses were small. It is said, too, that he came with a good appetite after those long hours on horseback in the open country, and he stayed for days and perhaps weeks, wrestling with problems of soul's salvation. Proctor's famous statue of the Circuit Rider which stands on the Capitol grounds at Salem is a fine and inspiring one, remindful of the early days when religion was, as it is now, a needed thing in the lives of busy men and women; recalling those days when the lonely man rode into their lives and out again, leaving behind him peace, and serenity, comfort and promise.

When old Joab Powell, one of the earliest and best known of the Circuit Riders, traveled up and down the valley he liked to preach out in the open under the trees. He had a mighty voice that, it was claimed, was so loud and powerful it could be heard a mile and a half away. It was said too that he could convert almost anyone because of his great persuasive powers, but there was a question as to whether or not such redemption was to last. Though Joab was a favorite minister, the ladies didn't approve or appreciate some of his more worldly habits. After his hours of strenuous preaching he liked to settle down for a rest and leaning against a stout forest tree, he would take from his pocket a plug of chewing tobacco, bite off a chunk and chew contentedly for awhile, then, sure and true, he'd send the geyser of brown juice a proud far distance to spray a fountain of dust from the road where it landed.

It was said Joab could neither read nor write and that the young German girl he married, who was no more gifted than he, had to put her mind to it and learn quickly so that she could read to him. He'd listen with closed eyes and in that way he learned by heart most of the Books of the Bible, as well as verse after verse of the Church hymns which later, at services, he'd roar through with his mighty voice.

Perhaps a few years would cover the time of the Circuit Rider's trips through the valley. Then one day he was to ride away, to be seen no more, to leave behind him only a lengthening shadow cast by his wide swinging cape and the broad hat pulled low over sunfilled eyes. But the shadows of the churches had already come to take his place.

First, in spirit only, these shadows began to form in the minds and hearts of people, to grow gradually into definite shape as the valley folks met in small groups and organized for informal services. At frequent intervals the meetings were held in homes for talk and prayer and singing. Later, as the town grew, such gatherings took place in schoolhouses or the Courthouse. In time those early organizations began to crystallize and to take the shape of things to come. Soon one church after another had its definite plan, and the town began to be the center of that early religious development that was to grow continuously until, at the present time, Eugene has more than thirty churches of every denomination, filling special needs of a growing population.

Before the churches were actually built the Courthouse was the scene of a great many activities which in these days we scarcely think of as suitable to courthouses. In 1868 temperance lectures were delivered there. At one time the ministers of various churches held a course of such lectures. Old timers remember when the churches held their concerts there. We can find no reason for this, but are tempted to guess that early day religion being as strict as it was, a concert, or anything classed as entertainment, was considered far too worldly to be a part of the regular church plan—but very useful, never the less, as a means for raising money to aid in furthering church causes.

Mr. C. B. Moores, writing in 1923, said:

"The Church is so completely interwoven with the various interests of society that it appears prominently on almost every page of history. Some of the greatest, sweetest and most inspiring memories of our whole history cluster 'round about the walls of our old churches, Old South Church, Christ Church, St. Johns Church. The lives of the men who laid the foundations of these Churches nearly fifty years ago in Oregon were full of romance and adventure. The hardships and trials which they underwent in order to establish a footing here for the Church of their choice were greater perhaps than those undergone by any of their predecessors in other quarters of the globe."

To go back to the origin of Oregon's first missions, in 1832 as the story has often been told and written, four Flathead Indians made the long journey across the mountains from their far away Oregon home as far east as St. Louis. They went in search of the white man's Bible and the white man's God. The story of that journey and the reason for it at last reached the New York papers, and in 1833 the New York Journal published an account of it. At once this information aroused great interest among its readers, and a desire to help these Indian people find the answers to their questions.

The Rev. Jason Lee of Stanshed, Canada, was asked to go to the far West and establish an Indian Mission. In Boston he was to meet his brother Daniel Lee and Cyrus Shepard, the two men who were to go with him on his long journey. From New England they started their western trek in 1834. They reached their destination in the Willamette valley after weary months of travel and all the hardships endured by the thousands who were to follow in their path. In October of that year they began a small mission, the first one located near Salem, and there they were soon teaching the white man's Bible to the Indians. They also taught them the early church hymns, and it is said that after the coming of Lee and the priests the Indians were singing their tribal songs to these tunes.

For two years Lee and his helpers preached to a strange congregation. From the infrequent ships coming up the Columbia there were sailors to be taught; there were stragglers from California, and the Indians from all the surrounding country. The missionaries preached in a tent on the banks of the Willamette river and built

a log school house for the young Indian children and soon established the first manual school.

That work of the early missionaries has made a lasting contribution to the early history of Oregon, and the name of Jason
Lee will be remembered as one foremost among them all. This
man whose career was to last so short a time gave so much that he
must be considered the founder of protestant religion for the
Pacific northwest and the valley of the Willamette, where Eugene
was one day to appear. And the influences of these first religious
meetings was to spread until all the scattered towns had their own
small churches. If Jason Lee could come back to the valley now,
perhaps he would look upon our imposing churches with their
plans and projects and programs and bow his young head in gratitude, remembering those early homes where morning prayers were
said and where families shared in thanks and blessing over the
evening meal; where having no churches at all, men knelt together
by a neighbor's fireside.

A letter from Rev. Nelson Clark written in 1909 said:

> "When I arrived in Eugene in the fall of 1855 it was a
> very small village having perhaps no more than 200 inhab-
> itants. Having no church and no school house we wor-
> shipped in a small building on east Tenth street and later
> on in a vacant store on Willamette street. By investigation
> I find I have preached in more than forty different places
> in this county including school houses, private dwellings,
> barns, shady groves and camp grounds."

Early churches did not confine their activities to preaching,
Sunday school and prayer meetings. They held Fairs in "Rhinehart's Hall" or in their own church buildings and they cooked up
church suppers for which they charged twenty five cents. There
were always special Thanksgiving services and on that day, each
year, the stores were closed at three o'clock in the afternoon so all
could attend. Families took time from busy lives to give thanks
for all the blessings they had received during the year.

Of the many services held in early times the New Years watch
parties were among the most impressive (to young children the
most awful and depressing affair). Members gathered in churches
late in the evening of the last day of the year. There were prayers,
and there was singing of hymns, and at midnight a quiet and

solemn farewell to the old year and a welcome of hope and promise for the one beginning. The tolling of the church bells added a solemnity to a thoughtful evening of contemplation of past and future.

There were Church Christmas celebrations for old and young, when beautiful Oregon evergreen trees filled platforms from edge to edge, leaving little room for the performers who sang and recited and played the organ for the entertainment of the congregation. All except the children who were there to receive their gifts and for no other purpose.

Revival meetings were popular. These were held during the winter months when spirits needed a re-birth and church-going may have lagged a bit through the dreary rainy Sundays. Those meetings were full of spirit and often brought new members into the church, as well as new enthusiasm and new hope to old members.

Camp meetings, much like the Revival meetings in spirit, were more recreational. They were held in the summer time, in beautiful groves or camp grounds near town for church members and anyone else who wanted to attend. People often took their tents and camped out for the entire week the meetings were to last. This was a chance to be with friends and to have a vacation; and they returned home with a new outlook on life, physically as well as spiritually.

The actual preaching was held in a large tent, or if the weather was good, services might be out under the trees in the grove. Leslie Scott wrote, "The longing for news, gossip, knowledge, and the interchange of ideas had to be almost completely satisfied at these historic Camp Meetings. Often, after a year's separation friends and neighbors from far away places in the valley met again to talk over those joys and sorrows and their many problems along a new Oregon frontier where they had found the land of their desires." And notes from an early diary mention "Those camp meetings where folks might warm by each other's fires", "Those meetings held in groves of evergreens or on the river bank among maples, where romance sometimes blossomed and weddings were held." "Camp fires were always kept burning to light up the stand, with extra lights of tallow candles for the preacher so he could see to read. Those glorious meetings gave us something to think about beside our hardships and our struggles."

Camp meetings however weren't always peaceful. Sometimes rowdies tried to break them up and, once at least, when Father Wilbur, one of the sturdiest of those early day ministers, was being harassed by unwanted onlookers, he left his platform, barged into the group, knocking them right and left with his bare fists. Then with face and shirt bloody he returned to finish his sermon.

Perhaps the churches' greatest influence of all their long and important history is their more recent activity on the campus of the University. There, religion is becoming more and more a real part of college life, and each year sees that influence increasing. Originally this University activity began with the interest of different denominations in the lives of their own students away from home, but it has grown into a religious pattern within the University itself.

The first such organization and one that has been in existence for thirty or more years is the Catholic Newman Club. The last and newest one is Friendly House, a Unitarian group recently organized. Wesley Foundation, one of the larger groups, was organized by the Methodist Church. It offers to students a well planned program of recreational, religious, and social gatherings. It established Wesley Church Study Club, and Wesley Players and is open to all students every day, as is also Westminister House, a Presbyterian group. This group sponsors a Sunday morning discussion class and on Friday night bridge and dancing and fireside talk. There is too, the Canterbury Club of St. Mary's Episcopal Church, Plymouth Club of the Congregational Church, as well as the Inter-University Christian fellowship and the Y.M and Y.W.C.A. "Religious Evaluation Week" is a program sponsored by the Council, and "Church Night" at the beginning of each school year is a part of the program as is also the Easter Sunrise service in McArthur Court.

A heap of crumbling stones in an open field on the old farm of Mahlon H. Harlow marks the place of the First Baptist Church altar in the valley. This altar was the hearthstone of that pioneer home located at the forks of the Willamette River. Here in July of 1852 a handful of people met to organize this first Church the small town of Eugene was to know. Mr. Harlow became the first Deacon.

In 1857 it was decided to hold services in town and for a time the members met in the "Red Top Tavern" in the hotel owned by Mr. Harlow located where the Osburn now stands. Later they moved to the Cumberland Presbyterian Church which had offered its building for the use of other denominations.

By 1864 the church made plans toward a building of its own but it was not until three years later, in 1867, that the congregation was able to move into the new meeting house. The new Church was first given the name of "The Willamette Forks Church of Jesus Christ." In time the name was changed to the "First Baptist Church of Eugene City." The first minister was R. G. Bond for whose service the church paid the sum of one hundred dollars per annum. There is no record of an increase in pay in all the years he remained but it is reported that he served faithfully and well. During the following years the Church was served by a number of ministers, and as late as 1883 it found itself again without a leader, but this small congregation of ninety members never gave up, and through the years the Baptist Church has held a proud place among churches of the town.

Under the name of "The Morrow Congregation" the Cumberland Presbyterian Church was organized in June of 1853. The first services were held in an old school house on what was later to be known as the prairie farm of Walker Young situated about a mile and a half Northeast of town. Rev. Jacob Gillespie was the first minister. We are told, "He wore home spun pants and shirt—even in the pulpit. He was a fine man and always lived up to his beliefs."

At the end of two years the school house was to be torn down and it became necessary to find another meeting place, so members transferred their services to the Bogart School during the completion of their new building. Mr. Gillespie gave land to the Church and the building was dedicated in 1857. He also presented the Church with a fine bell and the records seem to show that this same generous Mr. Gillespie helped in a substantial way in the building of the Church itself.

Part of the history of St. Mary's Episcopal Church is veiled in obscurity. The first service to be recorded was held by Bishop Scott in the courthouse in 1854. Eugene Skinner's wife Mary was one of its founders, and in the journal kept by the Bishop we read, "By the kindness of Mr. Eugene Skinner one of the proprietors of the townsite we have been presented with an acre of ground for a church." And he also tells us of the final payment of the church debt and of the purchase of more land where later a boys' school was begun "a project dear to the heart of Mr. Skinner."

In 1859 the new church was completed, being erected mainly by the citizens of the town. Rev. Johnson McCormac was placed in charge of the new church where he remained for ten years of faithful, arduous service. At this time the small congregation was raising money for the purchase of what was known as the "Cornelius School property" on the Butte, which consisted of four acres of land with a dwelling house, school house, garden and orchard. From this time on through a number of years St. Mary's was to get along with occasional ministers, though in 1872 a plan was made whereby Eugene was to have regular service on alternate Sundays; and in 1876 Rev. Lemuel Wells established headquarters here.

Between 1880 and 1883 many improvements were made. Sidewalks were built, roof repaired, new and more comfortable seats added. In 1886 Prof. Hawthorne of the State University acted as lay reader until the arrival of the new minister. The next year in the late eighties St. Mary's was organized as a Parish and for the first time in its history was to become an independent church.

In 1889 the corner stone of the new building was laid and that year the Church was consecrated. This new church was made possible by the generosity of Mrs. Hanchett, wife of Dr. Hanchett, the town's first physician. In 1938 the new Church was completed. It is located at Thirteenth and Pearl.

In 1854 in a small farm house at the cross roads of what is now Highway 99 and the Elmira road, was organized the First Methodist Church of Eugene. This farm was the home of Solomon Zumwalt. (In 1934 there was a marker placed at this historic spot and dedicated by a grandson of Mr. Zumwalt.)

In the beginning this Church was served by itinerant preachers. Rev. Noah Starr was the first regular minister. In the late fifties money was raised to build the first Church, and land at the corner of Tenth and Willamette was purchased for the sum of five dollars, "Provided it would always be used for Church purposes." Time seems to have erased that promise. The Church was built in the style of those days, a single room thirty by sixty feet filled with straight uncomfortable benches where faithful worshippers sat long hours listening to sermons of fear, and of promise.

The membership grew until there was a new Church needed, so the old building was sold and moved away, and later used as a school house. We have been told, though we prefer not to believe the story, that "In inglorious glory it went further down hill and was sold again to be used as a stable and eventually, to be torn down and given to college students to be burned at a football rally."

And so, Dust to Dust—those hand hewn timbers that Daniel Christian had made and fashioned into a Church.

Through gifts of money, livestock, farm produce, the sale of the old building AND a rumor of a gift in a certain will (the rumor was proven well founded) the contract for a new Church was given to Will Abrams and Nels Roney (Mr. Roney was later to be the builder of so many of our picturesque covered bridges). The new Church was to cost $5,175; the pulpit thirty, the fine ingrain carpet from wall to wall cost $159.70. The building was in the shape of a maltese cross and the pulpit was of white ash decorated in walnut. In 1886 the new Church bell rang out again for the dedication.

Accounts tell us that the church was paid one dollar a month for ringing the bell to notify the school children of assembly. That the pastor received seven hundred and fifty dollars a year. Four dollars and fifty cents went to the janitor, with an added twenty five cents in case there was an extra meeting. The Presiding Elder, Rev. I. D. Driver was paid one hundred dollars a year. Dr. Driver was a brilliant man who was to become famous all over the country after appearing as a member of a debating team against Robert Ingersoll and Dr. Watt of Montreal. Dwight Moody was Dr. Driver's debating partner and the debate concerned religion in general, Church beliefs, and the authenticity of the Bible. Ingersoll and Watt were badly beaten. Dr. Driver was later offered ten thousand dollars a year to go to Chicago but he refused because "he didn't want to be told what to say."

The day was to come when the Methodists would again outgrow the capacity of their Church building, and so the second one was torn down (to make way for a Theater after all) and in 1913 the new Church was completed. On a fine Sunday morning the members of the congregation, singing the "Hallelujah Chorus" marched in a body from the old church to the new.

A long journey but a proud one from the days of Jason Lee and the Circuit Rider.

Eugene Presbyterian Church was organized in 1855. For the first five years of its existence the Church appears, as far as records can be found, to have had no regular pastor though the names of many appear on the records as having served temporarily. In 1882 a fire occurred which for the time being ended all services there but a year later a new church was built and dedicated in February of 1883. Dr. E. R. Sims was its pastor. The original building was located at the corner of Eighth and Lincoln, later being moved one block west to Lawrence street. Eventually this Church building was to be sold to be used as a Chinese mission.

Frances Willard came here to organize Eugene's first W.C.T.U. The new Church was built on the Pearl Street site in 1908.

In the Lane County courthouse on the corner of Eighth and Oak streets the First Christian Church held their first services. (This was probably as early as 1862) but three years later in 1865 the church was formerly organized by Rev. Gilmore Callison. By the winter of 1868 it had its own meeting house on the north side of Ninth street not far from where Harrison Kincaid opened his newspaper office. This was for years to be known as "The Little Brick Church."

The building was rectangular in shape and carried a very tall steeple of wood. From those early days when the two hundred seats were more than adequate for the congregation the Church has grown until twice they have built new places of worship.

The first of these was completed in 1896, a large three story frame building on the corner of Eleventh and Willamette, but in the year 1911 a second move was necessary. The membership then built the fine Church they now occupy at Oak near Eleventh.

In 1947 St. Mary's Catholic Church celebrated its Diamond jubilee. It was in August, 1887, that Father Beck was appointed the first resident pastor of the Catholic parish. Previous to that year a number of missionary priests had attended to the spiritual needs of the few Catholic families in and near Eugene. Occasionally mass was said in private homes. As the homes became too small for the Catholic groups Father Gibney accepted the offer of the municipal authorities to say Mass in the old courthouse.

In February, 1873, the site at Eleventh and Willamette was purchased from George B. Dorris and in 1886 Father Metayer, who then had charge of the mission, purchased the old Methodist Church and had it moved to the new building site. In March the next year the Sentinel printed the notice, "Repair the Church building, put a fence around the Church property and start a school building next fall if the finances will allow."

Shortly after Father Beck's arrival in Eugene he returned to the Green Bay Diocese of Wisconsin to solicit funds and families for his new mission field, and in February, 1889, the new parish school was opened with seventy students under the guidance of the Benedictine Sisters. Father Beck was succeeded by Father James Black who, in 1896, built the first parish home on the north side of Eleventh Street, between Willamette and Oak. In 1907 the late Father Joseph O'Farrell built a new church at a cost of seven thousand dollars, at Willamette and Eleventh streets. Father John Moran (of Coos Bay) succeeded Father O'Farrell in 1912. During his pastorate he commenced the Catholic High School. Later the Church and school were moved to Eleventh and Lincoln.

In 1927 a contract for a new Church was let and in October of that year the fine new church building at Eleventh and Charnelton was dedicated. The Sisters of Mercy had opened Mercy Hospital and Nurses' training school in 1912. The Sisters of St. Joseph purchased Pacific Hospital in 1926. Sacred Heart Hospital was to be the latest of those established and run by the Catholic Church.

Among the thirty Churches (with their numerous branches) that followed the original five which shared in the life of the pioneer days in Eugene were:

Christian Science   **Unitarian**
Congregational   Temple Beth Israel
Lutheran   **First** Evangelical
Seventh Day Adventist   Light House Temple
Latter Day Saints   **Assembly of God**
Salvation Army

From the days of the Circuit Rider to the days of the Churches, God was here first and will be to the last.

Chapter VI

ONCE UPON A TIME

In the Willamette Valley, from its earliest settlement, trees played an important part. They added to its beauty and to its wealth. They affected its climate. But the trees along the river and on the hillsides were no more important than the family trees, planted in the Far South, Down East and in the old country and transplanted to grow and flourish under Oregon skies in a town so newly built.

Family life was a full one. They farmed, they danced, and went to church: they held meetings, these hot-headed southerners and stubborn Yankees. They bought and sold and bartered: they ran horse races and they studied. They saw floods and fires: and dressed up in frock coats and high silk hats to make New Year's calls. Sometimes they drank too much and had fights. They held fairs and torchlight parades. With little but farsightedness and courage and a pride that is a part of the town they struggled to build and to they built a great University. They held picnics and barn raisings. They went to camp meetings. They loved and were married and they raised children, and when they died they left behind them a spirit leave as a heritage to future generations.

THE vision that Eugene Skinner had on that day in 1846 has more than materialized. So pleasantly did his settlement expand from one cabin and one family to a population of nine hundred in 1864, to three thousand in 1884, that its early families expected it to remain a proper, modest town surrounded by its blue hills and secluded among its trees. They called it a pleasant place to live, easy going and quiet, but soon they began developing its more serious side by giving it good schools, a State University; dignified homes set back upon quarter-block areas in the manner of the times, houses with tall windows and iron grill work upon the roofs and with iron fences enclosing lawns and gardens. They gave it churches, a bank or two, a business block two stories high where farmers could trade potatoes, hides, and poultry for yard goods, seeds, farm implements. They gave it hotels where, along tree-shaded sidewalks, men often sat in comfortable lazy relaxation,

feet upon the rounds of chairs tilted back against the wall as they
discussed the news of the day.

At first it was bound to be stale news, brought by stage coaches
that dashed up to the shade of the huge maples, left passengers
and mail bags, drove around to the livery stable for a change of three
span of horses, then on down the dusty road along the bumping
way to Sacramento or Portland. After awhile the Pony Express
was to speed up the news. Then, excitingly, it came over telegraph
wires. Sometimes after that men scarcely had time to sit at all,
and the sidewalks past the St. Charles hotel were near deserted.

The Telegraph, (which was completed to California in 1861)
reached Eugene on February 14, 1864. On that day Joseph A. Gray,
president of the city council, sent the first dispatch to David Logan,
the mayor of Portland. Celebrations were held all over the state,
since news now could come from the east in twenty-four hours and
the pioneers felt their home folks much closer than at any time
since the first settlements were made.

It seemed no time, we suppose, until there were two blocks
of pavement along Willamette street, between Seventh and Ninth,
and a mule-drawn street car with happy black Wiley at the reins,
who daily, and when he felt like it, traveled the distance from the
railroad station to the University. Mr. Holden, a new resident, late
from Texas, was the builder of that first car system. The story is
told that he had been in town only two hours before he realized
its possibilities, hurried to purchase a block of real estate and two
weeks later had made arrangements with the city to construct a
railway. Sixty days later a line had been completed to cover a distance of three miles. Mr. Holden had imported two street cars from
Texas, along with three brindle mules to power them. In addition
to being proprietor of this railroad system he purchased property
at the southern terminus of the car route on the lower east slope
of College Hill which he fitted up as a pleasure park, to be known
as "City View Park."

We dislike quoting out-of-town papers but feel justified in
doing so if it helps paint a true word picture of "This Place" in
its struggling days. In 1892 the Roseburg Review said:

"Eugene has probably the most unique street car service in America. Whenever the cars are to make a trip the
proprietor advertises the fact several days ahead in the
newspapers, probably so nobody will be left behind when
the bell rings.—He is a Texas man and his imported mule

isn't acclimated yet, so that his sickness during the rainy season (there's that rain again!) causes business in that line to be at a standstill most of the time. The proprietor is also of a thrifty turn and takes outside contracts of excavating sewers and the like, which of course compels him to stop the cars while his mule assists him in carrying out his contract, as he did here on the sewage job last fall."

An early morning walk around the town was a pleasant thing and on such a walk you might have heard, down through the years, the voices of people, calling from cabin doors "Hi Neighbor", or on the campus of the new University "Hello" or from the streets a "Good Morning" to a stranger.

Eugene was a home town. From those first scattered cabins of logs to the fine stately homes on shaded streets, family life was the center of interest, the theme song in a new land, the reason for building and the dream come true.

After the real hardships of the very earliest homeseekers life was fairly comfortable and easy. In the early forties women had cooked over the open fire in great iron kettles hung from "cranes". They had made all the clothing—men's, women's and children's; had washed and carded and spun the yarn for socks and stockings. Sons as well as daughters had knitted socks on long winter evenings, and they knitted by the light from open fires. But there were other nights when they danced all night. Danced until fiddlers and callers were exhausted; and at midnight they stopped for supper, and then danced on until sun-up and breakfast.

By 1849 gold in California had made Oregon a boom state. She was producing much that California needed and could and would pay handsomely for. This meant the beginning of a less frugal time for those in the Oregon country. Especially was the climate conducive to comfortable living even in uncomfortable first houses. As a rule the summers were mild and dry. The winters were mild and wet, though there were those unusual years, as in the winter of 1870 when there was "fine skating on the mill pond" or in 1874 when "wells were frozen up. Seldom, if ever, had there been such bitter cold, snow seven inches deep." And at Christmas that same year: "The weather is beastly but the people are gay!" There were, even in early days, people who didn't think so well of the climate, for, to quote a Eugene paper of the time: "In Oregan it rains every month, but about five times more in the winter months than in the summer months. The winters are wet, cold, dismal and even sorrowful."

The pioneer, Mr. Ed Fronk, said:

"The winters of 1882 and 1884 were the coldest I ever remember. The Mill-race was frozen over and there was several days of skating. I remember they built big bonfires at the end of Seventh street and skated at night. In the winter of 1884 and 1885 was the heaviest snow we ever had here. It was from one to three feet deep and froze over hard enough to hold up a horse. Lee Matlock went on ice skates from Goshen all the way to Portland on top of the snow. The highest flood I ever saw in this part of the valley was in 1882. The river overflowed and came up on Willamette street. We lived where the Armory is now and water got up on our front porch but didn't get in the house. I rode in a skiff at Ninth and Willamette streets."

Apparently the only earthquake was in 1873. It was reported to "have stopped the clocks in Crain's jewelry store and caused a great deal of talk."

The first circus to visit Eugene came by stage route through Jacksonville and Roseburg. The tent was set up at the foot of Skinner's Butte where Manerud and Huntington's wood yard is now. This circus was a one ring affair and was quite an event.

There had been an election in 1864 and J. B. Underwood had been elected president of the council. The trustees were F. B. Dunn, Judge Walton, E. F. Skinner, J. H. McClung, and T. G. Hendricks.

Some improvements were taking place according to the *Journal* of September of that year.

"Two new public wells have just been completed on Ninth Street, one at 'Bristow's Corners'. This famous 'corners' was where the First National Bank is now located. The other well was at the crossing at the southeast corner of McClung's store. Chain pumps have been used in these wells as there are no cisterns in town to furnish water in case of fire. There should be a well on each business corner. However, the City Fathers, or 'common scoundrels' as some persist in calling them, are doing *Very* well and are always *Sure* if they are sometimes a little *Slow*. Before, there had been much complaint that 'nearly all wells in town are dry and travelers need them.'"

Definitely in those days Eugene was an unfinished town. The streets ran water all winter long (when they weren't clogged with mud) and, in the summer time those same streets were deep in a hazing, drifting dust that covered everything in sight. As late as 1875 the papers complained, "The road around Judkins Point is a disgrace to any community and that pine log across it, just this side of Springfield, has been there for two years and shows the narrowness of the Supervisor."

It may be in early days Roseburg didn't like us or perhaps the *Review* was short on news, but whatever it was we feel bound to quote their ideas of our nice busy streets:

> "The mud is as thick as boarding house custard and about the same color. In the middle of winter, horses on main street are not driven faster than a walk in order to prevent the stores from being splattered. Willamette is a pretty street too, and it is a shame that something is not done to remove that quivering sea of mud. The beauty of Eugene's summer streets excites the admiration of every visitor but if they stopped off there the day we were in town they'd leave by the first train of cars."

There were no streets south of Eleventh, and Alder was a country road meandering out toward Spencer's Butte. Travel down the valley was often by boat, on the decks of the old side-wheelers, apt to come to grief in the mud and the shallows, or to be snagged by huge trees along the bank. When a boat was stuck passengers would grab the low tree branches and help pull her across the gravel bar. This travel was seldom for pleasure and often only as far as Harrisburg for items that couldn't be found at home. Sometimes along the way when the boat tied up to the tree shadowed banks waiting for wood to be put aboard, some of the passengers cheered themselves by drinking what was called "BLUE RUIN."

Earliest hint of fall days in Eugene were the wood-piles along its sidewalks. Wood stoves and fireplaces were used for warmth and by September the supplies of four-foot oak and maple were being hauled into town and stacked in cord lots at the edge of board walks. And all through the early fall days the sound of the horse-drawn wood-saw and the good odor of fresh cut wood and new sawdust mingled intoxicatingly with the sharp air, the first rain on the dusty road, and the dampness of fallen maple leaves.

Those trees were priceless things in early days. People appreciated the ones already beautifying the site of their town and where there were none, Patterson's Island across the slough back of the tannery, supplied small ones for the planting. That same Ed Fronk, telling us so factually of early times, said, "My father bought the corner where the Armory now stands and the big maple trees (that were there before the Armory was built) were the very ones my father and I carried on our backs from Patterson's Island and planted."

In the spring of 1877, with progress the program of the city council, it demanded that "lamp posts be placed at the corner of Friendly's, Hendricks', Peters' and Rankin's, and late that same year the *Journal* openly boasted, "There are fifteen hundred people in town. We are climbing! The Millenium is drawing near!"

That same year work was commenced on Hitching Post Square. Prices were getting out of hand. Mrs. Renfrew, then owner of the St. Charles Hotel, raised the price of meals from twenty-five to thirty-five cents. And more depressing news was that the city library was to be closed and "will probably be so for the next winter if other steps are not taken." It wasn't long before the city band was in proud uniform. There was a street sprinkler that added greatly to the comfort of the dusty summer days and there was a free coach running from the Astor House to the depot. Eugene could boast, a newspaper said, "More fine shade trees than any town its size in the valley."

The St. Charles Hotel had several owners or perhaps managers. Ed. Fronk tells us of his family running it in the early eighties when the Fronk family first moved to Eugene. Every old timer remembers when "Grandma Munray" presided over the dining room there. Grandma wore her gray hair in long ringlets that hung to her shoulders. When the curls were pushed back her garnet earrings sparkled, being very real ones. When the dinner hour was over Mrs. Munra would join her charming family and her friends for a visit around the fire. Following the time the Renfrews were managers and owners, the Hoffmans, Jim and Henry, bought the hotel and it became the Hoffman House. The Astor House of the seventies or early eighties became, or had been, the Baker hotel, and was later the quite fine expensive Smeed hotel of the 1900's. At the luxurious Smeed, Sunday dinners were as high as eighty-five cents and a room, if one were choosy, cost two dollars a night.

The first early restaurant to come to town advertised in this questionable manner:

"Come one, come all
Come once, you'll come again
And let your cry be, we're all coming
And when you go, you'll cry Enough."

There were two hotels then. The Renfrew (St. Charles) at the northeast corner of Ninth and Willamette and the Red Top Tavern on Eighth, about where the Osburn now stands, owned by James Heath but later taken over by Mr. Harlow.

When many more years had passed there had appeared the Encore hotel, along with its proprietor, Mr. Gaylord. A strange enough person who each day at train time appeared at the depot, a cane in one hand and a large bell in the other. He tapped his cane along the station platform and rang the bell with all his might as he called over and over again, "ENCORE HOTEL, SECOND HOTEL ON THE RIGHT! ENCORE HOTEL, SECOND HOTEL ON THE RIGHT." And when the trains came to a snorting stop passengers would appear and some of them, like sheep, followed Mr. Gaylord and his clanging bell down the street a block to the "second house on the right" hoping there to find supper and a place to rest.

Churches were important in the lives of pioneer builders. Religion was old fashioned and soul-satisfying. Ministers were God-fearing and outspoken and believed in God and the Devil and in a life to come. And it was a fine thing, people said, to have such a faith. Each argued the points of his own particular church, deeply loyal to his own choice, for, as the years passed and the Circuit Rider became a memory, denominations drew apart to choose independent roads to Heaven.

That road was not always a matter of denomination—at least in the case of one opportunist whose business was window washing. He was an expert in his line and in great demand by individuals as well as by the churches, but he wearied of trying to keep the windows of the Methodist Church clean under a roof that leaked badly; so he switched his bucket, along with his faith, to the Presbyterians who had just put on a new roof.

In pioneering days wives were helpmates without pay or allowance or share in worldly wealth. If a wife had a dowry from home so much the better. And it was fortunate for the men that in settlement of the valley, laws allowed equal acreage to husband

and wife when they staked out donation claims. When, and if, the land was later sold there is no record of the wife having received her financial share from the sale of the acreage acquired in her name.

Homemaking duties came early in the lives of the pioneers. Girls married at sixteen or seventeen and at twenty most young men had assumed the responsibilities of a family. They married for better, or for worse, as it sometimes turned out to be. If women were unhappy about married life they nevertheless put up with it as a rule, and the men, liking it or not, did likewise, except in a few reported cases where some "lost" their way in the gold fields and never returned. If we listen to rumors we are told of a case or two where a woman went off with some other's straying husband, but since gossip was no more to be depended on then than now rumors must remain rumors.

When it came to moral standards within the family, women were what they themselves termed "straight-laced." Men liked their women that way and were not, under usual circumstances, inclined to stray away from the home roof.

The town's females of questionable virtues dressed the part and could easily be distinguished from the ladies of the city, who passed them by with averted eyes and skirts held aside.

In later years when the male-female population had somewhat evened by the arrival of more women in the valley, there seemed to be a growing feeling of independence among the men. Notices began to appear in the weekly issues of the paper, "This is to warn all persons against harboring or trusting my wife as I will pay no more of her bills", (under a signature of the 1868 paper). And in the same issue we see among the comments, "For a man who has been ruined by woman there is no law or judge," and the Editor shows clearly his own ire by stating openly, "I am glad to receive marriage notices, but request that they be sent in soon after the ceremony and before divorce is applied for. I have had several notices spoiled that way."

So there were beginning to be rare cases of divorce and in the natural course of events there was a certain amount of scandal whispered about, handed down in one way or another, usually with names omitted. A few stories even came to life in print, and made amusing reading; but left the reader with a feeling that somehow something had been lost in the telling, as in this unfinished item: "A young man had spoken slightingly of a young lady of the highest respectability. She heard of it and, mounting her horse to go and chastise the slanderer, she found him, and while inflicting the punishment he so justly deserved, she fell from her horse and was slightly injured. We withhold names out of respect for one of the parties." By such means the talk may have been hushed so that folks could go calmly back to their store keeping, their plowing; to oyster suppers in the St. Charles hotel and their New Year's calls; or summer rides around the race track in the park.

The health of the town was no great worry. People became ill—or they didn't. They survived—or they didn't. Dr. Hanchett was the first doctor in town. He must have been a man then past middle age for he was described as having "very white hair." His medicine consisted of castor oil, liniment, Dover's powders, and quinine, and he said that he "could cure a cold in two weeks and God could cure it in a fortnight." Honest old Dr. Hanchett! He cured many things with the early day "cupping" treatment, an unpleasant sight but not too painful, as remembered by the older generation. Those same old people by choice "stuck to" their porous plasters. Almost all wore them for backache.

When later more doctors came to set up offices they had to travel long distances to care for patients. Dr. Tom Harris and Dr. Shelton were two of these, as was Dr. Sharples. Once, when a rider in search of a doctor stopped in front of a store in Springfield to water his lathering horse the owner of the store said to him, "What's the matter?" and the excited rider, galloping away, called back, "Pa broke a leg and I'm goin' for the doc!" Whereupon the merchant yelled after him, "Get Doc Owsley! Owsley owes me and I owe you. Get Doc Owsley!"

There was one dentist, the first, by name of Caldwell who pulled teeth with a "Turn-key" but no further description of its horrors could be found. Dentists were quite reasonable according to the advertisements of Dr. Russ who came along some time later.

"Set of teeth, in rubber—$12.00
Set of teeth, in celluloid—$10.00
Gold fillings—$2.00
Silver fillings—$1.00
Extraction, with gas—$1.00; without—50 cents
Office hours—all hours"

Situations did, however, improve with time. In 1876 the *Oregon State Journal* carried this: "All persons who have undergone the painful operation of having teeth extracted are of course interested in all the comforts that pertain thereto. Dr. Frank Welch, being of a compassionate nature accordingly has sent for an "Archer's Chair" to give an easy position while in your misery."

To counteract the misery of toothache and dentists, people were thoroughly enjoying the new fad of having their pictures taken. Mr. J. A. Winter (in 1869) one of Eugene's most popular and highly successful photographers advertised:

> "NEW DISCOVERY: Know all men, women, young ladies and boys, J. A. Winter has perfected a process by which he can take pictures without showing the freckles. This is a distinction sought for in vain for a long time. Come along in before the roads get too bad to travel."

There were no undertakers in those early days. Neighbor women "sat up" with the dead and the neighbor men came along also to aid and for protection. This was a task no neighbor could have wanted, but no neighbor shirked. In the deep of winter storms, in a setting of eerie candlelight and oil lamps, with creaking floors and few conveniences, preparing the dead for burial and comforting the bereaved family was one pioneer task which exacted the most from its doer. To bolster sad hearts and tired bodies, there was always plenty of food cooked in the house or brought in by neighbors, and a big pot of coffee on the hot kitchen stove or beside the fireplace.

The Old Settler was fortunate in that first cabin with its dirt floor for he thus escaped one of the most unpleasant things about early day family life. Spring house cleaning! It was a curseful time for the men folks. They had to take up the heavy carpets, carry out the now dusty straw from underneath them, and then beat and beat the heavy "Brussels" until there wasn't a sign of dirt left in it. After it was done the men sometimes left home to "attend to business" while the women went on alone to complete the task of cleaning windows, washing curtains, putting a shine on the brass kettle beside the fire. With these things finished peace settled down for another year and with a clean start.

In time some fine houses appeared along the streets of the town—homes that for years to come were to be the center of family life. Dr. Shelton's fine mansion, now the McMurphey home, on the south slope of Skinner's Butte, to this day looks down in great dignity over a town that spreads out wide across the valley and climbs to the surrounding hills. Judge Walton's home was on the banks of the Mill-Race, "the slough", that in early days crossed the town and was crossed in turn by two wooden bridges. Still standing is the original Johnson home, the "President's House", it was called, at the northwest corner of Fifth and Lawrence Streets. President Johnson was the first to head the new University and another University professor, E. B. McElroy's home was on the next corner.

With its tall arched windows reaching from floor to ceiling, the J. L. Page home, still to be admired, was one of the popular ones in town. It stands on the northeast corner of Seventh and Washington. Another is the quaint home built for Mr. and Mrs. A. V. Peters, now located at 1611 Lincoln Street. There for years to come Mrs. Peters was to receive her callers on New Year's Day. Mrs. Peters loved cats, and as time passed the tall fir trees in her garden shaded the graves of her many pets. At 330 West Seventh Street is the fine old home of A. G. Hovey, our first banker.

There was the William Preston first home, which stood on the Southwest corner of Fifth and Pearl Streets. In that house, later on was to live the small boy, Sam Simpson, who grew up to be the poet who wrote the famous and much loved "Beautiful Willamette." Mrs. Preston remembers when the house was in the very outskirts of the town and when water stood below it the year around affording young couples boating in the summer and sometimes skating in the winter. That, she said, was "when Willamette Street had only board sidewalks and many trees."

In those days when home made ice cream was plentiful, made in hand-turned freezers, the ice was cut from Stowell's Pond or from the Mill Race where Eighth Street crosses.

Mrs. Preston remembers when the courthouse was moved so that Eighth Street could be opened—that first courthouse with its white fence and the "stile" that crossed it into the courtyard, and where right in front of it stood the pitcher pump with the regulation tomato can to drink from. When she was ten years old she came with her father from twenty miles away to see it. "It was a long trip the way the roads were, and it took almost all day, but I wanted more than anything to see the Courthouse. My grandpa had made the mill-sash for it. We stayed all night at Renfrew's Hotel and the next day it took all day to drive home again. We always counted on three days for the twenty-mile trip. I remember Carrie Rankin's store. There was positively never another one like it! Those beaded bonnets, the feathers, the plumes and the flowers that somehow never made their way out into the world, were still there, boxed up tight, as far back as I can remember." Miss Carrie in her long gored skirt which swept the old splintered floor, and her high lace collar that rose behind her ears, would get the boxes out for you if she was "a mind to" but, if she wasn't, there just wasn't a thing she could show you. Mrs. Preston told us about their original house that had moved one door south so that they could build a fine new one "while they were young". Searching through her scrap book she went on: "Those cards? Why they are the ones the gentlemen left when they came calling on New Year's Day. Handsome, aren't they? The men always looked handsome too in their high hats and their long-tailed coats. Your papa, and Will Abrams and John Church and Elmer Cleaver and Ben and George Dorris. William Stowall came and J. C. Judkins, Charlie Lauer, Mark Bailey and a lot of them. C. C. Croner came along with Tom Hendricks and David Cherry and Mr. Friendly. I can't remember them all. Ladies along? My goodness no. We stayed home and served them things to eat and drink."

We mentioned that some one had said the gentlemen sometimes rode quite high on coffee. She laughed.

"A few of them drank coffee", she admitted, "but coffee was just the same then as now, and so were people."

There was a bright fire in Mrs. Preston's fireplace, and it reflected warmly on the first piano ever brought to Eugene—a handsome rosewood square grand bought by Judge Walton for his daughter, Iula, and shipped across the Isthmus then far north to Eugene.

Mrs. E. J. Frasier met us at the door of the house the highway has tried to push away from East Broadway. She was not worried, except when they cut her maple trees.

"I miss the trees," she said. "I brought them from out on the Coburg road and planted them there before my girls were born. But nobody is interested in that." We were, but there were other things. Questions. "Eugene was the oddest town I'd ever seen," she told us. "I came here in 1892 and I couldn't get women to talk about themselves. They seemed ingrown; and I love to know all about people! I'd been living in California where it was different." Recognizing her deep-south ancestry we suggested that her yen to hear all about uncles and aunts was the South coming out in her.

She laughed a little. "I wonder. The first social upheaval in town was Mrs. Chapman, President Chapman's wife. She dared to wear heavy shoes right into the best homes while other women wore rubbers and took them off from dainty shoes. Mrs. Minnie Washburn and Mrs. Laura Harris were the two most interested in politics. Mrs. Peters called on me. She was French, you know."

That was the cute Mrs. Peters with the glass eye, whose yard was a cat cemetery. "I was so dressed up when I returned her call—I remember exactly what I had on, but I don't know why. My dress was black surah silk with a puff all around the hem, and a train. My hat had pink chrysanthemums and violets on it, and chantilly lace that came off the back in a cascade and fastened with a beautiful pin on the front of my dress." A plumb pretty picture to anyone remembering Mrs. Frasier through a part of those years! "When I went up the little path between the cinnamon pinks I held up my train."

With our everlasting craving to know more about the Peters we heard of Mrs. Peters' charm, and of Mr. Peters' interest in art and music. "He had only one eye, too," Mrs. Frasier said, and we all fell to wondering about that. "Someone told Mrs. Peters it was sad that they hadn't been able to afford clapboards on their house, but must use battens instead. She was very frank. She told me, laughing, that she and Mr. Peters had gone to great lengths to manage battens, which they both preferred."

Another old timer, Miss Whiteaker, remembers little about the town before she came here to the University, because, as she reminded us, her home was too far away for the family to see Eugene more than once a year. Her father remained on his farm through the years of his term as first governor of Oregon. "There was no state house, and no need to be away for anything but the legislature," she explained. The Whiteakers lived in Portland for a time, while their home was being built in Eugene.

"Did you ever hear of the Union Club?" we wanted to know.

She looked surprised. "Never."

"Your father was a good Democrat, so he wouldn't have belonged to it."

"That's right," she said, and we told her then that we kept running onto the statement that Governor Whiteaker issued a proclamation for secession. "He didn't as far as I know," she told us. "He was rabid about freeing the negro without sending him back to Africa, though. He was afraid of the future."

Miss Ann was cooking fine-smelling venison for her supper.

From one old timer came the reminiscent story of the "McGibbeny" family.

Woodsheds, barns and "backhouses" were as much a part of community equipment as were many more aesthetic things. The last mentioned but popular building was often in early days made more endurable by bright reading material, and in Eugene at least, by a particularly large and handsome lithograph entitled "Mrs. McGibbeny of the McGibbeny Family Telling the Story to the Little Ones." The picture was a good three feet square, making a cozy looking door to gaze upon in idle moments. In the handsome group were Mrs. McGibbeny and her five—or was it seven?—lovely children.

The McGibbenys were a charming family of touring musicians who often stopped in town to give concerts, and Eugene grew so fond of them that once when the show business hadn't been doing so well the town gave a benefit. A lengthy notice in the paper exhorted the townsfolk to come out and do their bit for the "popular, talented and charming family."

Since we are quoting early residents, there is Lester Hulin who has delved much into the history of the valley. Mr. Hulin cleared up one or two disputed points for us. "Leonora Skinner was surely the first white child born in Lane County," he said, "not the Spores child. And Judge Risdon's home was the first in Eugene. Mr. Walling says the first house 'after the location' was probably the Spencer Rogers home, on the later Joel Ware property."

We were glad to have that explained, since Mr. Walling had seemed to refute his own statement concerning the Risdon's first house. Asked about Dr. I. D. Driver, Mr. Hulin grew excited;

He was the smartest man the county ever saw. He believed that no man need forget anything he ever learned. Dr. Driver completely finished off Robert Ingersoll in a week!

Dr. Patterson's home was another fine one. And not far from the Preston's was the finest house in town, the elegant home of the Underwoods (he who was the town council's first president) where the charm and beauty of the three daughters made it a gay and popular meeting place for the younger generation.

The S. H. Friendly and the George B. Dorris homes on Willamette near Tenth were both famous for their hospitality. The Charles Lauer house was one of the largest, and stood across from the Underwood home on north Willamette. The Dr. T. W. Harris home and that of S. B. Eakin were the proud owners of windmills. Mrs. Harris told us, in a pleasant afternoon of remembering, that "on the warm summer days people came from all over town to look at and enjoy the fine cool green lawns and gardens."

Behind other houses, on an alley between Fourteenth and Fifteenth streets, near Pearl, there still stands the quaint house once owned by "Doc Owsley." Its lines are more graceful than those of houses built after the "eighties", and its Monterey balcony once looked down on the west sidewalk on Willamette street, between Tenth and Eleventh.

There was the early Hendricks' home built on the northwest corner of Ninth and Charnelton streets, a neighborhood to be known for years as the "Four Corners." The other houses soon to be built there were the Marion Wilkins home, the S. D. Holt's, the Horace Crain's. Quiet, dignified homes built on the "square" of what is now Broadway and Charnelton. They were the center of much that was the happy early life of the town. Now all are gone except in memories, and the "Four Corners" house a parking lot, a filling station, a public market and a grocery store.

Eugene liked her days of celebration and July Fourth was one of the best. Along with religion these pioneers took their freedom and their politics seriously. Some had been members of the "Union Club", that secret wartime organization, and though they were far from the realities of that bitter struggle, many of them were of the South and strong and firm in their convictions "fur" and "agin" slavery.

In those days one Fourth of July was much like another. On such a day, in the early morning when the sun had burned off the cool blanket of fog that hung over the valley, every street was filled with excitement. People were out early dressed up and waiting for the day to begin. Flags waved from housetops. Small girls in starched dresses with red, white and blue sashes sat on the edge of the board sidewalks looking longingly down the street where the parade would pass.

There was the sound of distant music, tramping, thrilling, martial music as the band swung into sight hunting its place in line. There were four military companies in the parade that marched so gaily down the dusty street. There was the proud Eugene City Infantry. The Lancaster Cavalry from down the valley and the McKenzie Light Horse Cavalry. And that perhaps is more of a varied military display than we could turn out in our present day parades.

What a sight it must have been! Flags snapping in the breeze. "Hurrahs" filling the air! The "Battle Hymn of the Republic" echoing and re-echoing against the hillside where the Old Settler had first sensed the freedom of the valley. The Fourth of July salute

was fired from an anvil on the top of Skinner's Butte. Horses
galloped down the main street raising clouds of dust to cling to the
hot faces and sticky hands of children following along as best they
could. Flags were presented to military companies and responded
to by volleys fired by the infantry.

The parade over, the whole town went to the grove near the
river. Here the women presided over long tables set in the cool
shade of the trees. When every one had been fed there was an hour
of fervid speechmaking and it has been told by an eye witness
that when the day was over many of the men went to the saloons
to finish the celebration, while the weary women and crying children went to the stores where they waited for their men, and from
where, later on, the horses took them safely home.

Horse racing was popular. On holidays and sometimes on Sunday, (though that was frowned upon by the Churches) there were
races. From children, riding their ponies bareback, racing down
the road to school, these men had grown up to love fine horses
and the sport of contest. But on the streets of the town fast riding
was frowned upon, and in 1867 the "danger was so great" that a
new law was passed prohibiting "more than six miles an hour on
our city streets." "Every day drivers and riders go at a breakneck
speed. Where IS our Marshall", wailed the *Journal*. Where indeed
was he? And where is he today, as "Hot Rods" filled with youngsters,
restless business men homeward bound, and touring motorists tear
through our city at a speed that would part the very whiskers of
the old pioneers dared they raise their heads.

Runaways were frequent and often serious, many times fatal.
Almost every issue of the paper told of at least one such occurrence.
We read of one on a June day when "A team broke loose at 'Bristow's
Corners', ran as far as the stage barn and up Eighth street to the
fence around the public square, and tore to pieces a buggy tied up
there." Of "one party whose team ran away on the dangerous
McKenzie road throwing them all over the cliff, killing a child,
breaking a leg of one of the ladies of the party, injuring all concerned." But the item went on to state that the "fishing was very
good at the end of the trip" and, a week later, "There were only
two runaways on Monday. A farmer in town whose horses took a
dash around the block, and Vich Behvens dray horse, not to be
outdone by a team from the country, started out and mowed down
nearly all the signs and awnings as far as Bristow's."

Some years later a "Gentlemen's Driving Club" was organized.
The members owned many fine blooded horses and Dr. Tom Harris,

with a group of his driving friends, built a halfmile track and grandstand for their own use, and on racing day all were out early hitching a favorite horse to a sulky. For the racing, as for the New Year's calls, the men were properly dressed. They wore linen dusters and cloth caps pulled down low to shade their eyes and gauntlet gloves that grasped the best whip money could buy. With these pearl or ivory handled whips held threateningly over the backs of horses, drivers headed west of town to the track that lay among a forest of tall evergreen trees. Later on there was the Huddleston track in the same location to be followed by the one at Merriaus Park on the River Road near what is now Santa Clara, for many years a favorite place for picnics and dancing as well as for racing.

Most homes had their own barns where men kept their horses, but there were many who patronized the livery stables, the town already boasting two fine ones. One of these which became famous among storytellers was owned by "Jack-Ass" Brown. He had imported jack-asses from Kentucky for breeding. Great consternation arose when a gentleman and his wife, who ran a select boarding-house nearby for young ladies, discovered the intention of Mr. J. A. Brown. These people complained to the city fathers, who, rather hesitatingly passed on the complaint to the owner. They asked that he stop the breeding business. And Mr. Brown, a husky red-faced man, declared that he was "mad as tophit!" and roared at them, "Gentlemen, as soon as I heerd them folks didn't like it I built me a high board fence, and they still didn't like it and so I built a higher one. But, so help me God, when Mrs. B's girls insist on a-climbing to the attic to look over I give up. I can't keep on buildin' higher."

If there was one thing the people in the valley loved more than another it was a fair. Any kind of a fair pleased them because it was something the town folks and the country folks could get together on and they did—often. The west park block had a round bandstand in the center of it and the band used to give concerts there sometimes in the summer evenings. The first few County Fairs were held there too and during that time there were barbecues, where great quantities of fine meat were cooked to a turn in long pits dug in the ground. There nowadays the games of horseshoe pitching go on.

In 1881 a meeting was held in the courthouse for the purpose of discussing the plans for holding a fair. A committee was appointed to look into the advisability of such an organization and, it seems, in no time at all and with very little opposition the first

"Agriculture Society" was formed and one hundred shares at twenty-five dollars each were sold. The second hundred was expected to be "easily secured" and an option was taken on a tract of land a short distance from town. Optimism was reflected in an editorial in the paper stating, "It is not likely that the State Fair will be held at Salem many years longer and when we have suitable conveniences we may ask for it and expect it at Eugene." But there followed many years of uncertainty and no fairs. It was much later that Mr. E. M. Warren, Amos, Jasper and Marion Wilkins took an option on a tract of land owned by "Jim" Huddleston, which they held until the town was ready to go ahead with its plan and the County Fair was eventually established as a regular and important part of community activities. That Huddleston tract is its present site. Until their own fairs were under way Eugene and the county continued to be satisfied with the State Fair at Salem.

Before State Fair time came people talked about it for days. The mother of the family sewed from morning until night getting the children's clothes ready, for this was the last real vacation before school. If "Pa" were a member of the Fair Board he was a privileged man with his own cabin inside the grounds. That made for fine visiting among all his family who gathered there, and it also made a daily entrance fee unnecessary and left many dimes and nickels to be spent on other things. If "Pa" were not a board member his family camped in its tents outside the gate.

Fair week, perhaps the most exciting and upsetting event valley towns experienced from one year's end to another, found a family up before daylight on a September morning. Children were on their best strained behavior in mortal fear of being left behind—a fear that ended only with the actual start from home. We can picture them making ready to go. On the quiet streets lights are still burning because it is long before the first suggestion of sunrise from over the eastern hills. Lighted candles or coal oil lamps flit from room to room or burn in the window of the kitchen where food is being packed. These Fair-goers carried with them everything they would need for the entire week of camping. Flour, sugar, rice, coffee, with dried fruit for pies and home-made jams and jellies, home-baked bread, fried and roasted chickens, baked ham, cakes, and always the big coffee pot and the syrup keg went along.

There was bedding to be packed, and a small cook stove, and, if the weather held in the way of a rainless week, the stove was set up outside the cabin or tent, and there meals were cooked out in the open and in plain sight of those hurrying along the path to the Fair buildings. Some old-timers can and still do talk about those meals, when, as children, they lay huddled under patchwork quilts waiting for the call to breakfast as they watched the smoke from frying bacon drifting up through the leaves of the oak trees beyond an open door. After breakfast in the crisp air of the fall morning the youngsters departed in every direction, dimes and nickles held close in nervous hands, and the day stretched away ahead of them like a path of dreams.

They weren't seen again until hunger drove them home at dusk. Then, almost before darkness settled down they were fed and tumbled into bed to sleep the pleasant exhausted sleep of children until another day came and the sun streamed into the cabin.

Camp beds were made of straw stuffed into bed ticks, then the deep filled beds were laid on the straw covered floor. Long ropes were stretched from end to end of the cabin or tent like a ridge pole, with cross ropes from side to side from which were hung long calico curtains, so that each family group might have its own private sleeping space easily arranged according to its size, one bed, two beds or three beds. For "Pa's" big family, State Fair was reunion time. From farm and town they were together this one week in the year.

A man spent the mornings around the stock pens, in the machine sheds, or among the farm exhibits, proud to strutting when he found a blue ribbon or even a red one on his own five-foot grain or grasses or on a favorite fat hog in the pens. In the afternoon this horse-loving lot of men naturally drifted toward the race track. Women did their share to make the fair a success and loved it as much as did the men. They baked and sewed and painted. They made patchwork quilts and were no less proud than the men when they too won prizes. At least one Eugene baby who celebrated her first birthday at the fair was cold all the week long while her best little coat and bonnet hung proudly on the wall in the main pavilion with a wide blue ribbon pinned to its satin streamers.

Old and young loved their fair. To the last days of memory they talked about it.

Eugene knew one early day custom that was most unpopular with the women and children, and, since the men took up the subject and passed a law about it perhaps they themselves didn't approve. It seems there was far too much bell ringing going on! There was a satisfying significance to the Sunday morning Church bell they said, and the fire bell was an excitement to be enjoyed

THE FIRST CITY COUNCIL AND MAYOR, THEN CALLED
THE BOARD OF TRUSTEES AND THE PRESIDENT, 1864:

1. J.B. Underwood, President
2. F. P. Dunn
3. Eugene F. Skinner
4. W. T. Osburn
5. C. C. Croner
6. J. H. McClung
7. T. G. Hendricks

OVERVIEW OF EUGENE, LITHOGRAPH, CA. 1890

as long as the sparks didn't light on a man's own roof. It was the tolling of that same bell that bothered them.

And what a custom it was! The bell was tolled dismally for every death in town, one note for each year the deceased had lived, and so, knowing the age of almost everybody, one could imagine with horror whose death had occurred.

There was a time when fires were too frequent even for the most enthusiastic fire-goer to enjoy and the City Council offered a reward of "one hundred dollars for the arrest and conviction of any person committing or attempting to commit arson within the city limits," a fund was created and a committee was appointed to "select and buy a hand engine, a hose cart and hose for the fire department not to cost more than $2500." The committe appeared at the county court asking "that a lease be given to the city for fifty years at the price of one dollar per year to keep the sidewalks and streets adjacent to said lot at all times in good repair." The city also to "build a cistern at the corner of Eighth and Oak streets of sufficient capacity to be of utility in case the buildings should at any time be on fire."

Until this time fires were fought in the best way that seemed handy at the moment. There was a family living out on the slope of Skinners' Butte who had emptied the straw from a bed when somehow the straw took fire. They didn't have any luck that day fighting the fire because the hero of the hour, starting from Willamette street with two buckets of water "found the slough so high in the north part of town that he experienced great difficulty in getting over without emptying his buckets."

George Midgley's partner in the planing mill was Will Disinger who was a member of the fire department. There was a rule that if any member was in town and didn't go to the fire when the bell rang he would be fined one dollar. One day Disinger was hunting out on College Hill. He heard the fire bell but he was out of the city limits and he figured the fire would be out anyway before he could get there so he kept on hunting. When he got back to town he learned it was his planing mill that had been on fire.

By the early eighties there were three fire companies. All had hand pulled carts, no uniforms, but bright red helmets and hand axes. Old timers tell of the "big fire", as near as memory recalls, about 1883. Fire broke out near the Astor House on Willamette street, where the Smeed now stands. There was a brisk mid-morning breeze and the hand pumps were manned as quickly as possible but the fire swept southward while men and boys pumped until exhausted. A group of young rowdies suddenly thought of the Chinese laundries. There was "Him's" down the street and beside it another, so both small shops were raided for Chinese who came running with pig-tails flying to pump as they protested. But in spite of drafted aid the fire destroyed a part of the business district.

The most spectacular fire was the burning of Dr. Shelton's "castle" on the south slope of Skinner's Butte. The house had not yet been completed and there was a rumor that it had been set by a jealous builder.

In other homes, like the Sheltons', whose locations have been lost with the passing of time, were carried on many of the traditions of early Eugene life. One of these was that charming custom of New Year's calls. Fancy seeing the gentlemen on a January first, a day of snow and blustering winds, or it might have been a day of clear, crisp sunshine. They gathered in groups soon after noon in the St. Charles hotel to wait for the hour of calling to begin. They were dressed properly for such an event in long frock coats and with tall hats of beaver or of silk, and many carried goldheaded canes. As they talked and waited to start they smiled from under well-waxed mustaches or from behind full wide whiskers or romantic sideburns. The crowns of their tall hats were deep and straight-sided and shining as a flock of wet seals. The vests under the long coats were of silk brocade in black, or plush in golden brown or green, and across the fronts of the vests watch chains dangled, often with gold nuggets adding to the glory of them.

Wives had remained at home to receive their guests. The callers arrived in twos or tens or alone, and were welcomed graciously, leaving high hats and canes upon the bed in the company bedroom or on the sofa in the long hallway, and they strolled from parlor to parlor, eating and drinking and paying compliments. The ladies were dressed elegantly, too, in "tea gowns" of "surrah" satin or brocade or velvet in fine rich colors of dark green, red, or plum—gowns with small trains and with lace ruffled sleeves, worn with broaches and earrings and bracelets of jet or garnet or of gold. And all during the afternoon each hostess served graciously and generously wonderful food of salads and cakes and eggnog, and it has been said by some attending that when calling ended on New Year's Day, "the sun went down on a happier and gayer 'Upper Crust' than had been seen since New Year's a year back."

A fine old custom lost with the years.

Those were full days. Women cooked, ironed, churned, spent

long hours with their children, sewed—sometimes on fine embroidery—and there was painting too, which every woman tried a little on silk and velvet, on tin and canvas. "Hired girls" were the rule in many homes, and sometimes they ate "at table." Along with home tending there were outside diversions.

There was Lane's Opera House. It had been Lane's Hall when it was first built in 1869. Its original form was a simple hall with benches; its location the north side of Eighth street west of Willamette. Rinehart's Hall was at the corner of Ninth and Oak streets and was built in 1884, with its formal opening on the Fourth of July in that year. In the early nineties it was rebuilt as an exciting real "theater", red velvet curtains, boxes, etc., and the *Journal* of that summer, "It was a most successful venture when Clara Morris appeared with her excellent company in '*Renee de Morey*'. The house was filled at one dollar and fifty cents each and it was a financial success even for a place of this size and was one of the best entertainments ever given in Eugene." And after the play was over many of the enchanted audience went next door to "Pool's Ice Cream Parlor" for that fine plate of oysters at twenty-five cents.

In that same theater they saw John Drew in *Rosemary*. They saw Shakespearean plays. Olga Nethersole came; and there were the Boston String Players and many other fine things, as well as Wizard Oil and Minstrel shows. Eugene saw fine plays because traveling companies made it a one night stop to break the long trip between Portland and San Francisco.

We are informed by the notices and advertisements in the early papers that people were reading the *London Times, The Illustrated Weekly, Country Gentleman, Godey's Lady's Book*, San Francisco's *Overland Monthly* of which Mark Twain and Bret Hart were editors. They were reading Dickens and Washington Irving, Scott, George Eliot and Hawthorne as well as the popular "subscription books" which agents were selling, such as *Everyman His Own Lawyer, History of the Secret Service, Bancroft's Map of the Pacific States.*

In the later days women lecturers were a popular form of entertainment. At least they were numerous, and often reported in the paper as having lectured in the Courthouse. Often those same papers cut short their reports to the dissatisfaction of many readers. "Mrs. Logan gave her lecture, full of spice and poetry on 'The relations man sustains to women, legally, socially and morally'."

Good living was pleasantly cheap in early days and it is interesting to compare prices in the Sixties with those of the present

time. Potatoes were sixty cents a bushel, butter fifteen cents a pound
and eggs were the same a dozen. You could buy a DOZEN chickens
for two dollars and a quarter. Beef cost six to ten cents a pound,
pork fifteen and mutton, honestly called such, was to be had for
ten cents. Strawberries were plentiful at nine cents a pound and
"Arctic Soda" was something new as Mr. Robinson now advertised
that he was "Serving in the best possible style ice cream and 'Arctic
Soda' at his confectionery stand, a truly pleasant place these warm
evenings."

There were plenty of places to spend money, even a small
amount of it. The general stores carried an assorted collection
of merchandise and there were also special stores. Sam Ashley made
fine harness at his shop. There were feed and grain and hardware
stores. Mr. Belshaw, one of the first druggists in town, paid his
helper fifteen dollars a month and the young man needed it for
he had to pay eight of that for house rent. Later that same young
Marion Wilkins was to open his own drugstore. There for many
years Dr. Shelton and Dr. T. W. Harris, two of Eugene's earliest
and best loved family doctors, were to make their headquarters.
In that drugstore there was often free candy for youngsters, and
there was blackberry cordial for the doctors after a long cold ride
into the country to set a broken leg or perhaps "born" a new
citizen.

Behind every butcher shop was a smoke house, though many
people did their own butchering and "curing". It was a real deal,
to travel out to the country, get a fat "porker" and in one's own
woodshed cut the animal up, hanging sides of meat to the rafters
above a smouldering oak fire. The remainder was put down in
brine for winter's use.

For local news everybody subscribed to the Portland *Oregonian*
and the *Oregon State Journal* which Harrison Kincaid was publishing in his small office on Ninth street. One permanent "Ad"
carried by the *Journal* promised "Anyone owing the paper can pay
in good oak, ash, or maple wood."

Though there were seldom any hot days, valley people went
to Florence or to Newport to escape the rare ones that might come
—or just to escape. There, with chattering teeth and blue lips, they
bathed in the icy waters of the Pacific, and reveled in feasts of fine
sea food, rock oysters, giant crabs and deep sea flounder and tom
cod. Newport had its home talent shows and dances, its campfires
on the beach, candy pulls at the Ocean House, with singing in the
moonlight; and each summer there was a contest to see who could

gain the most weight. Curves were liked then and were worth fighting for! Sometimes families went instead to the mountain "Springs", famous resorts for tourists and invalids. A hack or stage was run from Eugene up the McKenzie to "Belknap" Springs and to "Foley". The driver (an expert, he said) was S. S. Pepiot and he "guaranteed a safe trip from town in sixteen hours."

Down through the years as the town grew, outlying districts changed little. Farmers still got up before daylight, hitched teams by the glow from swinging lanterns and drove into town with produce to sell or barter. The women went along to do their buying and to visit friends until the lamplighter came at dusk to light the street lamps. The women had often to wait for their husbands who liked to stop for a game of horseshoe pitching in "Hitching Post Square." Horses and teams waited too, pawing in the dust, their tails switching flies as they stood tied nose to nose along the fence inclosing the square.

A hundred years have passed and Hitching Post Square has changed. Dusty cars and shining ones are parked, and overparked beside meter machines. The only horse rack left is a special one for the mounts of the police officers. Willamette street is a blaze of neon lights reflecting like rainbows in the shining wet pavement. And the many cross streets are filled with hustling, bustling activity. "This Place" has grown—may one day be a great city, but it will always be a Home town.

PART TWO

Chapter VII

LAW AND DISORDER

On March 18, 1876, John Quincy Adams Brown, escaping from a thoroughly inadequate jail, left this parting letter to pay respects to his jailers: "Eugene, Lane Co. Oregon March 12 I am agoin to git out of this if I kin I dont do this for any ill will to anybody but because I can't git any money to defend myself this is the first crime ever I done and it will be the last if I aint coat I think I have been here long enuf for what I done I have no ill will at any one in town they all treted me well I leve my sincer regards for you for ben so kind to me while in jale S. B. and C. H. and if I ant coat I wont let whisky git me in jale agin."

So he unscrewed the bolts on the door, and walked out.

THE little Leonora Skinner, first white child born in Eugene and Lane county, had scarcely doffed her swaddling clothes when law and order began to move into the new township of Eugene City.

Perhaps she even had to move out of her cradle to clear a spot, for the polling place was Skinner's cabin in that spring of 1849.

Word had gone round that the United States Congress had officially recognized Oregon Territory, had organized a government for it, and that the people themselves were to elect a delegate to Congress, so excitement ran high. There were mighty few men to vote, most of the really able-bodied having hit the California mining country, but every man eligible was there to proudly cast his ballot. Twelve or fifteen in all they were, from the county of Lane, which then contained part of the present Benton county.

Rather quickly following that early election, as we have already seen, the first courts were formed and the very first bits of legal business were transacted within the new town.

Mr. John T. Gilfrey was the first county judge in Lane county, doing business, we suppose, in one of the tiny cubbyholes of the raw little street, and later assuming his legal dignity in the shiny newness of the courthouse. There again records are meager, but things did happen and one of the first items we note is a poll tax of $1.50 passed in about 1855 or earlier—which was later reduced to one dollar, so that voting was less expensive than at first. Let us look into the archives a moment and discover the names of those men who served on our first grand jury and so were charged with the legal tasks of the first court term: Gideon Richardson, Thomas Hinton, Steven Jenkins, Henry Owens, Parker Byran, Joseph Bailey, W. H. Brice, Wm. McCabe, Wm. McCall, James Hendricks, Thomas Clark, James Robertson, Milton Riggs, "Old Man" Gay, G. B. Hayes, Samuel Zumwalt, Thos. Cady, R. E. Harper, Wm. M. Stevens, Cornelius Hill, W. A. Masterson, Presley and C. Morris.

It is said on good authority that the first actual account of a crime in the town limits appeared in 1861. This was the stoning to death of aged Hugh Feeney by Mat Bledsoe, a ruffian of the day. Bledsoe first felled his victim with a well-aimed sling shot, then stoned him about the head until he died. The brutal and violent killing occurred on the main street, and by some quirk of mistaken identity a William Crowley was accused by the court and sent up for life imprisonment.

Many crimes, of course, were the results of long-abiding feuds, dating perhaps from trying months crossing the plains under bitter hardships. Some were family troubles and personal hatreds, but whatever the cause, out-and-out murder seemed to be the quickest answer, and the law of the land held. Over a period of twenty-two years, eleven cold-blooded murders were known of in the county which must have been drama enough for even the most rugged— and a source of fear and terror to the lonely women and children.

Incorporation, first talked in 1862, stirred much argument. Eugene had not grown up enough to take on the dignity of "civic honors" some said, and besides, incorporation would mean more taxes. The *State Republican* held this point of view:

> Some of our citizens are striving to have Eugene City incorporated. Their reasons for their move is that they wish to banish the common nuisances, hogs and grog-shops. . . . We would suggest that the whiskey shops can be abolished by cutting off the southern portion of the precinct which extends away out into Africa. . . . As to maintaining a city government merely to get rid of a few old sows . . . that would be a very expensive way of accomplishing a small amount of good. . . . There are always persons in every little village anxious to have it a city, and they are . . . successful in getting the towns incorporated before they have . . . population or wealth to maintain a city government.

In spite of these sentiments the town did make itself an incorporated city on October 17th, 1862. In no time at all she had decided that she wished to change her name to the City of Eugene, and on October the 22nd, 1864, she voted the adoption of the new name, and in November a new charter, making new boundaries. But there was small interest shown in the matter. There were twenty-seven votes for and one against the new charter. The town's boundaries at this time are worth noting. The northeast corner was about where Fourth street and "the slough" came together. The line ran west along the south side of Fourth street to where Olive intersected, then south to the south side of Fifth street and along that line westward to take in the area as far as Elias Stewart's farm, or about to our Lawrence street. From there the line ran south to a point "eight chains south of the south boundary of the town plat", then eastward "to Gardiner's" and north to the east bank of the millrace, and so along the millrace to the point of beginning. In 1876 the southwest corner ran as far as about Thirteenth and Lawrence as we know our present streets, and stretched a little eastward to take in "Doc Patterson's barn," (near Alder street) and north to the railroad, along the railroad to the west line of Ferry street, and "west to the tailrace." In other words, it eliminated some portion of the original plat of the town, but ran further west and south than that first plat.

The first President of the Council was J. B. Underwood, with these members of that council: J. H. McClung, F. B. Dunn, C. C. Croner, Wm. T. Osburn and T. G. Hendricks.

The *Oregon State Journal* began publishing under that title soon, and we read in its columns that a petition signed by many citizens repealed the three-mill tax to pay for a watchman; that, in June of 1869 the "Eugene Water Ditch Co." was incorporated for the purpose of "bringing a ditch of water into town from a point on the river two and one half miles above this place." Shares at $250 each. "When completed it will be," said the *Journal,* "of great value to the place for manufacturing as well as irrigation." This is a little confusing, since five years earlier the new town boundary chart had swung from "slough" to "millrace." Under whatever name, it at least had water in it, which is more than we can lay claim to in 1948.

Now that Eugene had a water supply she went in for fire protection, organizing teams of volunteers to pull small carts, and such equipment, added to the watering troughs of which there were at least two on the main street, made citizens feel quite secure. The

City Hall was new, with its own tower and a firebell, and if you were not a volunteer in a fireman's hat still you could hurry into the frightening melee of flaming roof, shouting men and barking dogs.

A great many of the old county court records are handwritten and still in the courthouse, but a large number of the city records proper were destroyed in one of the numerous fires which plagued early days.

Indians from many tribes and many areas were a common sight from the first, their colorful and quaint garb contrasted against the drab wooden buildings and the dusty streets. Squaws, braves, maidens and papooses from the Siletz (from the coast area) and the Grande Ronde (Eastern Oregon) tribes were so plentiful as to be a nuisance at times, and in 1871 a petition went to the council praying for the removal of Indians from the streets and stating they were a detriment to youthful morals.

'Way back in 1874, the little woman was rising up and talking about her rights. Certainly they had earned the right to talk, standing beside their men and raising their families through the thick of immigration hardships, claim-proving, and rigorous pioneer living. So in April of that year, a brief newspaper story relates that a meeting for the cause of women's suffrage was held in the courthouse with a large number of people attending. "Mrs. Perkins, Mrs. Hanchett and Mrs. Jennings addressed the meeting and there was much enthusiasm."

An interesting law case of early days was known as the Harris vs. Burr test case. The suit was brought by the plaintiff, against Eugene, to test whether women could be prevented from voting for school director. The case was finally taken to the Supreme court, where it was decided in favor of the women.

Probably the earliest law suit important to the whole town was that brought to determine ownership of a 34-foot strip surrounding the present park blocks. In brief, a history of the case was this: Charnel Mulligan's claim was immediately south of Eugene Skinner's and bordered on what is now the south side of Eighth street. When time came for voting on location of the county seat, both men offered tracts of land should Eugene be chosen; and when it was chosen, they both deeded the promised land, which shows in old maps as "Skinner's donation to Lane county" and "Mulligan's Donation to Lane county." When these tracts were platted, they showed the parks, and the streets bordering the parks were called Park street, their width to be 100 feet. This made the lots on Main street only 126 feet deep rather than the regular 160, so all the stores backing on Park street took their extra 34 feet by erecting woodsheds on the outer edge of the street. A lawsuit to determine ownership of the 34 feet was decided in favor of the county. And they promptly deeded it back to the private owners. Hence the narrowness of Park street.

Very naturally, many of the game laws passed were a long time in coming, since wild life of all kinds was so plentiful as to be troublesome to crops, and the many predatory animals threatened early settlers' meager supply of livestock. Consequently not until about 1888 do we find the killing of grouse, partridge, quail and pheasant prohibited, and the closed season ran from January to July, only.

Female deer were protected from November to August, while the male had protection only until July. Open season on duck and swan ran from September to May. Horn and Paine seem to have owned the most popular "Sportsmen's Emporium", and their advertisement claimed that guns would be loaned and ammunition furnished.

The nature of that particular store makes us suspect it may have been quite a gathering spot for the boys, since Virgil Johnson, son of President Johnson of the University, once wrote, "Many stories used to float around the University regarding the stern discipline administered by the first president. In fact, little that ever happened passed his watchful eye, so that students used to wonder at father's sources of information. My own private theory was that he always secured a good deal of information regarding the pranks of students from the little group of Eugene citizens who used to gather in the rear of Horn and Paine's Gun Store to swap yarns of hunting and fishing. This was really Eugene's first club——" Wonderful, nostalgic, long-lost days of abounding deer and bear and winged creatures, of red-hot stoves, of cracker barrels, of creaking leather and sturdy buckskin, and a faithful horse tethered outside!

Of lynchings there were plenty around the nearby county when men took law into their own hands, but the first legal hanging in Lane county took place on May 12, 1899 when one Claude Branton paid the penalty for murder. One lynching took place practically under the eyes of a marshal had there been one about, when a convenient maple tree beside the St. Charles hotel was used for stringing up a man who had shot the sheriff. Many troubles and hates were settled by old fashioned fisticuffs and "wrassling", and we read with amusement that some of the bitterest rivalries and hates arose over the horse races of those days. There was a murder near the present Country club golf course, called the "Potato Patch" murder.

Many fines were levied for selling liquor without a license, or on a Sunday, which was also an illegal day for grocery stores to remain open. Livestock was a precious and costly commodity, and the malicious killing of a neighbor's horse extracted $50 in penalty from one violator. "Assault with intent to kill" seems to have been open to several interpretations and was accordingly frequently used in complaints. Even the loser in a duel might proclaim such a charge, obtain a conviction, and so save his reputation as well as his own skin. Men of the law were sparsely scattered about the wide-open spaces of a broad valley, however, and if any culprit managed to get out of town he was very apt to go free.

After schools became well-established, a truant law went into effect—but its effect sometimes took hold in strange places. One instance on record relates the story of a thoroughly irate husband whose wife was threatened by the law. On the point of starting a lawsuit over it he sputtered "the doggoned old fool of an officer wanted to get the wife took to school." Questioned further, he explained why she hadn't gone—"When you *sent* the notice she was fifteen years old; when she *got* it she was sixteen, and my wife, by cracky!"

One item of great interest is not connected directly with the local laws of early times, but is a little-known fact about the present Oregon laws. The original "Oregon code" was enacted in 1853, during Territorial days, and those first books were bound in New York City. When the time came for shipping them into this far-west country, two hundred copies were sent across the Isthmus of Panama and arrived safely after their long journey. The remainder were shipped around the Horn, presumably lost in one of the terrific storms which always made the seas journey so hazardous, and never reached their destination. The '53 code is extremely rare, and the University of Oregon law library has but one copy, presented by Judge Lawrence T. Harris. Next came the code of 1855 which was something of a stopgap to fill out lacking supplies, and the next full state code was set up in 1862. Meanwhile, the Territorial legislature authorized Lafayette Rhodes to gather up and complete the writing of all records of meetings or any other matter pertaining to government and this document was called the "Archives of Oregon." It is extremely old and valuable, holds records not to be found anywhere else, and is also among the price-less volumes in the law library.

Although the Oregon Territory was dry when it came under provisional government in 1848, it did not remain so for long. Dis-tilled spirits were very important to the pioneers, and in hundreds of emergencies that life-giving stimulant was all the medicine they had.

The lighter side of life was perhaps uppermost in the minds of Eugene City's fathers, however, when before too many years they legalized a distillery for a license fee of $1600 per year. Located in the northeast part of town (which would be within the original few blocks platted) the distillery boasted of the most "modern" equipment, turned out the goodly sum of 1800 gallons of head-aches, health and cheer each month, and its product was considered a class A article. Since it netted approximately $900 each month, its $12,000 annual revenue to the county equalled all other sources of income put together.

Results must not have been too bad, however, for in March of the '78-'79 year we find record of only fifteen arrests, twelve for drunkenness and three for assault, not excessive for a frontier com-munity it would seem.

That same year a law was passed to tax dogs within the city limits one dollar; and the "marshal" as he was called, could collect and sell goods and chattels from all those with unpaid taxes. Laws were soon passed prohibiting the sale of liquor to students, for-bidding minors under eighteen to loiter or assemble on the streets at night, posting rewards for arrest of arsonists, and organizing a fire department to man the brand-new, shiny red Button model hose cart. An ordinance had been passed declaring laundries a public nuisance when located in blocks seven, eight, eleven and twelve of Skinner's and Mulligan's donations.

B. F. Dorris, president of the city council in 1876, wrote this in his annual report:

> Within the last month, complaints have been made to me against the marshal for non-performance of duty in permitting the hogs belonging to the mill company to run at large. I have long since discovered that it is much easier to find fault with an officer than it is to perform his duties. The difficulties of the marshal in this case are not well un-derstood. While the law makes it his duty to take up certain animals found running at large, it also contemplates some

provision in the way of a pound to put them into and
none has been made, so if censure is deserved, and I think
it is, it should attach to the council and not to the marshal.
In order to obviate the recurrence of this complaint and
meet another want greatly felt, I would suggest that permission be obtained of the county court to inclose the
block fronting the jail, this inclosure to be used as a
pound, and also by farmers when they come to town with
their wagons. By this provision we would prevent animals
running at large and the farmer from the depredations of
the herds of cows that swarm through our streets from
one year's end to another. If we will not prevent cows
from running at large, justice demands protection to the
farmer.

Two months later a novel resolution was passed in the council:

Whereas it having become a universal custom to toll
the courthouse or public bell on the death of any or all
persons, even in the silent hours of the night, and even
when others are languishing on sick beds, when every
stroke of the bell causes a shock to their weak nerves, and
in many instances is a serious injury to them, to say
nothing of the many timid women and children who
experienced terrible feelings at the tolling of the bell; therefore be it *Resolved,* That the tolling of the bell at the death
of a person is a custom unknown anywhere else, except on
extraordinary occasions, and we condemn the practice.

It is easy for a lively imagination to conjure up the feeling
that gruesome night sound must have given the sick and lonely,
and how great the terror of the children must have been. Even
considering the whole idea from the vantage point of 1948, one
feels somehow grateful to the author of such a humane resolution.

With the war at hand, the deep-seated feeling between pro-
and anti-slavery forces again came to sharp notice, with the passing
of a law which forbade those citizens engaged in a rebellion to cast
their votes. At about the same time regulations were laid upon
"hurdy-gurdy dance houses" requiring a monthly license fee of
fifty dollars, and it became a punishable offense to adulterate gold
dust. Convicts were encouraged toward good behavior, Indians
and half-breeds were forbidden to run at large and a law was passed

COVERED BRIDGE, BLUE RIVER, 1905

WILLAMETTE STREET, LOOKING NORTH,
POSSIBLY EARLIEST KNOWN PHOTOGRAPH OF EUGENE, 1867

making the acts of county clerks valid. One of the strange laws passed as the new town and county developed was that permitting a man to take up 160 acres of swamp land, provided he would sign an affidavit declaring he had gone over it in a boat. Inevitably it led to land frauds, and one man who swore he had gone over practically dry land in a red skiff was long known as the Swamp Angel— his skiff had been mounted on a wagon.

Judge Risdon was probably the first lawyer in Eugene, receiving his license to practice at the first convening of the district court. In addition to the already mentioned Mr. Gilfrey, others soon came and in 1869 the new law firm of Underwood and Fitch was announced. From items noted the following year, this seems to have been timely. For instance, under the heading of: Let Us Have Peace: "Sheriff Meador has deputized nearly all of a large band of Indians camping near town to assist him in maintaining order. They will receive fifty cents apiece for every arrest they make." Then: "There is someone in town who is in the habit of laying down fences and letting stock into grain fields near town. The individual is being watched and may have opposition in business if he continues;" and in 1872, the *Oregon State Journal* made these terse comments: "Eugene is becoming a fast place; there is more gambling than ever before; men, intoxicated, can't navigate a six foot sidewalk; laws are not being enforced."

One of the most faithful of the town's drinkers walked right off the Willamette river bridge one day and dropped onto a bed of heavy boulders. There he lay, until some kindly passersby hauled him up with ropes and he walked off, unscathed and still very, very pleased with life.

It seems to be the case that Linn county laws as well as those of other surrounding counties were more rigidly enforced than our own. The old saying, commonly quoted in early days, tells a tale: "If I had you in Lane county I'd shoot you." It was a poor place to let someone cherishing a hate catch up with you.

Another very early lawyer to locate in Eugene was Hon. John M. Thompson of the firm of Thompson and Bean. He was active throughout many years and later became a regent of the University, of which he was always a most loyal supporter. The firm was one of the most prominent in the new state. Within a short time others came, and in 1877 Eugene City could spread her legal business around among seven lawyers.

Pioneers have been accorded the attribute of having been good, practical State builders, well qualified to govern themselves; and furthermore, they had practical means of finding out what the populace wanted and of carrying out those wants. If the common laws were a bit rugged it seemed a good thing for that day—perhaps, who can say, for any day. But the statute laws were wise and just for the most part, and have proven themselves so through the years.

In the olden days of the law profession in Eugene there were others, too. Men like Judge J. J. Walton, George B. Dorris, Lark Bilyeu, all of whom came here before 1885. In five more years E. O. Potter had arrived. Shortly after that came the quaint person of A. C. Woodcock—kindly, uncommunicative. During the last years of his career, he was often a little mellow as he meandered back and forth from his office. His worn old hat might be a bit awry, but underneath it his rosy face always wore a half smile, and his mind and wit were like a steel trap.

The year 1895 marked a beginning for one of Eugene's most distinguished law careers—that of Judge G. F. Skipworth. After studying in his brother's law office, the young barrister passed the Oregon Bar in that year and came at once to Eugene and was soon made deputy district attorney which post he held for four years. A turn at the city attorneyship was his next step, and following that he was appointed judge of the Circuit Court of the Second Judicial District, which place of honor he has held since that time. Known throughout the state as well as in his own district as an impartial administrator and an authority on law, he has likewise a reputation as a hard taskmaster which has made him one of the most respected judges ever to serve in Oregon. He brooks no carelessness from attorneys, jurors or others involved in the law, and demands smooth procedures in his court. Interested in civic affairs as well as the moral tone of the community, one of his finest contributions to Eugene and the state at large has been his deep interest in helping to lead youthful offenders away from institutional reform and into a path of useful, honest, and worthwhile citizenship.

Three years later there was to return to Eugene, a shining new law degree from the University of Michigan tucked in his pocket, another man who would wield broad influence throughout the state—Lawrence T. Harris. Born in Albany, young Harris had been educated in the public schools of Eugene, and had graduated from the University in 1893. After a brief period of law practice here, he was appointed circuit judge of the Second Judicial District, embracing Coos, Curry, Douglas, Lane, Benton and Lincoln counties, and upon serving out that term was nominated (by both parties) for a second term and, later on, a third term. Beginning in 1915, he served for ten years as an associate justice of the state Supreme Court. He had served Lane county in the state legislature in 1901 and 1903, and as speaker of the house during the latter term. Possessed of a fine legal mind, throughout his years of law in Eugene he has established a reputation for unswerving honesty and fairness which have won him an enviable place of honor throughout the state.

With A. A. Skinner of the earliest years, George M. Miller in the '80's, and Judge C. A. Wintermeier of the late 1890's we close a half-century of professional life on a new frontier.

Some ten or twelve precincts had been established by law in the town at this period, and by 1881 we read that "everything is quite peaceful and civilized." Business was mostly done by the barter and trade system so robbery was a minor vice in the good old days. Most citizens were good citizens and peaceful relationships seemed to be a large aim of their lives. As someone once wrote of the western settlement, "there is something in the freshness, freedom, and expansion of a new country that enlarges and intensifies human sympathy. The pioneers were notably kind and generous to each other." Marital infidelity was rare, divorce almost unknown in those early days in the valley, and observance of the golden rule was widespread as the result of their rigorous self-discipline and toil.

There are some seventy attorneys listed for Eugene in the present time, but rapid growth of the area indicates quite definitely that soon many more expert trial and litigation lawyers will find their way to a county which comprises as many square miles as Delaware, Connecticut and Rhode Island combined, and the big politics of which have barely found their beginnings.

The Chinook wind ruffled bright autumn leaves, and from far down the valley the siren of a long yellow Diesel echoed through the foothills and over Ya-po'-ah. Seems like living's getting more and more complicated, the Old Settler thought. The more folks, the more laws. Some good, some bad. Seems like a body don't get along with neighbors if things come too easy. Good folks down there, though, through the years. Town's spread out some more; trees coming all over the hills now. It's almost another century, he thought. And wondered.

Chapter VIII

PIONEER POLITICS

Just as the Willamette valley was the first part of the Oregon country to attract settlers because of its equable climate and fertile soil, so it was the first place to feel the pull of political parties and loyalties, because of that population. By 1856 what is now western Oregon was so fully occupied by the great donation land claims that the most desirable lands were taken. Eastern Oregon population was almost nothing, and there were as yet no permanent settlers in the distant fringe of land called by the Indians "Ee-dah-how" (Idaho) which was Shoshone for "the sun coming down the mountain at sunrise." There was not even a school around the Puget Sound part of Oregon Territory, save one small private institution at Olympia. Settlements spread from the valley to the remainder of this northwest.

And while we speak of "Willamette", it is interesting to note that the first known application of that name to the great river was made by a David Thompson in the year 1811. Six years later the same spelling is found on a map prepared by William Rector, U. S. surveyor, and Peter Skene Ogden uses it in his journal. In other places the spelling appears as everything from Wilarbet to Walla Matta and Wahlamath, and for many years the controversy raged over our lovely valley and its gently rolling river.

POLITICS "as she is played" started in the new Territory the moment Joseph Lane was made its first governor and arrived from Indiana, and has been making a name for itself since that day.

Only the first few isolated years had passed by when strong feeling growing between North and South began to manifest itself and men discussed their convictions openly. The "Long Tom Confederacy" as it was called by the old timers, waxed eloquent in the cause of the South, and serious troubles might easily have arisen out there had not organized troops quickly put down any uprisings. This hotbed of rebellion took in all the small settlements along the old Territorial road to the west, comprising what is now Smithfield, Franklin and all nearby areas.

At one time the Confederate flag was raised there, and a group of the more rabid supporters headed by John Mulkey came swaggering into town offering to fight any so-and-so who didn't like it. Several men showed up who definitely didn't like it, and a militia officer spirited the southern enthusiast off across the ferry to Coburg, (in a buggy accompanied by Judge Risdon, Mr. Pengra and Mr. Underwood) and thence to Vancouver Barracks for safe keeping. They took the long way round to avoid a group of shooting Democrats awaiting them on the northern road out of town, but the Long Tommers called it a "dirty Yankee trick" and used up their bullets until government troops from Vancouver arrived with a small cannon and quelled the trouble.

All political activities for many years had their background in the pro- and anti-slavery movements, but the general majority of the new Territory residents were opposed to slavery and to secession. This fact alone proves how free-thinking were the pioneers, since by far the greater numbers had come either from the southern states, or were from families whose roots were deep in the southland. Many had close relatives fighting as Confederates when the war finally broke. There was great discussion among the young bloods, many of whom chafed to get into the fray on their chosen side. But the great prairies and mountains stretched between them and the battlefields and lay as a forbidding barrier which brought terror to even young hearts. All in all, the cause must have seemed rather far away to most families, concerned with making a good life in a wild new country.

In actuality, politics surrounding the slavery question had held up governmental recognition of Oregon's cries for a government of her own. We read in a letter from Sen. Thomas H. Benton of Missouri, (who had for thirty years loyally supported claims and needs of the far western area) to Mr. Shively, one of three new officials appointed to maintain order in the northwest, under the date of March 1847: "The house of representatives, as early as the middle of January, had passed the bill to give you a territorial government and in that bill had sanctioned and legalized your provisional organic act, one of the clauses of which forever prohibited the existence of slavery in Oregon. An amendment from the senate's committee to which this bill was referred, proposed to abrogate that prohibition, and in the delays and vexations to which that amendment gave rise, the whole bill was laid upon the table and lost for the session. . . . But do not be alarmed or desperate. You will not be outlawed for not admitting slavery. . . . A home agitation, for election and disunion purposes, is all that is intended by thrusting this firebrand question into your bill; and, at the next session, when it is thrust in again, we will scourge it out! and pass your bill as it ought to be. . . ."

Most prominent among the Democrats living near Eugene was John M. Whiteaker, farmer and stock raiser of the valley. After the Territorial government had been at long last established and it was found after ten years a ripe time to change to a sovereign state government, the Democratic forces rallied round this honest farmer and he was elected to be the first governor of Oregon. Many authors have reminisced at length, and attempted to evaluate Governor Whiteaker. Some have remembered him as the fiery presiding officer of a Democratic convention, who laid his big gold watch and high hat on the table and opened the convention with a mighty bang of his gold headed cane; some have remembered him as having been deeply sympathetic with the southern cause and the idea of secession.

But most have remembered him as the honest farmer, the man who loved the outdoors with its hunting and fishing, who believed one hundred per cent in the Democratic party and states' rights, who kept a negro man on his farm, who displayed a fiery temper on occasion,—and who made a good governor for the newest state of Oregon. In looks, Governor Whiteaker had rather wide set, questioning eyes, sparse hair which shows white in most of the pictures available, and a fringe of whiskers and mustache completely surrounding his face. H. R. Kincaid recalls, in his memoirs, the alleged Thanksgiving proclamation issued by the Governor, which he turned into something of a protest against Yankee institutions. He also recalls that the gentleman enjoyed a bit of old fashioned "snakebite" on his outdoor expeditions; and that once during his term in Congress he chartered a locomotive in Sacramento in order to reach Washington quickly and aid in organizing the Democratic contingent in the lower house. Some historians feel that his sentiments became more mellow as time passed and war wounds healed.

Born in Indiana in 1820, the young John Whiteaker went to California to seek gold in 1849 but returned to his first interest of farming when he came back to Oregon in 1852 with his wife, after serving as captain of the wagon train of that year. His political service to Oregon was long and loyal, and when he died in 1902, one of the interesting figures of valley history had disappeared.

Anti-slavery agitation and pro-slavery propaganda were more important in Eugene and the valley than in many other areas, because we find there was "actual and well-grounded fear that an attempt would be made to effect the secession of the Pacific Coast States", according to Hon. T. T. Geer, author of "Fifty Years in Oregon." Many people in the new state were openly anxious for a Southern victory. Governor Whiteaker himself did not like the Union meetings which were constantly held all over the state, for he seems to have believed in the divine right of slavery and therefore in the cause of the secessionists. His address in the first year of the war intimated that Oregon would not join in the war on the South, in which premise he was right so far as active fighting went.

Elections, no matter what the issue, always roused great partisanship in Eugene, and existing newspapers were always filled with sly digs at the opposing side. This is a typical one: "A large, half-starved hound came down on Friday's train bearing a tag with this inscription 'One of Tilden's supporters looking for office.'"

And this: "Ben Hayden has put on a clean shirt and started out speechmaking. He is a model Democratic orator and is doubtless after a nomination. Ben's chances we think are slim and he is apt to be slaughtered this time, as heretofore."

Eugene City reached a state of great excitement over the approaching visit of President Rutherford B. Hayes, and party wheelhorses dusted off their best silk hats and gathered 'round to lend support.

Considering how far away from the capitol the west coast was, it is interesting to note the great tributes paid the two martyred presidents. To quote: "On Wednesday, April 19, 1865, the day of the late President Lincoln's obsequies, Judge Stratton adjourned the circuit court which was then in session; the business houses were draped in deep mourning; the bells tolled and a profound gloom seemed to overshadow the land. At one o'clock a large impromptu meeting was held at the courthouse, Dr. Hanchett presiding.—The ceremonies are described as the most solemn and impressive ever witnessed in the community." Sixteen years later a like ceremony was observed following the assassination of President Garfield. At that time it was written that "no party spirit arose to mar the ceremonies, and all was the result of a holy spirit to honor the memory of a noble man."

Politicians were frequently dressy in those days, but among the really dapper figures of the time was Mr. Sherwood Burr, a gentleman of the South but an avowed Republican. For many years he was a prominent political figure, always meticulously dressed in his pearl-colored spats, top hat, and cane. He remained in the office of county clerk for a long period of time, trading votes around as was the custom of the day—or perhaps any day. Political leaders made definite attempts to keep politics clean; and simple, straightforward vote-trading seemed one means of keeping things out in the open.

Every man who was willing to step out from the furrow behind his plow, or away from the fences he was always having to repair, found a ready call for his services in the political and business developments of his chosen town. So it would be utterly impossible to list all of those who held a prominent place in the commonwealth's growth. One of the oldest and most far-seeing pioneers in Eugene, questioned some years ago as to who was who in Oregon answered quickly "the pioneers who settled it, who saved this country for the United States; who established its statehood and who set up the original laws of its constitution—." And so it is with the city of Eugene. Those early day men who were its councils, courts, mayors, school superintendents, commissioners, legislators and public servants in general are the ones who led the way and to whom we do honor.

The Old Settler shook himself, and blinked a canny eye at the goings on. Politics, ho-hum—wasn't much of it when I left, he thought. Folks are wasting a mighty lot of breath, telling the other fellow how to drive his oxen. A mighty lot of breath without much doing. Some folks are doers, some folks are sitters, he thought; some folks like to hoe their corn and find it good, and sound and right, when the harvest time comes and winter sets in. Then some folks don't seem to bother if it's small, and no good and right wormy, so long as other folks hoe it and feed it to them and their bellies are full to busting. Everybody's got to be broke to double harness, he said to himself; everybody ought to pull a little share going over the scariest part of the trail. Seems like mostly they forget where we aimed, he thought. Politics—hmmm. And he tried to remember what it was like in the past, and to see what it would be like in the future, but he could not.

WILLAMETTE STREET, LOOKING SOUTH FROM BETWEEN 6TH & 7TH, CA. 1910

GIRLS ON TRICYCLES IN FRONT OF T.G. HENDRICKS' HOUSE
northwest corner of Charnelton and 9th (Broadway), ca. 1890

Chapter IX

THE LAND AND THE TREES

That black walnut? Yes, it was planted the year Eugene began. There's a gnarled cherry tree over on Sixth street that was a switch when the first frame house went up. That oak was big and old when the old settler came along. Maples like this one mark a pioneer path from here north across two rivers. And do you see that redwood? That one reaching high above all the rest? It was planted in 1882, and topped back twice. And it's a hundred and fifty feet high if it's an inch. God grows trees big in this country. And man——

You say you can't see those trees? Not even after I've pointed them out? Well, let me finish my sentence. God grows trees big, but man cuts them down.

LONG before man, this valley of the Willamette was a vast ocean, one with the Pacific ocean that we know. In those geological eons that ordinary man can scarcely imagine, the earth's crust "up-folded" in a great line north and south, parallel to our coast line. This ledge, high and then higher through the ages, is our Cascade Mountain range in all its rugged beauty. Followed its building-up, another age-long period of "quiet", and then much the same up-lifting occurred further to the westward, in the north and south line that came to be our Coast Range. Each, as it grew, blocked off portions of the ocean, holding it prisoner inland.

Dr. Thomas Condon, that factual, clear-minded geologist who pioneered to Oregon as a missionary in the state's very young days, knew its geological patterns and knew how to make those patterns readable for the simple layman. He named the inland sea that had covered the great area held between the two mountain ranges "Willamette Sound", and likened it to the Puget Sound of Washington state. Each had, he said, its high, rugged, surrounding mountains with their snow-capped peaks—Puget Sound its Mt. Rainier, Mt. Adams, Mt. Baker, the Olympics; Willamette Sound its Mt. Hood, Mt. Jefferson, Mt. Mazama, The Three Sisters. There was one difference of vast import. Puget Sound had no Columbia River. Where the ocean waters and the Columbia met, the waterway of the river was wide and long and deep—deep. Glacial flood waters from the Cascades and the Rocky Mountains advanced toward the

81

ocean beaches, which were much higher than now; these flood
waters were pushed back, until the Columbia and Willamette val-
leys were floors beneath seas whose waters rode high above the
cities of today.

Each up-folding of the earth's surface left, Dr. Condon wrote,
corresponding troughs. Such a trough was the line of the Willamette valley. Coming to periods of volcanic activity, erosion, rain,
snow, the picture is more real. We can visualize the ages of "trough
drainage", with rivers beginning to cut their ways down from mountain sides, through the still wet high lands and low, until the valley
floor lay in the sun, drying itself through those periods that geologists know. Upon some of that floor lay in deep places the fine,
granite-laden, rich silt of the ages. It is now soil of many kinds. Our
valley is a map of these prairie lands, some of them quite priceless
in this time, but some not so fertile.

Very soon it became evident that not all of the Willamette
Valley was good land. Veins of gravel and of yellow clay ran underneath parts of its surface like destructive moles. Low land, where
white and blue forget-me-nots thrived, was cracked swale at certain
times of the year. More technical terms explain some of these soils,
but under any name they mean poor land for cultivation. It was
just as well, the first landowners said, that their claims were wide;
and they moved from swale to prairie and from clay to hillside
slope where orchards and gardens thrived.

For the valley's prairie lands were mellow. Low, rolling hills
were easy of cultivation. River bottom was rich, black soil that lent
itself to such crops as potatoes, beans, peas, hops; higher lands
were, after a few years, beginning to yield the finest apples, plums,
pears, cherries. Filbert orchards and walnuts of a special strain
have in later times taken the place of some hop yards. And always,
there lies the land rich for many kinds of grain.

Mr. Walling, writing a full history of Lane County in 1884,
declared Lane County land plentiful, and actually not too high at
five to fifty dollars an acre! Because, he said, its real value was
proved in assured fine yearly crops. That hop land, berry land,
orchard and wheat land now brings a thousand or two thousand
dollars an acre, say real estate men; and a city building lot costs,
in this chin-up period, from seven to fifteen hundred dollars, with
choice lots running and jumping upward to two or three thousand.
A dim echo of the day old church members recall when the town
sold, from the goodness of its heart and the heart of its main street,
building sites for churches at five dollars a lot.

Eugene has been proud, and different, and envied because of her trees. They line old streets, particularly in the western portion of the town—great maples, black walnut and English walnut trees, locust, Carolina poplars, cutleaf birch; an occasional tall old fir or cedar. There are silver maples that were here when the place was young; and now, on newer streets, bright leaved plum and Norway maples color dark days. There are some Lombardy poplars which, it must be admitted, make trouble for walks and pavement, but they grow well along the strips of poorer soil. Sadly enough, the town has had an epidemic of tree cutting in its effort to be grown-up. Business, say those experts who know about such things, cannot thrive where there is a tree. And so, while anxious middle-westerners carry water in buckets to their drouth stricken Chinese elms, and while even Los Angeles adds trees to its main thorough-fares, Eugene would seem to be attempting a raw look.

Long ago the young maples by the St. Charles hotel gave shade to the tipped-back chairs of men who didn't feel that a maple tree can be ruinous to business, men who knew what the beauty of a city could mean. Naturally, no one wishes to go back to a tipped chair and the St. Charles hotel any more than one would welcome old Wiley and the mule-drawn streetcars, or a six-man fire cart, or streets deep in mud. But our trees need not all go tumbling in the name of progress. Those that came from our founders and builders as our most precious heritage are disappearing. You can hear them crashing down many streets. The pioneer path that they marked could have been cherished; and some day, when we have grown old and high and broad enough to appreciate dignity and age we might have looked up through their branches at the sky and the future and the past, and we might have said, "Smart, wasn't it, to put a fence around an old timer like that and save it? Says here it was planted in 1850. Hm. . . . This is two thousand and forty-five. Makes it a good hundred and ninety-five years old. It could have been that men sat under its shade to talk about Lee's surrender, and the first airplane, and the new atomic bomb." And we might have been glad that its shade was still there.

It is even now, as it was in 1888 when Eugene's *Oregon State Journal* fought against the unnecessary cutting of an honored old oak at the corner of Ninth street and Pearl. "It had stood for a hundred years," said the *Journal's* editor, Mr. Kincaid, "and it might have stood for another hundred years to beautify our town."

There was a man who, as park board member and president for thirty years, and as earlier school board member, instigated the planting of rows of trees, and then did battle to save them. Pioneer school yards, and now other school grounds, are shaded because of him; many of our spreading maples and walnuts and evergreens, defended over a period of years, still beautify our streets because of him. With deep pride, we, his daughters, acknowledge the debt of Eugene to Marion Wilkins, who fathered its trees.

Chapter X

CAME SEPTEMBER

The pattern small red schoolhouse never found Eugene. "Select schools" soon dotted the new town and children of every age, from very young to too old, paddled through the mud and rain or kicked through the leaves when school bells were rung. Academies and private high schools followed the first tiny select schools, all, taken together, amounting to a prophecy. They distinctly showed the way the twig of the town would be bent. The people who believed in them and sent their children to be taught in them were a type to whom educational advantages were a must—would always be a must.

Already these builders were glimpsing ahead a university, perhaps not consciously in the beginning, but a dim blueprint was there, and in those years when the private and select schools were emerging in odd places, the foundations of a broad educational structure were being laid. The cornerstone was the district school, but the first spindling pillars and steps, the first bright glass windows through which the future shone, were those private schools.

THE hand of the Old Settler had barely sworn to the validity of the town's first survey and plat when Miss Sarah Ann Moore opened a "select school" at a place designated as "point of the hills", on land of the Fielding McMurry donation claim. The spot was presumably near the present Masonic cemetery, and rattlesnakes in the area made life unhappy for Sarah Ann Moore and her pupils. The house was of logs, with a puncheon floor not guaranteed against snakes, skunks or owls. Its aloofness from the town is surprising until one stops to realize that there was no town, but only the dream for one in the minds of those families in scattered cabins. The small Irena Dunn (Mrs. C. S. Williams, mother of Mrs. Howard Hall) went to Miss Moore's school in 1853, and soon after that Elizabeth Kincaid (later Mrs. J. N. Gale and the mother of Mrs. E. A. Barette) was a pupil there. Mrs. Barette recalls that her mother told a story of a wildly exciting day in the school at point of the hills. A rattlesnake intruded in the midst of 'rithmetic and bit a young man named Matlock. There was shrieking, and

85

running, and much advice. The young Matlock administered his own cure and the only one at hand—a pocket-knife cut, and strenuous sucking to get rid of the poison. He didn't die, but readin' and writin' and 'rithmetic did, and the pupils scurried over the hills homeward. Records fail to tell how long the school continued, but since this event happened in the late fifties it might be guessed that Miss Moore closed the log door, and soon, and latched it behind her with a sense of relief.

According to the best records obtainable this school was Eugene's first educational venture.

Her first gift of land for public school purposes came, as has been said, and fittingly enough, from Eugene Skinner who offered lots "5 and 8 in block 24" of his town. The earliest plat shows that this would have placed a school at the northwest corner of Eighth and High streets, at the south edge of the Skinner land claim. This site was not accepted by the district, but another one was chosen at what was to be the southeast corner of Eleventh street at Olive. This offer was in the form of a challenge. Two lots would be sold for ten dollars with the proviso that a school would be built within two years. That was in 1856. The town responded at once by putting up a small building that same summer. It wasn't much of a building. It was of logs, with a dirt floor at first where horses pulled into it the big backlogs for the fireplace. There were no desks, but a shelf that edged the room, with benches running their uncomfortable way beside the shelf, so that the pupils could face the light! The fireplace gave real warmth, however, and the first teacher to preside over such elegance was probably J. H. Rogers, or, some say, G. R. Caton. There is no available list of the children who went there.

There was a County School Superintendent now, and Eugene was the Fourth district. The county tax was two mills for the support of all schools. In *nine years, 80 pupils were in this District school*. There were 110 females, 124 males of school age in the town.

Other private schools followed that of Miss Moore's like a parade of hatching ducks. Between 1850 and 1870 no less than ten were "hatched", some taught by young Eugene women, some by "schoolmasters" arrived for the purpose. One at least was called an Academy, some were called Select Schools, two were high schools designated as private; all were private in the sense that they were privately supported and run. In the middle 'sixties five were holding classes simultaneously, attended by what the records call "children of well-to-do families." As to dates, it will be noted that most of these schools waited until the District School had had its chance, and it may be suspected, if not assumed, that somewhere underneath all of this boiling up of effort was a dissatisfaction about the "learning" being handed out.

There was probably, in the early fifties, another small private school, that of Miss Moss, in a vacant house at the corner of Eleventh street and Pearl; Columbia College was built in 1855; late in the fifties Professor Cornelius established the Eugene Academy following the abandonment of that Columbia College, but the Academy, too, was shortlived. In 1862 Miss Boise opened a school in the building of the District school when its term ended; the next year Cornelia Killingsworth started classes in a small building between Eighth and Ninth streets, back of what is now Miller's mercantile store. Two came into being in 1864, that of Mrs. Odell in the north part of town at the east end of the butte, opening October 5th for the winter term, and one begun by J. L. Gilbert in "Gillespie Church."

In June of 1865 (the year there were eighty pupils in the District School) two charming Eugene young ladies opened their Select School in the building of the Presbyterian Church, a small church on the corner of Eighth and Lincoln where the newer and larger church later stood. These young ladies, Miss Anna Underwood and Miss Lizzie Gale, found themselves with sixty-five students. (This school was later moved one block west and became a Chinese mission school, where Miss Mary McCornack was to teach.)

In 1866 Professor E. P. (Uncle Pinkey) Henderson, started a private high school about where the Osburn Hotel stands. Miss Alice Stowell was one of the teachers here. Professor Henderson had been the first president of that early school, Columbia College, which had given up and closed its life after many troubles. His high school on Eighth street was taken over as an annex to the District school in 1875, and Molly Bushnell (Mrs. M. M. Davis) and Emma Fisher (Mrs. J. J. Walton) were assistant teachers to Mr. Frank Grubb who was principal. It was known as the Red Top Tavern Annex. John Arnold and Robert Veatch opened a private school in 1870, and we find in a newspaper of 1873 that "We now have three schools in successful operation: the public school under Professor Grubb, Professor Arnold's school, and the select school taught by Miss Maggie Patton. All are in a flourishing condition." By which we gather that the select school of Anna Underwood and Lizzie

Gale had ceased to exist, along with a select school begun in 1868 by Miss Kate Andrew and Miss Leona Iles. Then we find almost at once that the school of Mr. Arnold and Mr. Veatch, who had been announced by the *Oregon State Journal* as "gentlemen of great experience" lasted but one term and that term short. That could have been because the Rev. D. McManus opened the St. John High School in a building known as the Skinner Butte Academy on Feb. 1st. "Rev. McManus," said the *Journal,* "is late from the east and well recommended," then listed the following rates: "Per term of four months, Reading, Writing, Grammar and Arithmetic, $10. Algebra, Geometry and Trigonometry, $12. Latin, Greek and French, $15."

In this same year, 1870, Marietta Henderson opened a select school in the Academy building formerly occupied by Professor Henderson near the courthouse. The next year I. Allen McCrum, a schoolmaster from Pittsburgh, Pa., started his select school, making a charge of $3 a month for "a liberal education. All things necessary for college entrance or business." On October 28th of that same year Miss Leonora Goltra opened a private school in Mr. Henderson's building. Professor Blake commenced a private school in the Butte Academy January, 1872, which may have been a business school, for one opened at about this time.

Concerning the Academy building the *Journal* wailed in 1873, "Where has the money gone? The money subscribed by the citizens of this place seven years ago to purchase the Skinner Butte Academy building with the understanding that the school would soon be open. The building is becoming dilapidated. Can anybody throw any light on the subject?"

With the private schools of Miss Pinkham in 1874 and Miss Lizzie Geary in the following year, the flame of the select schools had burned itself out, but it had been bright in some places, feeble in others through twenty-five years.

None had lasted long, but each had its part in a needed program, unconscious for the most part that it was doing more than that. Most had only meager funds, but many were efficiently taught. The youngsters who trailed to them in high buttoned shoes and pigtails and pinafores, in mannish long pants and coats and, from pictures, even in bowler hats, made quite fair starts as young sprouts who would be the builders of a cultural community.

While these schools were carrying on the District school acquired new "wings—additions about completed," the *Journal* said, in 1869. It was even working itself up to the point of a new building. And why not? By 1876 the town held 225 males between the ages of four and twenty, and 222 females between four and twenty. There were 295 legal voters and an average school attendance of 180, with 125 in the private schools, 100 in no schools at all; there were five private teachers and five in the public school.

It had been thirty years since the Old Settler had first looked upon the valley. The original school building, with its added wings, had served for twenty-two years, during which time the Red Top Tavern Annex had been used. Mr. R. G. Callison had been complaining bitterly from his chair of school superintendent that the county's school facilities were "a disgrace." Eugene, where one-eighth of the pupils in the county were educated, "or herded," a more suitable word, said Mr. Callison, had equipment "more calculated to send upon the world a band of barbarians . . . than students." And so came the need for a new school.

Now look more closely. This was in the year that the University opened! Its first class would graduate in 1878—the year the new and handsome Central School was opened. These things seem impossible to believe.

The Central (district) School rose on Eleventh street, midway between Olive and Willamette streets, with grounds covering most of the block's length. At first the building was but one story, which cost the taxpayers four thousand dollars. Eugene had a population of 3,306 in that year of 1878, twelve of whom were Chinese, one a Japanese and one an Indian. Two hundred and fifty-six families made up the town.

When the Central School had been crowned by its second story, and stood solidly upon wide grounds where a very tall pole flew a very fine flag it became a center of activity for all of Eugene. On that playground city boys learned to ride the strange, ungraceful high bicycles of the period; the militia drilled there, and the band practiced marching to its own music. Biased speeches of Republican and Democrat were allowed on the high platform with unbiased fairness, and pupils clattered down the wooden steps to hear them, understanding little of what they said but glad to leave desks for the open air. There were 300 legal voters now to digest the political speeches, and more than 300 pupils to listen without digesting.

A list of County School Superintendents carries names of some of the voters, and likely enough, names of some of the speakers. The years include 1851-1886, incomplete.

Robert Robe, 1851-55   Nathan Hull, 1864-66
R. H. Parsons, 1855-56   J. W. Skaggs, 1868-70
D. M. Risdon, 1856-57   Thomas Grundy Hendricks, 1870-74
J. H. D. Henderson, 1858-60   R. G. Callison, 1875
Daniel Locke, 1860-62   Ben Underwood, 1862-64
                A. W. Patterson, 1882-86

Because Eugene school records were destroyed in a fire in 1910 we are deeply grateful to Mr. Walling, who so painstakingly searched through those records for data printed in his history of the county in 1884. In that year, Mr. Walling tells us, the Central School had over 400 pupils and was manned by six teachers.

There were two other schools known as pioneer schools, the Geary, named for Dr. Geary, an early minister, and the Patterson, named for the family of the early Eugene physician who left off doctoring to survey the townsite. The Geary School (our present Vocational School), built in 1890, stands on West Fourth street at Madison, still in fair fettle and showing its ornate nineties origin. Both the Geary and the Patterson, which was built a few years later on Alder street at Thirteenth, wore bell towers and gingerbread trimmings. The Central School was square, grey and stolid to the end of its days, with walnut trees edging the grounds. It was the best loved of all because it had been the first loved, and had belonged to all of the town. Down its broad steps the sleds of youngsters flew on snowy Saturdays when teachers were not looking—sleds that needn't stop until they had dashed all the way across Eleventh street to bump the wooden sidewalk. From its playground youngsters stared across at the newly occupied Catholic school where nuns in somber black garb rang handbells to call to classes what seemed a different, strange kind of children. Sometimes, outside the picket fence that enclosed the small church and school there were whisperings about guns and ammunition hidden away in dark of Catholic basements against a day of—well, against a day of something. One really didn't know what. The street that ran between the two schools was as wide as the world. And very exciting. Some day, the children whispered, there might be a battle. Then the picket fence would have to come down! Then the nuns would probably take flight, and the black-robed priest would never again go up the steps of the little pink church.

And then, one day, came Father O'Hara. With his coming the whole mystery faded into nothing. Imagined guns came from imagined basements, and the children beyond the picket fence were just children going to school. And the battleground—well, it was only Main street again.

At Central it was cross, scowling Professor Reed to whose admonition pupils listened, or did not listen. Then there were gentler principals like J. M. Williams, and handsome ones like E. D. Ressler.

There were teachers like Miss Emma Chase to whom some pupils went in the first grade, again in the top grades, and finally met up with over solid geometry in the new high school. Patient, kind and wise Emma Chase!

The Central School building was gently moved to the original school corner on Olive street to make a place for the first high school. Eugene High School, built grandly of red brick with a "belfry", with classrooms in the basement and an assembly room on its second floor, thrilled the town in 1903. That building is now the City Hall.

To go back to that Columbia College. In 1855, that year in which Eugene City built a courthouse and laid out Hitching Post Square, it also saw the building of a college. That was only two years after Mr. Skinner had marked off his land in a town plat. It is necessary to keep recalling these dates and figures because they seem pretty illogical in spite of the fact that they stand in brown ink on yellowed paper in the shelves of the courthouse. It isn't so important that someone built a college on a hillside above the town in 1855. What is important is the fact that the town was a mere pup of two years and that it wanted anything as pretentious as a college on its hands.

The site for this remarkable idea was chosen on what we know as College Hill, south then from the townsite, but now a part of one of our most sitely residence sections. The backing for the college was somewhat churchy, very political minded, and thoroughly divided upon the question of slavery. That question was continually lifting its head in this valley, and was everywhere bitterly and furiously argued, as we have said before, and must continue to say, because it explains a number of otherwise strange things.

As for instance the fate of Columbia College. The college opened in 1856, with E. P. Henderson, who had a master's degree from Waynesburg College in Pennsylvania, its president. The spanking new building burned after four days of classes. Professor Henderson gathered his fifty-two students together in a private home made available near-by and went on teaching while a new structure was being built. For a year after it was completed, classes

carried on there with an enrollment of one hundred students—
young men who were to be important to the state in later years.
Then, just before the end of the first year, the second building
burned. Firebugs, the town said. That's what it was. Just firebugs.
It shook its head, and whispered. Then it talked out loud, and
made plans for a third attempt. It doesn't appear to be too clear
just who was doing all of this building and re-building. If the Cumberland Presbyterian Church kept up its spirit through this trial
by fire, its faith was strong indeed. For meanwhile its own members were in disagreement, and about slavery! From that they fell
to disagreeing about what kind of building to put up this third
time.

Professor Henderson disagreed with everybody, and resigned.
The next president, one Ryan, was a rabid Southerner. And you
were a Southern Democrat and for slavery—maybe for secession—or
you were a Republican upholding the Union. In the Willamette
Valley there were few men sitting atop a rail fence on the issue.
The Union League disapproved violently of Professor Ryan. One
of Ryan's students was young Harrison Kincaid, a reporter for the
Republican paper, the *People's Press*. When Mr. Ryan wrote an
article for the *Democratic Herald* defending slavery and signed it
Vindex, Harrison Kincaid answered in the *People's Press* and signed
himself Anti-Vindex. One article brought on another, until Mr.
Ryan, in a huff, went to the drugstore of Ellsworth and Belshaw
and there, finding B. J. Pengra, editor of the *People's Press*, took
a shot in his direction. Some say it missed entirely, others that
Pengra was wounded. However it was, Professor Ryan fled the
country. At that point the board of directors of the college gave
up. Columbia College was through. Mr. Ryan later appeared in
the Confederate Army of Virginia; Harrison Kincaid was to edit
Eugene's great newspaper, the *Oregon State Journal*, and to continue as its owner and editor for more than forty-five years. Mr.
Pengra survived his wound, if wound there was, for he was afterward appointed Surveyor General of Oregon by President Lincoln.

So there would be no Columbia College after all. Its list of
students held such names as J. J. Walton, Harrison Kincaid, the
Joaquin Miller who became the famous "poet of the Sierras", James
and Henry and Lewis Rinehart, and R. G. Callison, all Eugene
lads, and others destined to make their names prominent in several
counties.

A younger generation was led to College Hill and the scattered
stones of Columbia's foundations. Eying the tall firs, they wondered

what carelessness had allowed a school in their shade to burn to the ground; they wondered why it was never rebuilt. That wonder has turned now to amazement that so young a town should have attempted a college at all, and on a hillside so far out of its reach. And then it remembers the probable hand of an incendiary, but nowhere the means to combat fire. And it feels a little pride that Eugene had heart left for the battle to build a state university. It suspects that not for all the grain and gold and pigs and produce traded in to build that university would its founders have dared think of locating it upon the ill-fated College Hill site.

Northwest Christian College opened in 1895 as the Eugene Divinity School. Backed in spirit and with funds by a citizens' committee, it purchased land adjoining the campus of the State University. Its first president was E. C. Sanderson, whose brainchild this school actually was. Mr. Sanderson believed that there was but one way for Bible schools to survive. Liberal Arts schools of church origin were having their struggles financially, and he thought that Bible schools, working in a cooperative fashion with and beside the universities, would not only save themselves money but would bring a certain degree of religious influence into those universities. The working committee seemed willing to agree with Mr. Sanderson in this and to go along with him in the building and support of a Divinity School.

In the fall of 1895 a board of regents was named by the Oregon Christian Mission Convention, an organization within the Christian Church, and in 1897 Rehm Hall was put up, partially financed by Mrs. L. E. Rehm. In its first year the school had from five to seven students training for the ministry of the Christian Church. By 1908 the Divinity School had become the Eugene Bible School, and in 1933 was re-named Eugene Bible College when it affiliated with Spokane Bible College of the Inland Empire. The latter, a liberal arts school in part, had run into financial difficulties.

And so, after awhile, did the Eugene Bible College. Out-reaching and over-spreading its activities with far too much enthusiasm, it lost most of its property and was faced with the need of reorganization.

The school today is new. It is freshly incorporated, with a new Board; with no assets and no liabilities left over from the Eugene Bible College. As Northwest Christian College it was enabled to buy back its lost properties, with thirteen years to meet payment.

This it accomplished in six years. Kendall Burke, a graduate of the college in 1919, became its president in 1936, and was followed at the time of his death by Ross J. Griffith, the present head, who is a Doctor of Philosophy, Yale University.

Those who know about the school tell us that to Kendall Burke, to Judge U. E. Harmon of Tacoma, and to Dean Victor Morris, School of Business Administration on the University of Oregon campus, must go most of the credit for the successful reorganization of the present Northwest Christian College.

The Eugene Vocational School is a practical school for practical men and women. Occupying the pioneer Geary School building on Fourth street at Madison, it stands surrounded by the maple trees planted there when the building was put up in 1890. Outwardly the place looks as always, except for additional shops. Indoors, corridors are polished neat as a pin and pleasant office girls are ready to tell you how the school can be of help in your business or housekeeping life. And the ways are many. This, the only regional school of its kind in Oregon, offers a man anything from repair of automobiles and radio servicing to electrical knowledge, photography, and aircraft engine technicalities. It will teach him how to do business and how to sell what he wishes to sell. It will perfect him in the art of meat cutting, plumbing, carpentry, painting, dairying, poultry raising; it will give him courses in creative design, diesel mechanics and cabinet making. He may learn to be a power lineman, a machine shop expert, or improve the knowledge he already has in these crafts.

And men are not the whole story—even veterans, although veteran on-the-job training is featured. For women there is the fun of tailoring, dressmaking, decorating, upholstery, slip covering; children's clothing and food preparation. And from photographs lining the walls of the shining hallways, the girls are as camera crazy as the men, and as good at technique.

The school started with three instructors. It now has forty-six, all of whom must have had three years' trade experience beyond the "learning period" in a chosen trade. This means in all about seven years of equipping oneself to instruct here.

Vocational School has been conducted over a period of ten years, has turned out 8,235 trainees to go into industries, fifty percent of them to permanent positions. Federal funds have matched local funds, and the school is approved for veteran rehabilitation. The following example is more impressive than typical perhaps, but there are others of the same sort: that of a young student coming from his home at Pleasant Hill every day for three years, mostly by the hitch-hiking method, to finish with a permanent job as a journeyman carpenter. His three year tuition, he states, cost $1,500, but he knows his blueprints and how to read them, and he is a better builder, he thinks, than some of the men under whom he used to work. He thinks, too, that the Vocational School is tops.

Enrollment for January, 1948 was 646, forty percent of whom were veterans.

Another business school is the Eugene Business College. Its building is at 364 East Broadway. A. E. Roberts, who heads it, handed us a brochure of classes and courses and fees, with no sidelights. Those we had to pick up on the outside.

The school was started in 1901, we do not know by whom. We do not know its present enrollment. There are stenographic, bookkeeping and junior accounting, secretarial and executive secretarial courses, of which the student may have his choice; or if he desires to put all time on one or more studies he may do so under a special arrangement. There are night school sessions from September through the winter, two evenings a week. The matter of textbooks is taken care of from the office.

Mr. Robert's office is not at all the sort of office one would expect to find, and certainly not the type he discusses in his classes, but the building is small and space is limited.

Fees are twenty dollars a month in advance, whether one is part-time student or full time. An employment bureau is free to present and past students, its object to be of assistance in job finding. Time required for the courses varies from 810 hours to 1,458. The regular secretarial course is full preparation for stenographic or typist Civil Service examination.

"It's a good school," the brochure slogans, and promises to back up its statement if a student is thorough.

That Catholic School where Central Schoolers used to stare through and over the picket fence, is a full-blown fine one now, with Father Francis Leipzig at its head. It occupies the block on Eleventh street and Lincoln, near St. Mary's Catholic Church. Father Leipzig had some interesting things to tell. Since its beginning in 1889, at which time Father F. S. Beck was in charge, St.

Mary's school has grown from the handful of youngsters who trooped up those pink steps when the handbell was rung to a student body of over seven hundred. This past year's increase alone is more than a hundred. In the matter of grading it follows the pattern of the State schools; its high school was set up in the fall of 1918, a four year course with a present enrollment of more than two hundred. This leaves about five hundred in the elementary grades.

Ten young men have gone out from this parish to the priesthood, and thirty young women to be nuns.

In the matter of religious tolerance Father Leipzig speaks warmly of Oregon. Ours is the only state, he tells us, that admits a Catholic priest to its board for the regulation of high school activities. This five man board, elected by superintendents and principals of state high schools, considers questions pertaining to high school athletics, debate, elocution, music; and it is a fine thing, Father Leipzig thinks, that Oregon has taken her broad stand—an expression of an ideal toward religious understanding and integration.

That Father O'Hara whom we glimpsed much earlier in this story as the priest of the first small parish at Willamette and Eleventh streets, was destined to be an influential and rather a great man. While in this parish he undertook, in 1921, to establish what he named a "Religious Vacation Week." In Cottage Grove, Harrisburg and Springfield he conducted a two-week period of purely religious study for children of either Catholic or non-Catholic homes. He had at first some forty pupils in this vacation school. Father O'Hara, now Bishop of Kansas City, Mo., was not content to let the matter stop short of organization on a national scale. This he accomplished, and four years ago there were three-quarters of a million young people on the rolls of the vacation school.

"Catholics and non-Catholics?" it seemed a fair question since we still do our Catholic research through a fence. Over the telephone there was a hint of a smile in the Father's pleasant voice.

"Both," he said. "Naturally, most of those who attend are Catholics." He told us then that he had been the first priest to give this sort of training where there already existed a regular Catholic Parish. This was in the Corvallis parish in 1922, where he taught sixty-two summer students.

In the past months a $40,000 program of expansion has made an extra classroom for students, additional housing for the twenty-two nuns teaching here, and provided a memorial chapel to the late Father Daniel P. Curley.

MILLRACE, UNIVERSITY OF OREGON

SPANISH-AMERICAN WAR VETERANS, COMPANY C, WILLAMETTE STREET
BETWEEN 10TH AND 11TH, CA. 1898
Photographer: C.L. Winter

The head of St. Mary's now has two assistants, will soon have a third, in addition to the priest whose duties are within the Sacred Heart Hospital. Father Leipzig has been in Eugene twenty years— a third of the life of St. Mary's. Which would seem to be another piece of luck for the Old Settler!

There is another school for children's Bible study. It is the Week-day School of Religious Education sponsored by the Eugene Ministerial Association, and now in its twenty-fourth year. It conducts one-hour classes once a week "on released time as allowed by Oregon law," its teaching interdenominational.

Eugene has now two high schools, Eugene High and University High; three junior ones, Woodrow Wilson, Theodore Roosevelt and Colin Kelley Junior Highs. With a half dozen grade schools in the town area and another half dozen which are district schools in outlying places, she has at no point enough of room, teachers, equipment to handle the in-rush of children brought by the wake of war, by tremendous lumber activity and—well, just brought, let us say, by the stork.

Children are everywhere, in schools and out, just as parents are everywhere, in houses and out of them. Oregon's population has increased all at once by more than forty percent, the second largest state increase in the nation, and there is an immediate necessity for a two hundred percent expansion in the school system. The school board is breathless in its attempt to keep up with the little fellows loosed in our midst. Faced with a fall term, 1948, enrollment totaling 3306 elementary pupils, 1310 Junior High and 1375 Senior High School students the board warned Eugene that her predicament would be much worse before it could be improved, even were she to do something at once, such as voting a heavy bond issue and a tax levy besides. Because of this warning a special election was held. It provides for a five-year program of construction that will further bear down upon the already wearied shoulders of the taxpayers. They promise a high school to cost $250,000; they voted a bond issue of $2,500,000; they laid upon themselves a $250,000-a-year cash levy over a five-year period. With the new high school at top of the list, other buildings will be remodeled upward, making much additional space for elementary grades. There will be new classrooms and equipment for present buildings, new heating units for a part. The entire bill foots to something like $4,250,000.

It foots to a large sample of the same generosity and sacrifice that enabled Eugene's early families to build a University and to hang onto it in spite of tremendous obstacles. But accomplishment will mean that the town of the present has not fallen on its face in its allegiance to the past, but that it is stepping eagerly along, where already it has left indestructible markers on a road from the small Fielding McMurry school at "point of the hills" to the campus of a State University.

Mature minds have the privilege, but not the need, to rust in this town of Eugene. Programs for education bristle at adults from every direction, town and campus. The Vocational School already mentioned is but a small part of the town program for grown-ups.

There are the High School classes for those who wish high school diplomas; a course in citizenship for aliens; a course in driving. There is, or was, a class in lip reading which may be continued another year. Aside from high school work there are the classes for adults at Wesley and Westminster Houses on the campus, sponsored by the Methodist and Presbyterian churches. Lighthouse Temple conducts a three-year course for religious leadership and youth training, supplying for the most part the needs of its ministry. The Y.W.C.A. has its own program. A School of Nursing goes on at Sacred Heart Hospital, and Dr. Michell gives instruction for Boy Scout leadership. Of course the Red Cross has, at proper seasons, its classes in first aid and swimming and life saving—a fine thing with Eugene's new swimming pool now open. The P.T.A. sponsors forums for discussion and study of home and school training problems.

Some of the churches have seen fit to set up courses for young marrieds and young parents, dealing with home and nursery troubles. Banks have their required courses for employees and a few retail stores conduct classes of the same sort.

Mr. Gillett, who heads the public school program of adult education for Eugene, feels that one of its most important features is that of home groups which meet, with instructors or without, to discuss hobbies and to work at the things they look upon as avocational fun, from gardening and wood working to sewing and cooking. No doubt some of these home classes stem from the groundwork of the Vocational School.

And there is nothing earthbound in this adult study. Mr.

Gillett does not hesitate to mention the four flying services which give instruction, and the Modern Beauty College; the School of the Dance which deals in ballroom, toe, adagio, acrobatic, ballet technique; and, as a final fillip, Stage Door Studios, which will make one poised on platform feet, calm before a microphone, at home in a stage setting, or impressive over a radio network.

Mom and Dad needn't stay at home or on the ground more than just the hours necessary to put into practice the things they learn.

You may as well face it. Education will get you in Oregon if you don't watch out! From the campus side of the adult picture the Oregon State System of Higher Education will see to it that you learn anything you desire to learn, from business to pleasure, for credit or for no credit; for your own rich enjoyment, or for the serious job of living the fullest and most helpful life it. is possible for one to live. If all of this misses you entirely, mark our words, you are past master at dodging, or you never have read about the Oregon System of Higher Education!

The fact that you may be logging off land needn't stop you from coming down from your tree and tuning into the radio to learn about business administration or how to interpret Dante or the myths of the Greeks. A "whistle punk", that amusingly titled man who has an important job with the small logging company not yet graduated from its donkey engine, may as well be learning Spanish or Latin—or his own mother tongue. The fact that a lineman is installing a telephone for the new executive on Main street should not close his eyes to the miles of educational films that stretch across Oregon from Astoria to French Glen and from Gold Beach to the Wallowa Mountains. A home-making career, nor an established business need not deter one from writing a novel or working for an engineering degree. If there is the urge, and if there is a pen or a typewriter at hand, then a correspondence course or an evening class in your own community may be available.

"The State is the Campus." At least so says Mr. Viron Moore from the Eugene office of the General Extension Division.

As every old timer in Oregon knows, and most of the new timers by now, under the relatively recent set-up, five state institutions are combined to make up the State System of Higher Education: The State University, the State College, and the three colleges of Education. From these five campuses, instructors, bona fide, and qualified to teach upon those campuses, go out every week to conduct classes and direct education for those who cannot reach the colleges and university in person. Numerous extension centers have been activated—Portland Extension Center the largest because there are grouped the most people (3,300 now). That center and the Vanport Extension Center (now holding classes in Portland) serve a total of 4,500 students a term. Aside from the centers, there are classes in any town asking for them and supplying enough students to justify the set-up for a desired study. Fees are the same as college fees and such classes meet once a week for two or three hours of work under instructors approved by heads of departments, or in cases of special requests, where possible by the instructor named in the request letter to the Department of State-Wide Classes, General Extension Division.

It is from this manner of class arrangement that we in Eugene may benefit. Here, because we are campus-situated, the number necessary for the formation of a class is much smaller. Such a class meets in a room properly designated within a university building; and, as stated earlier, study may be for credit or not, as desired. There are from eighteen to twenty such classes in town at this time, second largest number in the state.

Directly under the State Board of Higher Education is Chancellor Paul C. Packer to whom Dr. J. F. Cramer, Dean-Director of the Extension Division, is responsible. Because the General Extension Division is inter-institutional Dr. Cramer is responsible to the Chancellor and the Board in much the same manner as a college president. The Division is thus enabled to serve all campuses equally well.

Under Dean Cramer there are eight departments: the state radio station KOAC, and Department of Visual Instruction both at Corvallis. Under Visual Instruction a large library of educational films and slides is available for use of club organizations and schools, along with a running patter of explanation of film or slides. Radio station KOAC is Oregon owned, State Board managed, and State College operated. Its 5000 watts send entertainment and educational information over the state—programs originating in studios at the University and the State College. The station was licensed in 1922, under the Physics department of Oregon Agricultural College, now Oregon State College.

Departments three and four are Portland Extension Center, undergraduate and graduate work, and Vanport Extension Center, with lower division classes to be followed by advanced training in one of the state system institutions.

Fifth, the correspondence courses. These offer work at high

school and college levels, meeting certain graduation requirements in many departments. This department had more than 4,500 registrations for 1947-8.

Sixth, any adult state-wide classes which are not a part of the college day—those of evening or other off-campus hours (this carried 4200 registrants).

Seven, the Institute of International Affairs, a setup for forums among and for the people of the state for the purpose of discussing questions of the day. "The Institute does no proselyting and has no ax to grind," Mr. Moore said, and he should know, because this is handled through his office. "The state," he added, "pays for this." Such forums reached 40,000 persons during the last two years. The aim of the Institute is to build understanding among nations; its beginnings were made before the United Nations conference was a reality. At this point I was given a bulletin of the Extension Division which says "The Institute follows the thesis that only when the people of all nations understand the problems and appreciate the cultures of other nations, can any awareness of international interdependence and world-wide integration for the benefit of the whole be imparted." My goodness. And just above this was a silhouette of North America (the nose being Florida) shaking hands with our neighbor on the south.

The eighth department is the last one added, in 1948. It is a Committee on High School Relations. The Committee, of which Dr. Cramer is chairman, is its head and soul. Its body is Dean Anderson who hurries over the state to interest young Oregonians in the education idea. His duty is to enthuse young people across the state concerning the advantages to be gained from four years at one or another of the state campuses.

Dr. Cramer's faculty list is amazing. It might even be amazed at the task it is carrying forward. The more than 15,000 students taking work under its program would fill a large college. Whether you, an Oregonian, long for more credits and degrees, or merely wish to study for the joy of studying, or even if you only feel that your business or social life may be broadened by college work, you may as well get going. The starting is as easy as shooting a hunter in place of a deer.

It would be a pleasant thing if the spirits of that little group of five bearded men could step from the old building where they first talked about a State University, and look upon Oregon's gift of education to its people. We think they might take a second puzzled look, and then scratch a beard, gently.

Chapter XI

NEWS CAME TO TOWN

"The .county road between the University and Judkins Point is the liveliest road in Lane county. From ten to fifteen wagons can be counted on the road at any time of the day." (Oregon State Journal, *October 25, 1890.*)

"Cemetery lots are generally three by six. If you don't want to occupy one, be sure to secure a healthy, well drained lot for your home. That will fetch you to Fairmount, which place has not a single unpleasant feature about it." (Oregon State Journal, *November 1, 1890.*)

"Sleighing and skating. Three ladies and seventeen gentlemen went by steeds to Camas Swale. They left at 9½ and arrived at 12. The day was cold and clear." (Oregon State Journal, *January 21, 1873.*)

"All who intend to attend what will no doubt be the greatest theatrical treat ever offered the citizens of Eugene, the performance of Clara Morris at Rhinehart's Saturday evening . . . should be in their seats at seven o'clock . . . as the company are to proceed on their journey south on the 11 o'clock train." (Oregon State Journal, *1890.*)

"Renew your youth, enjoy life, die happy, and start to heaven from the best town on earth—Eugene." (Anybody's Magazine.)

EARLIEST gesture toward a newspaper for Eugene seems to have been *The News*. First printed in 1858 it barely survived the year. Its publisher was John B. Alexander who appears in the town's beginning, 1852, and the paper was not the immature idea of a college boy, as were some of the later sheets, for John Alexander was thirty-six years old at the time. Eleven years later he was to begin publishing the *Guard*, a paper for, and faithful to, the democrats hereabouts over a long period of time.

The *Pacific Journal* followed *The News* in 1858, and the untrammeled views of men in a new and untrammeled country were to breed fiery news sheets throughout the years of the war between the states. It does no harm to stress again the fact that Oregon fought the Civil War in its heart. And newspapers were the medium through which spokesmen accomplished the airing of deep and sincere beliefs on both sides. The slavery issue for Oregon rode the presses day and night.

The *Pacific Journal* soon became *The People's Press* with B. J. Pengra its publisher. He was that Pengra who ruffled the political feathers of President Ryan of Columbia College—a story told elsewhere. *The People's Press* did not soft-pedal its stand against the Confederacy, and the young journalist Harrison Kincaid joined in the melee with vigor. Joel Ware, an early Eugene figure who was soon to work with Kincaid at the office of the long-lived *Oregon State Journal*, followed Pengra as editor of the *Press*.

The very next year, in 1859, the *Democratic Herald* sprang to arms under the editorship of Joaquin Miller, a poetically inclined young man filled with unpoetic fire for the Confederacy. Joaquin Miller's father was Hulins Miller who had come to Oregon, a Quaker bearing an unloaded musket, from school teaching in a log cabin in Randolph County, Indiana. The honest Hulins Miller believed, and said, that the land west belonged to the Indians; but he was a poor man, and he saw others off to Oregon and heard the talk of a new land. The young Joaquin could not contain himself until they were on their way. Hulins Miller found land on a slope below the Coburg hills.

"It was a miry, muddy road away up to the Willamette Forks" Joaquin wrote later, "with neighbors forty miles distant from one another in places, and no bridges, a few ferries across the swift, deep river; but we got there at last, and the spare neighbors, as was the custom, came to the 'raising', and in a few days we had a home—a house such as it was—let us call it a palace. For never was nobleman of high degree with all his house so happy in his castle as was proud, brave, dear papa." The land law had been "meanly changed" while they were en route, he wrote, slicing the six hundred and forty acres they had planned upon to half that number, but no one complained.

Joaquin, born, and as yet Cincinnatus Hiner Miller, 'tended to his farming for awhile, but his pen arm tired of pitching hay and planting. Joaquin's mother watched her men folks bringing trees and logs from the high hills, cutting rails for fences, planting and harvesting a garden, fishing in what Joaquin called the "sweet, swift river", and said to them, "I tell you, boys, things are just a-humming!" Joaquin, aged fourteen, put on his shoes and ran away from home.

With a neighbor boy, Will Willoughby, he crossed the ferry

on the McKenzie and headed straight for the mining camps of California. Stories about him are confusing, but Harr Wagner, writing the delightful book, *Joaquin Miller and His Other Self,* says that the boy's first job after leaving home was that of cook in one of the mining camps. "I cooked all winter for twenty-seven men, and every man was alive in the spring," Joaquin boasted with some right and much amusement. But his own cooking made him ill, and he soon left the camp on the Klamath River. It was in this camp that he wrote his first poem, and it wasn't much of a poem, but a ditty that the men liked to sing. So far there was no sign that Joaquin would ever be famous as the "Poet of the Sierras," with London printing his words.

It was now that young Miller appeared in Eugene, and in time for a session of Columbia College before its close. He watched the battle of words between Mr. Pengra's newspaper and President Ryan, then opened the office of the *Democratic Herald* to say his own say.

But his government decided that Joaquin Miller wrote things that should be barred from the mails, and so barred them; it decided that his hot-headed paper should be stopped, and stopped it—several times. Printer Bud Thompson said, "These little vacations came so regularly that I began to enjoy them. I would go hunting. There was talk of providing Mr. Miller a residence at Ft. Alcatraz. . . ." And so Joaquin left to ride for the Pony Express in the wild Indian country of Idaho and eastern Oregon, but Eugene would see him again as editor of another newspaper.

Meanwhile our old friend Hilyard Shaw of the first sawmill began the publishing of the *State Republican,* 1861. It was on this paper that Harrison Kincaid worked, taking his pay in land that Hilyard Shaw turned over to him from the Shaw donation claim. Our early Kincaid football field, an area where university buildings now line the south side of Thirteenth street between the Faculty Club and Kincaid, is a part of this newspaper-earned land. The *State Republican* was later turned over to J. N. Gale, who took it to Salem.

The Eugene days of the *State Republican* are interesting. Young Kincaid was the printer. James Newton Gale had reached Oregon from Posey County, Indiana, in 1853. He married Harrison Kincaid's sister, Elizabeth, and after quitting a mill business he had established, he joined with his four brothers to learn the printing trade. When he took over the *State Republican* from Hilyard Shaw he taught his wife to set type. They lived just back of the small

office on the north side of Ninth street between Oak and Pearl, so
that it was possible for the young bride to attend to her household
duties and at the same time see that she made the "deadline." When
Mr. Gale had built a house she boarded the office printer, made her
soap, and baked her saltrising bread over her fireplace, leaving the
typesetting to the men.

The secessionists declared that they would hang Mr. Gale for
his abolitionist views and throw his printing press in the river; but
he paid them little mind, and had his say. After awhile he took the
Republican to Salem, continuing it there as the *Argus Republican.*

There were other early papers doing battle over the slave issue:
The *Herald Reform,* a monthly, the *Eugene City Review,* which
Joaquin Miller came back to edit; and in 1864, March 12th, Harrison Kincaid printed the first issue of the *Oregon State Journal,*
a weekly that was to shape opinion in Lane county for almost forty
years.

During the war years the *Union Crusader and Copperhead
Killer* was edited by Reverend A. C. Edmunds. Mr. Pengra and
Judge Stratton wished to rid the town of it. They urged Harrison
Kincaid to buy out Edmunds. If he would do so, they promised,
they in turn would buy him out. Joel Ware, publisher of the
People's Press, agreed to go in, and the two took over the *Copperhead Killer.* Mr. Kincaid's personal memoirs, *"Sunshine and
Shadow,"* tell us that they never did receive the promised money,
but started the *Oregon Journal,* and Mr. Kincaid managed to "pay
up the editor's note and let Ware out at the end of the year." After
that Ware only set type in the evenings, being occupied in the land
office.

Mr. Kincaid says that the pioneer editor's task was long and
hard; men had nothing to lean upon. They had to build for themselves—and for each other. And then he tells us:

"For five years," (presumably the first five years of the *Journal,*
or until 1859 or 1860) "news was received by horse stage from
Yreka, California, to which place it came by telegraph." In this Mr.
Kincaid's memoirs were in error, because there was no telegraph
to California until 1861, according to his next paragraph and history. Goodness could only know the slow route by which happenings in "the States" would find their way to the coast prior to 1860,
when the thrilling advent of the Pony Express first brought letters
and news in the brash new time of ten days. The Pony Express
continued little more than a year, so we must take up Mr. Kincaid's
news story at the point of the first telegraph line which reached

California in 1861, writing "thirty" at the end of the Pony Express story.

The distance from Yreka to Portland was four hundred miles by horse stage and required four and a half days. Getting news by this route cost money. Sending ten words from San Francisco to Chicago in 1861 cost $4.55. News could come by boat from San Francisco in a matter of four or five days. If it left Sacramento by mail stage it reached Portland in six to seven days. In 1865, Portland to New York, ten words cost $7.50. The publisher who sat up all night to get the scoops was high in public favor, no matter how poor he might be in funds.

The press of the *Union Crusader and Copperhead Killer* was used for four years to print the *Journal*. In 1868 the "Pioneer Press" was brought to Eugene from the *Oregon Spectator* at Oregon City. Making the trip by boat up the Willamette river it was ship-wrecked, and for some time it lay under water, which, however, did not prevent it from printing the sheets of the *Journal* for many years. Even now it is in use at the University of Oregon as an auxiliary proof press, and in fair shape. The press is a model patented by Samuel Rust in 1829 and built by R. Hoe and Company of New York City.

Actually there were two pioneer presses in the Northwest, that one which had been used by the missionaries in the then Sandwich Islands to print a Hawaiian spelling book (1822) and sent to the Spalding mission at Lapwai in the Oregon Country, (1839); and this Washington press of, first the *Oregon Spectator* at Oregon City, and then the *Journal* in Eugene. Certainly the Washington press was the pioneer on the coast. In 1849 a Ramage press was putting out the *Alta California* in San Francisco, and about a year later it was printing the *Oregonian* in Portland.

"The Washington press was superior to the Ramage press," Mr. Kincaid wrote. "Perhaps as many as one hundred tramp printers from all over the United States have used it since it was brought to Eugene in 1868."

Looking over the history of these old presses we find that the Ramage went to Olympia from the *Oregonian* to print the *Columbian*, first newspaper in the Oregon Country north of the Columbia river. The Sandwich Island press, en route from Lapwai mission to the Whitmans' at Waiilatpu mission, rolled, with a packhorse, from a mountain trail to the foot of a steep precipice, was rescued, and did years of service as a press for the printing of Indian language books.

In 1867 the first issue of the *Guard* appeared in Eugene with that same Mr. Alexander who had started the list with *The News*, as editor, and an old-timer in press business. J. M. "Bud" Thompson as printer. J. W. Skaggs soon took over the *Guard*, and made high tariffs and the national banking system his targets and roared for States' rights. He roared, too, for Bud Thompson to take over, offering to give him his hand press plus type, two bundles of paper and two cords of wood. Mr. Skaggs then quit.

Now the *Guard* and the *Oregon State Journal* were to run neck and neck and side by side, Democrat to the core and Republican to the hilt, into the middle years of Eugene. Mr. Kincaid never had other associates (except hired help he tells us) than his two brothers, John S. and George S. Kincaid, who carried on the paper while he spent some years in Washington, D. C. From his point of vantage in Washington, New York and Boston, and later in Europe, Harrison Kincaid wrote of things national and big; he gave the little town in the far west an over-all picture that few such towns had, and he was widely quoted and widely known and admired. He made the *Journal* a Republican paper of great influence.

While Mr. Kincaid occupied his cozy office on Ninth street the *Guard* had moved into a new location "next to Mrs. Woodruff's millinery store", or so the ad said, on Willamette street. When the *Journal* had installed a new press that made 1200 impressions an hour it went quite high-hat with the "West Side." It said, "The west side came to us asking if we were too hightoned to exchange papers? We may ask the west side now if he is too hightoned to wash his roller and make a decent looking paper. There is no excuse for publishing such a dirty thing."

Mr. Thompson said that he had been given the *Guard* on his promise to keep breath in it, and this he managed, then sold out a year and a half later with a profit of $1200. His big fight during that time was for a new school for District Four, and by talking all the time about the odor of skunks which pervaded the old school, he embarrassed Eugene's business and school heads no end.

George J. Buys followed Thompson and Victor (the Victor half of the masthead remains obscure) in December, 1869, and published the paper for eight years.

In 1878 Eugene was busy and prosperous, with her new University graduating its first class and her new public school opened. The *Guard* was in its eleventh year, the *Journal* in its fourteenth. Harvey Scott, after an absence from Portland's *Oregonian*, was back at its desk as editor, and his papers were coming to valley towns on the new train from Portland to Eugene in any time from six to eight hours, depending upon weather, cows on the track, and other emergencies. The *Oregonian* was Eugene's one source of daily news and welcomed at two o'clock each afternoon.

The *Guard* in its eleventh year was bought by Ira Campbell and his brother John, who were to own it for thirty years. Ira was only twenty, the paper only a four-page weekly. The following year it was doubled to eight pages, and in 1890 became a daily. Ira Campbell was sure, about that time, that in ten years Eugene would have twenty thousand people. He was a ponderous man, in not too good health, and he died in 1904.

In the latter 'eighties a small boy, Herbert Condon, was carrying Portland papers in Eugene.

"I had a new bicycle, nickel plated," Mr. Condon, Dean of students at the University of Washington, tells us. "It was one of those fifty-two inch high bicycles, and its owner, Clay Humphrey, had just brought it from Portland. I was on the school ground when he mounted it the first time. It threw him, and he said he would sell it for seventy-five dollars. Seventy-five dollars was what I paid for it, and I was immensely pleased with my purchase. I carried *Oregonians* out Humphrey Row, a row of small houses on south Willamette street short of College Hill and the Amazon, and from there to J. B. Underwood's big home on north Willamette. Then I rode west to Lawrence just beyond the Presbyterian church; and I rode east to Chichester's, by the campus. I always met the two o'clock train in the afternoon and Sterling Hill was the agent. Sometimes a part of the town met the train, too. I sat on my high bicycle on a day in 1886, leaning against an oak tree on the campus, and watched the laying of the cornerstone of Villard Hall."

Another newsboy was carrying *Guards* somewhat later. He was Herbert Cox, who, in 1901 and 1902, delivered papers "all over mud flats" where he had more than a hundred subscribers. Mud Flats was that area north of the Geary School and west of Skinner's Butte. (Eugene had its Mud Flats and its Fairmount Flats!) There were four carriers, and each one, says Mr. Cox, was paid fifty cents a week. For his fifty cents he carried a hundred and twenty-five papers. He does not add, but we will, that he is a lumber executive now.

When, after thirty years of ownership, the two Campbells were out of the *Guard*, there followed several quick changes at its desk. Charles Fisher came from Roseburg via a paper in Boise, Idaho, but went after three years to the Salem *Statesman*. E. J. Finneran, following, had his troubles. The *Guard* went into receivership, and Mr. Fisher reappeared with Mr. J. E. Shelton in as editor and manager. Mr. Fisher continued the *Statesman* for five years, came back to Eugene, where three years later he died.

It was about this time that Carl Washburn backed the *Guard*. Mr. Washburn, a partner in the McMorran and Washburn dry-goods establishment, brought as editor Paul S. Kelty from the *Oregonian*, and for three years Mr. Kelty and his son, Eugene S. Kelty, published the paper.

The present owner of the *Register Guard* came from the *Cleveland Plain Dealer* to the *Guard* on March 1st, 1927. He soon sent for his young star reporter, William Tugman, who took on his new job on Friday, the 13th of May. Under these two, the pioneer newspaper that had begun within the Alexander family when the town was young, finished its seven decades of service in its own right and moved forward to the present, arm in arm with its rival, the *Eugene Register*, as the *Eugene Register-Guard*.

The *Eugene Register* had been the idea of S. M. Yoran, a prominent Republican and Mason who came to Eugene in 1883. In the following year he, with J. M. Hodson, opened the office of the *Register*, a semi-weekly. Mr. Yoran was forty-nine at this time, and soon turned the newspaper over to his sons, George and Will, who were later joined by the younger brother, Darwin. In 1892 Seymour Condon and Chester Edwards bought it and made it a morning daily; then the Gilstraps, Will and Frank and Otto, bought it from them. Under the Gilstrap family the paper grew strongly. Eugene had long wanted a Republican daily, and with this shot in the arm stimulating competition, the *Register* and the *Guard* pushed back their swivel chairs and made ready to provide the town with entertainment. Entertainment is an ill-chosen word. Show would be better; or circus. The fun of it continued until 1930 when Mr. Alton Baker came along and pushed them into each other's arms.

Politics, naturally, was the big issue; but in most things pertaining to their town one said yes and the other said no. A good many citizens read both sides. Numbers of them were strictly *Guard*-minded or *Register*-minded. In 1908 the Gilstraps installed the first press (a Cox duplex) to print paper from a roll.

Those years were marked by two really famous news reporters, Otto Gilstrap, who could put excitement into a fire, autumn color into a hillside, or ice cream and taffeta silk into a party with equal ease; and Horace Burnett, a tall and smiling Eugene boy back from the Spanish war, who has perhaps walked more miles and written more miles about his town than any reporter in its history. Umbrella on arm, Horace Burnett may still be seen walking straight-shouldered and with intent along the news lanes he finds it hard to give up for retirement. His hair has greyed a little; otherwise he is much like the person who covered the exciting new red brick high school and the San Francisco fire.

A man walked for his news then, rain or shine, up ladders and down alleys, and wherever a telephone line goes now. He walked, but he needn't run, at least in Eugene. Help was short in the office, with no girl society reporter, and in those brocaded days clubs had not pushed Society from the scene; and so a man shut his umbrella and went inside and sat awhile, and made lists which must be right, and sometimes he sipped tea and carefully applauded a concert number, balancing on a spindle-legged chair. Mr. Burnett had coped with the terrors of the Philippines, but this he didn't fancy. Mr. Gilstrap never flinched:

Last evening Mr. and Mrs. Blank celebrated the 25th anniversary of their marriage at their elegant home on West Ninth street, surrounded by their children and invited guests. It was a pleasant evening that will linger long in their memory.

Mr. Blank and Miss Blank were married in Lane County and have since resided here, Mr. Blank having been for the greater part of this time one of the prominent druggists of the state, and both himself and wife have been well known in church and social circles.

The rooms were charmingly decorated with potted flowers and the tints of autumn leaves. Music was rendered during the evening by Miss Nina Wilkins, violin; Harley Zeigler, mandolin, and Miss Winnie Smith, piano. Refreshments were served during the evening, the tables being presided over by Misses Wilkins, Hovey, Yoran and Kerns.

A numerous lot of elegant presents were tendered Mr. and Mrs. Blank. One very unique present was presented by Mr. A. J. Johnson to Mr. Blank. It was an old saddle, and on a card attached were the words: "Used by Mr. Blank while courting Miss Blank." The old relic will be highly prized.

Those present and invited were: Mr. and Mrs. F. M. Wilkins, Mr. and Mrs. T. G. Hendricks, Mr. and Mrs. S. M. Yoran, Dr. and Mrs. T. W. Harris, Mr. and Mrs. J. B. Chambers, Dr. and Mrs. F. W. Prentice, Mr. and Mrs. E. J. Frasier, Mr. and Mrs. Chas. Lauer, Mr. and Mrs. J. S. Luckey, Mr. and Mrs. H. E. Ankeny, Mr. and Mrs. A. J. Johnson, Mr. and Mrs. S. H. Friendly, Mr. and Mrs. Geo. B. Dorris, Prof. and Mrs. Thomas Condon, Mr. and Mrs. F. W. Osburn, Judge and Mrs. E. O. Potter, Prof. and Mrs. E. B. McElroy, Mr. and Mrs. G. R. Chrisman, Mr. and Mrs. I. L. Campbell, Mr. and Mrs. George T. Hall, Mr. and Mrs. P. Frank, Prof. and Mrs. F. G. Young, Prof. and Mrs. John Straub, Prof. Letcher, Mr. and Mrs. H. B. Miller, Prof. and Mrs. J. W. Johnson, Mr. and Mrs. S. H. Holt, Mr. and Mrs. J. W. Kays, President and Mrs. C. H. Chapman, Mr. and Mrs. R. McMurphy, Mr. and Mrs. E. C. Smith, Mr. and Mrs. J. H. McClung, Mr. and Mrs. J. F. Robinson, Mr. and Mrs. L. N. Roney, Mr. and Mrs. L. Bilyeu, Rev. and Mrs. W. S. Gilbert, Rev. and Mrs. J. T. Abbott, Mr. and Mrs. W. H. Abrams (Salem), Mr. and Mrs. W. H. Goltra (Albany), Prof. Luella Clay Carson, Mrs. Church, Mrs. Craig, Mrs. Shelton, Mrs. Williams, Carrie Hovey, Edith Kerns, Louise Yoran, Maude Wilkins. (The date, 1897.)

At the turn of the century the *West Shore* magazine was in print, a finely done piece of work showing the northwest—its scenery, its homes and its towns. The Kincaid paper offered that magazine and the *Journal* together for $5.50 a year, which seems a bargain, because the *West Shore* lithographs are priceless now and *Journal* writings about as suited to this time as to that. For instance: "I have been fighting for 22 years for the United States to shut out paupers and anarchists from our crowded and worn out nations. . . . They will eat out the substance of our people and harass them in a thousand ways until life would hardly be worth living." Nobody listened, Mr. Kincaid said, tho' he'd plead a thousand times, "there went up a continuous howl for more people. The Democrats favor them because they nearly always vote that ticket. They are worse than the cholera. They will multiply like Canadian thistle, and go on forever getting up strikes . . . and voting to make everything free."

Early journalists never pulled their punches. The Corvallis *Mercury*, viewing Mr. Kincaid's candidacy for State Printer, in a published card ". . . boils over with wrath at the rebel, Irish, copperhead, confederate, ignorant, dirty democracy of Oregon." And said Mr. Kincaid, "not a single word attributed to us and quoted was contained in the article in which this unscrupulous liar pretends to have found them."

Mr. Kincaid, like many good Republicans, stumbled over the issue of free silver, and the Republicans cast him to the Democrats in short order. He didn't mind. He thought free silver was best for the nation and said so. After more than forty years the famed editor, refusing to sell out to another, gathered up his books and files, sent his pioneer press to the University, locked the little Ninth street office door and went home.

Mr. Kincaid, out of his pioneer heritage, believed that: "Indolent people did not come to Oregon, for they were barred by distance, expense and hardship. All who had not endurance, perseverance, energy, were excluded. . . . It was the most terrible and dangerous part of a whole lifetime."

In 1910 Eugene's Commercial Club decided the terrible part was all in the past, and that the Willamette valley ought to have new blood, someone to whom it could show its scenery. With a gentleman named Dan Freeman newly hired as booster, it yoo-hooed to the middle west and to the east by means of a small magazine called *Anybody's*. It was anybody's guess how true some of the magazine's statements were, as note: "A walnut orchard is a bank that is in no danger of failing. The grower gets 15-18 cents, the dealer gets 25 cents." The same issue said that M. H. Harlow had produced 11,565 pounds of Royal Ann cherries, sold them at 4 cents a pound, netting him $462.60, and "he was thrilled."

The next spring it announced snowballs in Eugene, but only on trees; and "total destruction of crops by bad weather is unknown." Along with this went pictures of bare-foot boys in January, and apple orchards filled with bloom upon one page labeled "HERE," with a poor orchard just on the opposite page being ripped out of the ground by lightning and wind, and labeled, of course, "THERE." However, Mr. Freeman did very well, and people yoo-hooed back at him with letters, and after awhile with fare for railroad tickets and money for homes. Now, however, Mr.

Freeman and all of the real estate dealers were too busy to get out copies of *Anybody's*. And anyway, the need was past. Ho hum.

In 1918 Frank Jenkins became editor of the *Register,* with Ernest Gilstrap managing editor, Otto Gilstrap telegraph editor and Horace Burnett city news editor. Frank Jenkins was young and he gave the conservative *Morning Register* a touch of face lifting with his editorials and front page news column. At one time during his editorship Paul Kelty was associated with him—the same Paul Kelty who would later be editor of the *Guard.* During the war years the two papers ceased to fight each other, and in 1930 Mr. Alton Baker merged them into one.

In 1931 another news sheet appeared in Eugene. Joseph H. Koke, Thomas I. Chapman and Richard Horn opened up at 67 East Broadway with the *Eugene Daily News.* John Anderson was its editor, and the new morning daily eventually worked up a circulation of 11,000. One of its owners, asked for news of the *News* says only that it was something he'd "like to forget." However that may be, the paper "was a darned good paper," to quote one of those who wrote for it.

After Mr. Fred H. Chitty became publisher of the *News* both papers took up the battle-royal that was to save Spencer's butte the disgrace of a logging operation. Word got around that the butte was being sold to private interests for its timber, and that cutting had already started. The *News* said, "Until a few months ago few persons ever gave a thought to the ownership of Spencer's butte. The park was there . . . the woods were opened to picnickers . . . and through the years generation after generation had enjoyed it. . . . We have a notion most folk were surprised when it was suddenly made known . . . that the owners were on the point of selling the land to a logger. Logging was already under way. Unless the city undertook to buy the butte it would presently be denuded."

The issue was placed on a city ballot after both the *Register-Guard* and the *News* had stirred up the town to the realization that a naked Spencer would be a very sad sight indeed. That tree-happy pioneer F. M. Wilkins, president of the park board at the time, begged the town to cast its vote for a park area around the historic butte. "Remember," his letter to the *News* ended, "Eugene boys and girls will be climbing Spencer's butte fifty and one hundred years from today, to be inspired . . . by a city built out to the very foot of the butte." The Business and Professional Women's club pledged a hundred dollars toward the campaign. Other organizations followed their lead. The town cast its ballot wisely, and

Spencer is as it was in Hudson's Bay Company days; and it is ours to keep in beauty.

Before Mr. Chitty came from Olympia to take over the *News* it had been in the keeping of Sheldon Sackett, an editor with ideas about a newspaper empire. Mr. Chitty had ponderous plans too, and those, added to the Sackett ones, overwhelmed the paper completely. It attempted to become twins, with morning and evening editions. In spite of the fact that we are told that "Eugene had some very smart journalism at that time, with keen competition," the double play of the *News* was not financially successful, and the paper went to Arthur Priaulx. From Mr. Priaulx it moved on into the hands of two California brothers, the McDowells, who, right in the midst of doing all right for themselves and the town, in 1943 sold the *News* circulation to the *Register-Guard* and went back to the sunshine.

And so Eugene settled back in its easy chair to read one paper and only one, except, of course for the *Oregonian*. But it proves to be not so easy a chair, for this one newspaper is faced with quite an assignment. With a town grown well out of its britches, arms too long for its sleeves, hat too small for its head, and worst of all, shoes much too snug for its feet, our *Register-Guard* editor must turn tailor, mender, and cobbler all at once. William Tugman, coming here soon after the arrival of Mr. Baker, found Eugene growing fit to split, and has seen it continue to pop out in every direction. If it is eventually pushed, pulled and yanked back into its clothes the *Register-Guard* will have had a wise hand in the achievement, knowing that the garment will have to be an "outsize", and costly, and paid for on the credit plan.

Chapter XII

CLUBS—PROJECTS—AND PROBLEMS

We are joiners here in the valley. We join social, fraternal, religious, and patriotic clubs. We organize for health, against crime. We join clubs for pleasure, for politics, for profit, or for loss. New-comers meet to organize for fun or to cure homesickness. The town thrives on clubs. They are a large part of its life as a community as well as sharing in the lives of individuals, and they strongly influ-ence its political, educational and civic problems.

WHILE memory is here to recall for us the story of early days, we are able to visualize with the tellers a picture of a winter night and of a quiet half deserted street of this new small town. Lamps are burning in cabin windows, and bright lights from saloon doors make shining spots in the mud of the rain drenched street.

On such a night in 1865 a group of horsemen rode silently along the muddy road toward the hills northeast of town. The "plop" of mud on horses' flanks and on boot-clad legs and the beat-ing of rain on broad brimmed hats were the only sounds to be heard.

These men, members of the first "club" the valley was to know were headed for the deserted and mysterious house of James Daniels. Some rode alone like night riders. Some in silent groups. There were George Murch, R. G. Woodward, Tom Vaughn, Thomas Cady, Mitchell Wilkins, and others whose names are lost, members of the "Forks" first secret society, and they were off on a rendezvous for a secret purpose.

With them rode a young boy, quiet and frightened. The Civil war was far away and the meaning of the *"Union Club"* a dark mystery to him, but he knew why he was riding through the terrify-ing night. He was the only one of the company who knew all the words to the war time song *John Brown's Body Lies A'moldering in the Grave* and he was there to lead in the singing when the time came.

Through the early hours of the night the men and the boy rode on to the deserted cabin; horses were silently tied to trees near by and as each man entered the house, he took a candle from his pocket, lighted it and by the dimness of the sputtering tallow, the meeting was called to order.

Those were exciting days. War spirits were high, feelings bitter, and this was a way to talk it out among themselves, to hate the "Rebels" secretly and to say what they'd do if they could.

When the meeting was ended in the dimly lit room they sang, their voices low, the stirring words of the song; and the frightened boy was sworn to silence and reminded again of why he was allowed to go along. Finally candles were put out, and in the dark the men mounted horses and rode home with a sense of pent up feelings relieved, and of pride and satisfaction in the part they had taken, though secretly, for their country.

From the pioneer journal of that same young boy we read:

> Nights were sleepless, barking of dogs or any unusual noise upset us children with a feeling of horror. What would happen if our state did secede? Lane county Democrats grew so strong that troops were sent from Vancouver and with them they brought a little gun about as big as a man's leg and they set the war piece up in the corridor of the courthouse. I suppose they put it indoors so they could watch it for it must have looked much larger to them than it did to us. Among our first Rebels I seem to remember the Mulkeys—all of them—the Gibsons, Roberts, Calloways, Whitmans, Edmunsons, Gates, all deeply sincere in their allegiance to the South.

From this first Union Club perhaps came the idea of wanting to join something, to be a part of what was going on, to get together for a "cause". Small groups developed a favorite hobby and organized to help it along—counter groups organized to stop that particular project or to produce a better one. In the years to come clubs popped up like prairie dogs on the plains and grew like brush in the rain. Natural born leaders took their places, others were elected, and the pick and shovel folks went along to do the dull work and everybody, at least most everybody, was satisfied.

Early settlers were the first boosters of the town. They loved it with a stubborn devotion that refused to admit shortcomings, and though in the beginning actual organizations were few, they were in spirit forerunners of the many that came later on.

First Masonic Lodge in Eugene was organized on June 10th, 1856. Its charter officers were L. S. Rogers, S. A. Cox, W. W. Preston, Hiram Smith, A. A. Smith, J. E. Hall, E. W. Keith, Isaac Swearingen. Among the original ninety-eight members were many well-known names of Eugene's citizens.

The Masonic cemetery was the first one for the town.

The other early organization in Eugene was Spencer Butte Lodge No. 9, I.O.O.F. Instituted in 1860 by Samuel E. May, the charter members were, besides Mr. May as Worthy Grand Master, James Monroe, Enoch Smith, Garrett Bogart, Isaac Swearingen, James R. Phillips.

In a history of the lodge delivered by Judge Walton in 1879, he said, "Those were dark days in the small town for Spencer Butte Lodge, but all honor was due the few faithful who labored without ceasing in the hour of her greatest need; and who had that abiding faith that love and friendship and truth would prevail." Money was scarce and it took every cent they could rake and scrape together to pay rent and dues. In 1865 the Lodge financed the building of a second story on the new fireproof building of Bristow and Company at Willamette and Broadway where the First National Bank now stands. Eugene Skinner was one of the first members to be installed and he was the first to die. The present Odd Fellows Temple at Broadway and Oak was completed in 1907.

Other fraternal groups and clubs which followed were well aware that their young city had its crime problem and its need for aid and reform, and from that time forward such organizations have looked upon the moral and physical well being of Eugene as a driving need.

We are informed that serious poverty appeared in 1872, quoting from the *Journal,* "The expense of keeping paupers is increasing and amounts to one-seventh of the total expense of the county. This should be done as cheaply as possible and the county should own a farm near town as a home for these paupers where those who are able can work."

This plan years later was carried to completion by acquiring a sprawling white farm house under the shadow of the beautiful old maple trees on the county road. And the old gentlemen (we don't call them paupers now) seem to be comfortable and possibly near-happy as they work in the garden or rest on the benches near the door.

For many years reported cases of poverty were taken care of by "donation parties". Many of the churches made collections of clothing and supplies and school children responded enthusiastically on "donation day" with jars of home-canned food that mothers allowed them to take to their classrooms as their part in the day's program, though some children were sure to trade openly their jar of cherries for one of sweet pickles that could be eaten on the spot.

Nowadays for the normal run of needy cases we have our ever-present Community Chest and Red Cross, as well as many church clubs, all carrying on most efficiently in the heavy demands made on them.

Naturally there was crime. We must admit it along with our share of other shortcomings. Though we were probably no worse or better than any other far western community, a Salem newspaper said of us in 1872, "Eugene is the fastest town in the state. They have torch-light processions at which all hands wear 'Plug' hats and make their torches by setting fire to the 'Plugs', letting them burn down until the hair is scorched." No doubt Salem was jealous. But after all she did get the State Capitol and she did, in spite of Eugene's announced ambitions, keep her State Fair.

Our own newspaper stated openly, "If any man wants to kill another let him bring him into Lane County." And one old-timer admitted that "the town was not as wild as some but, nevertheless, pretty exciting in the early Sixties and Seventies when there was plenty of gold from the mines piled high on gambling tables."

The Long Tom saloon on Willamette street was the scene of the settlement of some personal problems, as was the dusty road in front of the St. Charles hotel and the "Shadow House" near by, though Eugene was frankly glad to escape being the setting of a double murder committed by a Calapooia Indian. His impatience to murder his two squaws made him commit the crime before the three of them got into town, but the news arrived ahead of him and the old man was caught and given a good sound horse-whipping and sent on his way to a healthier place. We hope this temper of Indian men was not the cause of the tribe decreasing in ten years from 380 to 165!

There must have been however a lighter, and some might say, a brighter side to the Indian situation, for in the early seventies the newspaper headed an item, "After Indians"! and went on to say, "An agent has been in town several days in search of stray Indians. It has been said that this particular locality would make a splendid reservation for female Indians if we may judge from the way they seem to prosper here. For several months it has been a very common thing to meet 'dusky maidens' on the street, dressed in the finest silks and gaiters, dashing along as though finances and camas were exceedingly plenty."

In spite of the acknowledged healthfulness of our climate the number of doctors increased and they were always busy. The town did have perhaps, along with other healthful localities, its share of disease. At two different times typhoid cursed the pleasant valley; and once, some travelers must have left smallpox germs around. Germs that grew and flourished in our fine mild weather and the horrible disease struck right and left, among rich and poor alike. There were plenty of these scourges along the valley but Eugene was never any good at covering up such stories, so while other towns escaped notice we admitted our germs honestly and prepared to cure the disease along with the cause.

Most years even the Old Settler escaped the troubles of illness. The winters were not often ones of ice and snow and blizzards, and the gentleness of the summer brought him no sunstroke or heat prostration to contend with. The old folks claimed the rain here was "sort of dry" and the present generation must for once agree with them, for along the streets of the town and on the campus of the University go throngs of healthy looking youngsters, this same dry rain glistening on uncovered heads and running in wet streams down bare legs.

Our hospitals are efficient if not sufficient. Our speed in growth is equalled by our speed on the highways and around blind corners, and so our accidents seem to take the place of some of the normal illnesses we have escaped. The fatal runaways of the early years are replaced by our hit-and-run drivers, and where once our nerves were momentarily shocked by those same runaways, now, on the highways, they are kept on edge permanently by our logging trucks that whiz by us with hundred-foot logs shivering on their elongated backs.

In 1888 political clubs were referred to as the "Republicans of South Eugene" and the "Republicans of North Eugene" with about twenty or thirty votes among them. The Democrats divided in about the same North and South manner, voting, some years, in about the same proportion. That year the Young Men's Republican Club was organized as was also the "Board of Trade." Mr. S. H. Friendly was President of the board and Mr. Snodgrass secretary-treasurer. Its other officers were F. B. Dunn, A. G. Hovey, F. M. Wilkins, T. G. Hendricks and J. A. Straight, and according to a news report of that month almost the first meeting was devoted to "authorizing ten thousand copies of a pamphlet to be published setting forth the advantages of living in this county!"

The Board of Trade at one time had more than a hundred working members as well as their own club rooms. Later on, larger political clubs followed the national pattern and quickly fell into place in the affairs of the town. With those, in early days feeling was bitter. Even the children took sides, especially at the time of a presidential election. They hated each other with a good healthy political hatred. They called names, pulled hair and threw rocks. They worked busily raking up great piles of leaves from under the big maple trees along the streets, leaves later to be burned in celebration of the election returns. But the bonfire of the defeated side was left to grey itself out in the ashes of dismay and hopelessness, as the children sneaked home to their beds. When the election was over the grown-ups could forget—almost—but the young ones carried it with them for days.

In 1883 the original Lane County Pioneer Society was founded, to commemorate the western immigration and to serve as a future starting point for reunions of old families. In that first society were three pioneers each from the wagon trains of '43 and '44, eleven from '45, eight from '46, twenty-eight from the great trek of '47, twenty-two from '48, twenty-six from the days of '49, thirty-six from the '50 train, forty-two who crossed in '51 and one hundred two and one hundred nineteen from the terrible cholera years of '52 and '53. John Whiteaker was the first president of this pioneer society, A. S. Patterson vice-president, Thomas G. Hendricks recording secretary, Judge Walton, Jr., the corresponding secretary and R. B. Cochran the treasurer.

Of civic groups the Chamber of Commerce was one of the earliest and most important ones, originating as the Commercial Club in 1902. Headed by Dr. D. A. Paine, R. C. McMurphy, F. M. McAlister, and W. W. Brown, the club was, in the beginning, more or less a social organization. Athletic to the extent of billiard and pool tables and a bowling alley, it served as an important recreational and social gathering place for the business men of the community. However, the function of the group as a promotional agency was soon realized and its first serious project was a plan to have Crater Lake set aside as a National Park. Interest in better roads followed this move and the program was begun for the improvement of the McKenzie route.

In 1905 the club grew more ambitious and planned an exhibit for the valley at the Portland Lewis and Clark Fair. They investigated the possibility of paving the length of Willamette street and of an electric street railway system as well as the problem of new street lighting, and they appropriated twenty-five dollars to advertise the county! Just following this period, the character of the club changed. It became essentially a booster organization, enlarged its membership, soon published a booster pamphlet titled "Anybody's Magazine," and hired the first paid promoter, Daniel J. Freeman.

In 1936 a major reorganization took place and the constitution was re-written. The object of the newly set-up Chamber of Commerce was to "Develop and perpetuate the civic welfare of the city of Eugene and region served by the community." Today a well-rounded program carried out through committees of business men guided by the board of directors and Fred M. Brenne investigates every phase of activity in Eugene and Lane County. Four decades of building a bigger and better city is the history of the Eugene Chamber of Commerce.

Away back yonder women were organizing! The first sewing circle called itself the Sunshine Club (the object, Mrs. Preston said, was to "freshen women up"). The Club started with "three darners and three guests." That didn't seem enough so each "darner" as well as each guest invited one other and the club officially got under way. Later on many of these women were to be among those who organized the "Women's Republican Patriotic League." Invited by the gentlemen to be guests at one of the political meetings much in vogue at the time the ladies were so delighted with the affair and the spirited conversation that they went home and promptly organized groups of their own.

Politically, their new club was much less important than its name would imply, since votes for women were as yet unknown, and because at least half the members were Democrats! "We never even *talked* politics," said Mrs. Preston, who was several times president of the club, though herself a loyal Democrat.

The men of the town could never understand it!

The earliest and most important of the women's serious organizations was the Fortnightly Club. The first meeting was held in 1893 by a group of young enthusiastic friends with the object of bringing together others interested in cultural and social pursuits. The first of their projects, and a very important one to the new town, was the donation of an assortment of books and the acquisition of a vacant room in a store building where they opened the first reading room.

In winter time these women, in their long skirts, trekked over muddy sidewalks and in the summer over dusty streets to reach that first meeting place in the small stove-heated room above a grocery store; women who reflected the character and purpose of those early settlers who so earnestly desired that higher educational standards be established in their western homes.

Later the Fortnightly Club took on its first major project, the definite plan to establish a library. This meant a great undertaking for the young club, and a huge one, actually, for the town; but the club's members believed so thoroughly in the need for such a building that they refused to doubt its possibility. They succeeded in interesting Andrew Carnegie, and the great project came to success with the completion of our present library building on the corner of Eleventh and Willamette streets.

At one time the Fortnightly club had ambitious plans for a clubhouse of its own, but because in those days the University was so badly in need of help the members unselfishly decided to present the sum as a rotating scholarship loan fund. Many years later they celebrated their golden anniversary and fifty years of service by establishing a fund for a scholarship in nursing, to be an outright gift to any young woman wanting to take up nursing as a career.

This club was influential in bringing to Eugene many well known speakers and fine concerts, and carried on its own active study group.

Now, in 1948, its newest and most ambitious project is sponsoring, through the "Century of Progress Club" a new library building so badly needed in our overgrown town. Charter members of Fortnightly Club were: Lizette Bailey, Margaret Bilyeu, Helen Bushnell, Idaho Campbell, Luella Clay Carson, Alice Hall Chapman, Sybil Collier, Cornelia Condon, Elma Eakin, Florence Gilbert, Mary Dorris Condon, Franc Hales, Lulu Sawyer Linn, Katherine McClung, Mary McCornack, Philura Murch, Addie Osburn, Minnie Washburne, Emma Goltra Wilkins, Irene Williams.

Early in 1900 another social club was organized which, before long, was to prove itself more than living up to its name.

This was the "Charity Club", a group of young married women, twelve in number, who met at first for social programs and their own pleasure. Later they were to take the first steps in planned help and aid for the crippled children of the community.

Four of the members journeyed to Salem to put before the Legislature their request for aid. It is unknown now just what the response was or whether they received any encouragement. Nevertheless the women went on with their efforts, personally accompanying the children to Portland where doctors provided care, and surgeons operated, without charge.

The first members, Lizzie Bryson, Emma Hardy, Mrs. Bruce Bogart, Jennie Harris, Lou Dunbar, Rosalie Hayes, and Blanche Willoughby, were the originators of this small club which did its pioneering share in a worthwhile and important work. The wife of the University president, Mrs. P. L. Campbell, took an active interest in their special project though she was not a member of the club. After many years the time came when the Charity Club was to end its activities; and now to carry out those early ideas in 1948 we have our newest and most important project the Hospital School for Crippled Children, the only one of its kind in the State.

Mrs. Carl Phetteplace first organized the board of directors and the school has been named the John Phetteplace Memorial Hospital in memory of the young son of Dr. and Mrs. Phetteplace. Support for the plan has been spontaneous and generous. The Sisters of Sacred Heart Hospital not only donated the two-story building to house the school but financed the remodeling of it. Private homes have been offered as foster homes for children from the country who are brought into the hospital for treatment so the needs of present capacity have been met, though originally an enrollment of only ten was possible.

The main purpose of the school is to teach handicapped children to live normal lives insofar as that living is possible. When its planned new building is complete the hospital will be able to care for children from other parts of the state. Almost daily requests for such care are coming in to the Board.

Since its beginning more than a year ago, almost every organization in Eugene and many from outlying districts have contributed to this newest project.

Moderns have formed another group which is following in the footsteps of the Charity Club. This is the Welfare League.

In 1930 a group of young matrons, each inviting a friend, met to officially organize the League. The expressed purpose of the new club was to "work in kindly cooperation with other agencies to aid in the financial and social problems of our community." From its first Christmas effort of packing scores of boxes of food and clothing and toys for the poor, to the sponsoring of the first public school nurse, a well baby clinic, medical aid to needy families, milk funds, and manning of the new Hospital School from its beginning, the Welfare League has worked at child welfare in its broadest sense.

Members have contributed over fifty thousand hours of entirely volunteer work. Proceeds from every League activity—bazaars, benefits, style shows, even dues—are now being turned over to the Hospital School and its future building. Charter members of Welfare League were: Mrs. W. D. Abel, Mrs. Martha Baker, Mrs. T. I. Chapman, Mrs. David B. Evans, Mrs. Howard Hall, Mrs. George Hopkins, Mrs. James King, Mrs. Will Moxley, Mrs. Lynn S. McCready, Mrs. Carlton Spencer, Mrs. Orville Waller, Mrs. H. W. White, while those added were Mrs. Waldo Adams, Mrs. Alton Baker, Mrs. Francis Callison, Mrs. Campbell Church, Mrs. Emma Briggs, Mrs. S. C. Endicott, Mrs. Gaven Dyott, Mrs. Walter Hummel, Mrs. Frank Jenkins, Mrs. W. H. Jewett, Mrs. C. R. Manerud, Mrs. Weir McDonald, Mrs. Mae Stannard, and Mrs. Harry Titus. Mrs. P. L. Campbell was an honorary member.

Our first Country Club should be listed among the older ones. In its young and struggling years the club was a small and exclusive affair with a nine-hole golf course spread out over the east slope of College Hill. Here the dry grass in the summer time was slick as a frozen pond and the greens were of sand from the river. About all that first group of golfers had was spirit and the tiny tumble down clubhouse across the street from the first tee. However, some of the folks still alive look back upon it as the finest Country Club the town ever had or ever will have.

Now our modern Country Club is also housed in an old farm house, but it is attractive, well-managed, and has a membership of more than four hundred. Its beautiful eighteen-hole course stretches away among fir trees, parts of old orchards—cherry, apple and pear, and huge walnut trees shade some of the most troublesome spots. The location of the Club is interesting since it occupies the original donation land claim of Mr. Gillespie where the pioneer Cal Young and Mrs. Young still live.

In 1920 a new club at once found itself busy with the special problems of welfare aid. This was "Kiwanis", a group of citizens especially interested in the younger generation. Kiwanis members are deep in an all-community service, but their own special contribution is the backing of the Four H clubs. For this group of future farmers Kiwanis sponsors the "auction" of stock following the County Fair where these 4-H workers bring fine blooded stock for exhibition and sale. The club also helps finance the trip of the Eugene boys and girls who win the coveted Four-H trip to the national convention.

"Rotary Club" was organized in 1923. Its program of work is

to encourage and foster "the Ideal of Service" and the application of that ideal in the members' personal and business life. Rotary offers a splendid opportunity for enlarging friendship and participating in the building of a community. This club has many committees for vocational and community service. In the latter, their Youth committee and Farm club committee (to interest and assist the rural youth in educational and agricultural activities) as well as the one for underprivileged children are busy and important ones. They have also a committee working especially in cooperation with the Children's Hospital School.

One of the busiest and hardest working clubs in the town is the Junior Chamber of Commerce. With an active membership of more than 150 its working plan is the practical one of investigating a project, and, finding it worth while, backing it with all their energy and young enthusiasm. Its members head the Red Cross disaster committee. They head and conduct the March of Dimes in Eugene. Another project is a continual traffic safety program, as well as fire prevention study in schools and town. Perhaps their most worthwhile and distinctive program is their "Americanization" one. Along this line they sponsor a weekly radio program. Besides these and other interests too numerous to give in detail Junior Chamber of Commerce shares in all Civic programs.

"Lions Club" of Eugene, one of the hundreds of branches of the National "Lions" organization is this year celebrating its twenty-fifth anniversary of service to the town. Its more than a hundred members are interested in many civic projects—Boy Scouts, parks and playgrounds and others, but their main interest and specially directed aid is for the blind.

With many purchases of needed equipment for those less fortunate, members of this club have found an important outlet for their desire to aid. "Sight Conservation" includes financial help in needy cases of children in the schools where eye examination and medical care are indicated.

Eugene "Active Club" is just what its name implies. A member of "Active International" which operates in Canada and Hawaii, as well as in the States, it is active in international affairs as well as those of purely local sphere.

Nationally the objectives of this group are several, but the most important one is the training of young men for the carrying of community responsibilities. Locally in "Active Club", the emphasis of work is on activities which help children. Its largest annual project is sponsorship of the State High School Basketball

Tournament each spring, and during the winter months it conducts a tournament for younger students. All admission fees for these games go into non-profit high school activities.

The Active club is committed to one money-raising project per year to help finance the new Hospital for Crippled Children. They have volunteered to raise ten thousand dollars for the Civic Stadium football field, have purchased playground equipment, and donated money for emergency care of needy pupils. Newest of all programs of Active is the planned purchase of uniforms for the Eugene High School Band.

One unique club which not every town can boast of is the "Lane County Look-Outs" and we pay them a special small tribute. Made up entirely of physically handicapped members who are unable to get about as do most of us they somehow have managed to find small ways of helping in community projects by telephone or mail committees, and in addition keep track of one another with the small friendly things which mean such a tremendous lift to shut-ins.

Sport clubs are numerous. "Obsidians, Inc.", a group of rugged and enthusiastic mountain climbers has been active for years, while the "Willamette Ski Patrol" is a newer one following the same route as it were. There is a Hunt Club for horse lovers and among the less strenuous forms of sport there are two public golf courses, bowling; and on our newly made Fern Ridge Lake we even have a Yacht Club.

Youth organizations are many. Among the most important, at least to the future of the town, are the Four-H clubs and their Association. These future farmers are already winning their place in national contests. The Boy and Girl Scouts are all active in local Scout affairs as are the young members of Y.W. and Y.M.C.A.

Besides our professional clubs for Bankers, Dental, Medical and bar associations, fraternal Clubs are many, all active in affairs of civic interest: Elks and L.O.E., Eagles and auxiliary, I.O.O.F., Rebekahs, Knights of Columbus, Catholic Daughters, Knights of Pythias (organized in 1883) and Pythian Sisters, Woodmen of the World, all Masonic orders from the Blue Lodge to Shrine club, Eastern Star and all Masonic auxiliaries, R.N.A., B'nai B'rith, Moose, Maccabees, and Neighbors of Woodcraft.

If yard beautification, or flower arranging or herb-gardening is a major interest in one's life the Garden Club is the group to join. Masculine members specialize in an annual camellia show.

There is the Optimist Club, for service, and the Eugene

Council of World Affairs, the latter one of the town's newer organizations and just now getting a healthy start among us. Two popular representatives of National Clubs are the Round Table and the Knife and Fork groups. Each of these feature dinner programs, often with guest speakers on national affairs.

Among national clubs for women represented by branches in Eugene are the Daughters of the American Revolution and the National League of American Pen Women.

The first of these is an important one among our patriotic organizations. This small group of women, descendants of military men of Revolutionary time, teaches first of all Americanism, and, locally, gives much time and thought to maintaining records of pioneer days, putting up markers at memorable locations of early homes and places of historical interest.

One of the major efforts of the D.A.R. was in the saving for a time at least of the famous battleship *Oregon*. In 1923 the Portland *Oregonian* announced that the *Oregon* was being sent on her last trip and was to be junked. This, it said "would be to the lasting disgrace of the State." The D.A.R. took up the fight to save the famous battleship and Mrs. F. M. Wilkins, Lewis and Clark Chapter, Eugene, who at the time was State Regent of the society, personally wrote letters to hundreds in the state carrying on a steady campaign to save the ship. She went to Bremerton to make a personal plea, and in 1925 the *Oregon* was brought home! (We must add here that "to the lasting disgrace of the State" this was to prove a hopeless fight, for the famous and proud old ship has again been forgotten in the passing of time.)

The second group, The National League of American Pen Women, was organized in 1945 by Cora Freer Hawkins, and is the only branch in the State. Other charter members were Lucia Wilkins Moore, Gwendolyn Lampshire Hayden, Louise Fitch and Nina Wilkins McCornack. This group of writers is especially interested in recording in books and story the early history of the West.

Among the civic minded organizations for women is the Business and Professional Women's club. The National was organized in 1919, and the Eugene's local in 1923. This club has been keenly interested in all things pertaining to the betterment of the city, particularly the out-door life of the community. It took an active part in helping to forestall the destruction of the timber on Spencer's Butte, and saving it for the all-time pleasure and beautification of the city. The club modernized and made usable the cottages in Skinner's Butte Park, and built the out-door fireplace for the hundreds of summer picnickers to enjoy. It was the first organization to offer a financial donation to the Park and Playground fund through the "Century of Progress." One pioneer said of this organization (and it would seem to apply to every prominent club in town): "As long as the spirit that is demonstrated by this group is in existence, there need be no fear for the future of the Nation."

The Eugene Quota Club was organized in 1941. Its program of special service has been work with children, medical aid for the handicapped, Girl Scout work, and a number of scholarships for University girls. Its program for the near future includes aid for underprivileged and the furnishing of a room in the new hospital for children.

The Eugene Zonta International was organized in 1936. A group of executive women in business, their main objectives are to encourage high ethical standards and to improve the professional status of women. They encourage and promote the organization of Zonta Clubs in all commercial centers.

American Association of University Women has its many study groups—and play ones, too—and a wide membership of University women from this and other colleges.

More and more clubs! They seem to grow and keep pace with the town. Hospitality Club is one especially for newcomers. Re-Active another busy auxiliary, Young Business Women's club, Beta Sigma Phi, an international non-collegiate study club, National League of Women Voters, and Eugene City Club, whose membership is open to all women in the town and vicinity.

On the campus of the University are many clubs for women. One can see why it is a saying among us that Eugene is probably the most "organized" small city in the west.

It is impossible to imagine anyone coming into Eugene and being unable to make pleasant contacts if there is a willingness to get the necessary information on these endless organizations. If you are in town you can scarcely escape joining something.

PART THREE

THE STORY OF

Eugene

IN PHOTOGRAPHS

The Story of Eugene, as depicted by the Wilkins sisters in this book, is the story of the Old Settler establishing roots in the fertile soil of the Willamette Valley just where the Willamette River passes by the once-treeless hill known as Skinner Butte (or Skinner's Butte, as it had been called for most of the city's history).

> From time to time the Old Settler looks in on the city he had founded, which has grown, fitfully and slowly at first, but then burgeoning like a gangly adolescent grown too big for his clothes. Then, suddenly there it is, today's modern city—which is to say 1946's city—sprawling beneath the Butte, lights flashing brightly on the main street, smoke rising from the mills, lots of "those doggoned engines on the track and the sky full of flying things," as the Old Settler expresses it. It seems a far cry from the sweet air of yesterday, the quiet trails, the leaves falling softly, and the wild critters close by. Eugene has grown up. Perhaps it is time to move along, the Old Settler decides.

Illustrating such a story is not always easy with the pictures available, plentiful though they are in the Lane County Historical Museum. How do you illustrate the unique and sometimes-contradictory nature

Overview of Eugene,
looking west from
Skinner Butte, ca. 1914

of its people? Photos don't show the political and social disagreements that have marked the history of Eugene. They often fail to show the spirit of the populace—its love of comfortable homes and gardens, of trees and greenery, of water in the nearby rivers and lakes and, yes, even in the misty rain. How can you show through photos the people's concern for education of the young?

Sometimes you don't—you opt for the thousand words instead.

What photographs do illustrate, though, are the external trappings of that spirit. The earliest photos show simple commercial ventures, the blacksmith shop of 1866, the machine shop of 1892. The early spirit shows in the civic gatherings, the parades on Willamette Street—even in overcoming adversity, such as the great Willamette River flood of 1890. Creation of the Millrace brought industrial growth which spawned more commercial and residential development, automobiles, road building. These, too, mark the *Story of Eugene*.

Page 1 photo: "When the 69th came home": Oregon Soldiers returning from WWI, Willamette between 6th and 7th, ca. 1919. Photographer: Chester Stevenson.

John M. Sloan Blacksmith
Shop, corner of 8th and
Olive, ca. 1866

Business of James M. Hendricks, agent for
Frank Bros. Co., dealing in agricultural implements,
southeast corner of Ninth (Broadway) and Oak, 1892

Early automobile,
possibly west 7th, ca.
1907

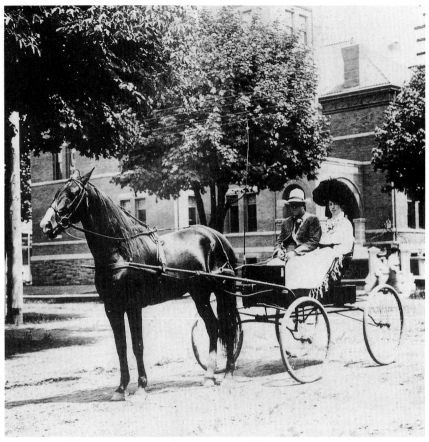

Couple with horse and buggy, in the front of the
Lane County Courthouse, northeast corner of
8th Avenue and Oak Street, 1903

Road race participants,
Broadway between Oak and
Pearl, July 13, 1909

Overview of Eugene from
Skinner Butte, ca. 1914

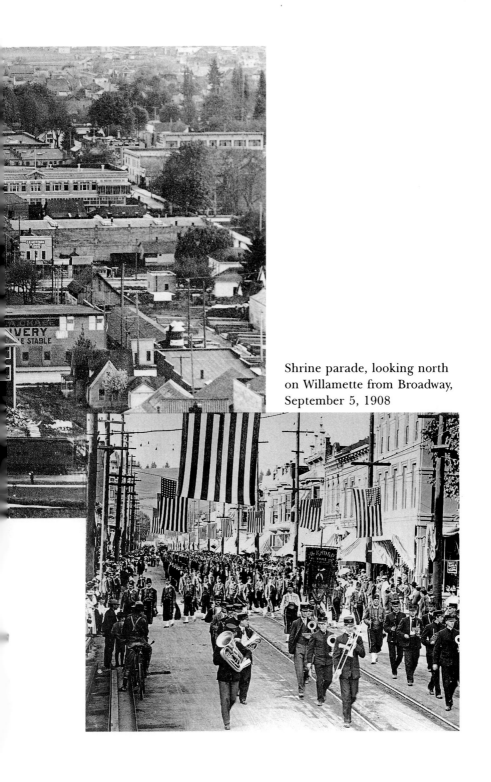

Shrine parade, looking north
on Willamette from Broadway,
September 5, 1908

Overview, looking northeast from Skinner Butte,
Ferry Street Bridge and flooding from Willamette
River, February 4, 1890

Rowboat on the
Willamette River,
Ferry Street Bridge in
background, ca. 1905

Shelton-McMurphey House
from Skinner Butte, ca. 1910

After the rains. 12th Avenue looking towards the
University from Hilyard Street. Deady Hall tower
in center background, ca. 1916

1st Grade Classroom,
Washington School,
1916/1917 School Year

Gathering in front of Central School, southeast corner of
11th and Olive, ca. 1895, Photographer: C.L. Winter

First football game at the U of O, Villard
& Deady Halls in background, 1893

The Millrace, looking east.
Left: Eugene Woolen Mill,
6th & Mill; Right: Eugene
Fruit Growers Association,
7th & Ferry, ca. 1915

The Millrace, looking north from the bridge at 8th Avenue. Left to right: Eugene Excelsior Company, Eugene Mill & Elevator, Eugene Woolen Mill, Midgeley Planing Mill, 1908

Truck mishap, Eugene Woolen Mill,
East 6th Avenue, ca. 1910

Street paving, looking west
on 8th from Olive, ca. 1910

Stone Quarry, west side of Skinner Butte, ca. 1908,
Photographer: A.A. Simmons

Eugene Sand and Gravel Plant, northeast
side of Skinner Butte at the north end of
High Street, ca. 1900

Contractors doing finishing work on house on east 11th;
later Alpha Phi Sorority House, ca. 1910

Mechanics in Bangs Garage, southeast
corner of 8th and Pearl, October 30, 1920

Vegetable stall in original Producer's Market, north side of 8th Avenue across from Park Street, ca. 1917

Log pond at Giustina Bros. Lumber Co., west 2nd, ca. 1945

Chapter XIII

THE UNIVERSITY OF OREGON

The first winter had gone on into spring in the little settlement, that spring into other seasons and other years.

The lone cabin of 1847 had become a cluster of small homes spread about the nearby valley, ranging out like spokes from a master wheel. Frightening distances had lessened a bit as trails became roads wide enough for wagon travel. Now the coyotes' howl came only from the far foothills; now the dusky Indians were scarcely more than memories. Pheasant and quail had become accustomed to their new neighbors, and nested happily close about the town, sharing slyly in the grain and fruit of new gardens. The sky was often dark with great flights of ducks and geese swinging overhead, calling the change of seasons when river willows showed their first rosy tips of spring, or autumn color flamed in the hills.

A decade went by, and then another. Small cabins gave way to comfortable homes. And stores. And schools.

The Old Settler was gone now, but he must have looked back and thought to himself it's a right fine place. He might have pondered long, and then whispered down the soft Chinook wind—it's a right fine place, and it's time for a big school, one to last through the ages.

And that was the spring of 1872.

1. Earliest Struggles—Construction—First Faculty
Early Student Body and Campus

THE first official, concentrated move to promote a state university in the township of Eugene came about with the organization of the Union University Association, formed in August of 1872, with a capital stock of $50,000.

The chief factor in crystallizing a long-debated subject was news that the state legislature of that year—which then convened in September—was to definitely locate the proposed institution.

It seems startling at first glance to realize that the grade schools and the university movement came at almost the same time; and it seems startling that more than twenty-five years had passed since the town was founded. But let's check the facts and map the cause.

131

Farm life was the rule in early day Oregon Territory. Grain, fruits and stock required long hours of labor by the entire family, and contacts with the widely scattered neighbors were few and far between. Actual dangers were also few, so far as every day life went, and that fact, plus mild climate and lush crops, gave the pioneer settlers a feeling of security and willingness to live largely to themselves. The nearest city was two thousand long and weary miles back over the mountains and prairies, and they had felt no great urge for higher education out here, or immediate need for it.

Consider the picture, too, from our vantage point of modern washing machines, oil furnaces, frozen food lockers, and the neighborhood store. In the earliest homes in Eugene and the surrounding valley, housewives made their own soap in enormous iron and brass kettles over an outside fire; spun their own yarn, and dyed it from vegetables and herbs brought from field and garden and brewed by themselves; wove their own materials; cooked the family meals over fireplaces; tended gardens and stock; bore children and raised them—without doctors for the most part. It seems astonishing to find that they ever remembered the needs of schooling.

Yet many families, before the public schools came into being, sent their sons and daughters to the various academies and denominational schools, of which there were seven in the valley: Christian College at Monmouth, the Presbyterian school called Albany College, Pacific University at Forest Grove (Congregational), Willamette University at Salem (Methodist), another Methodist college in Corvallis, the United Brethren called Philomath College, and a Baptist school in McMinnville. Eugene had Columbia college, even if briefly.

A government policy established in 1803 had declared the granting of two townships of land in each state entering the Union thereafter, for the purpose of establishing state universities. Then, by a Donation Land act of 1850, the Territory of Oregon was given a similar grant. The Territory at that time included also land north of the Columbia river. Three years later two separate areas were formed, creating Washington Territory, and in 1854 it, too, received the grant of two townships. So our own commonwealth was ready, in 1851, to select the land which would support her first institution of higher learning.

There is much background leading up to the Union University association.

With the earliest attempts at forming a state university coming in 1851, the whole matter promptly became a political football with pressure groups working in all directions, and that first year the state politicians handed the university to Corvallis, the penitentiary to Portland, and the capitol to Salem; the next move was to award the university to Jacksonville; then nothing further occurred until 1857 when it once more became a very live issue before the people of Oregon.

Strangely enough, one of the University's greatest benefactors in later years was to oppose its establishment at that time because he was, as a Southern party wheelhorse, much in favor of the parochial school system. His name was Matthew P. Deady. As president of the state constitutional convention of that year, his voice carried a good deal of weight. It was countered effectively, however, by R. P. Boise of Salem, who, with a large group of followers, felt that the state should have one non-denominational school of importance. They wanted a good school close by with lower fees than the sectarian institutions—and as northerners they opposed the southern viewpoint of the Deady group. Right or wrong, Judge Deady was sincere in his viewpoint. When, in later years, he saw the tremendous value of the state university, he was even more valiant in his strong and sympathetic support.

The dickering and discussion was most involved for quite a time. Then, following the impasse created by the opposition group, we have a long period of inactivity. We quote from Dr. H. D. Sheldon's *History of the University of Oregon:*

> Revival of interest in the state University endowment occurred in the early seventies. As the old plots and locations of the University lands were obsolete, the state land board at the suggestion of the governor, ordered the land re-located. The plots so prepared were approved by the local land offices and accepted at Washington, D. C. An amount of 10,935 acres was deeded and bonded in the biennial period ending in 1872, and the University endowment fund raised on paper at least from $10,055.09 to $41,979.74. Under the conditions of the time, this sum was an item of first importance, and the ten-year period after the adoption of the constitution having elapsed, active steps were taken to locate the University.

More than that, the issue suddenly became red-hot again.

So we had, on a warm July night in 1872, a group of five men sitting about discussing the need of more adequate schooling and of a state University. When dusk finally came in the sitting room of the old McFarland home on Charnelton street, the kerosene lamps' were lighted and the talk went on and on. They were good citizens all, these men with their old-fashioned whiskers, their serious faces, and their minds turned toward the good of future generations. When the talk was over they had a plan. Their names? Mr. B. F. Dorris, Mr. S. H. Spencer, Mr. John M. Thompson, Judge J. J. Walton, and Mr. John C. Arnold. Others came into the picture slightly later, and hundreds worked on the project throughout long years, but these five own credit for the first actual move toward higher education.

Thus came into being the Union University Association, from which we digressed for background material, and incorporators of the $50,000 investment were those five men plus Messrs. W. J. J. Scott, J. B. Underwood, J. J. Comstock, A. S. Patterson, E. L. Bristow, E. L. Applegate and Dr. A. W. Patterson.

First officers of the Association were John Thompson as president, T. G. Hendricks as secretary, B. F. Dorris, J. J. Walton, W. J. J. Scott and W. H. Abrams, and they formed the board of directors which presented to the September session of the state legislature a bill to permit purchase of a site and erection of a building worth $50,000—to be ready to turn over to the state by Jan. 7, 1874. The bill further provided for a board of regents of nine, six to be appointed by the governor and three by the association itself, specified that state scholarships should be awarded by counties, and forbade any sectarian religious tests for either students or instructors.

In the subsequent legislative skirmish, Albany came forth as a major opponent of the bill, but it was passed in the end—and so began what turned into a long and uphill battle. In reading detailed accounts of those ups and downs, it seems certain that nothing but the dauntless spirit of pioneers who had already accomplished tremendously in the face of untold hardships enabled them to carry through a project fraught with so much needless opposition and so many major problems. The way was treacherous, but the leaders were doughty—Judge Matthew P. Deady, L. L. McArthur, R. S. Strahan, George Humphrey and Messrs. Thompson, Hendricks, Walton, Dorris and Scott.

Immediately committees were appointed for selection of the best site and for raising money; and immediately personalities and desire for profit entered into the picture, between the east and west sides of town. The original site chosen was a five-acre tract east of

Oak street and south of Twelfth street (beginning at what is now the area surrounding St. Mary's Episcopal church) which was then the Amazon bottom land and very marshy. Ultimately the choice was left to the state board of commissioners and they met to canvass the situation, looked over the lovely view from "Henderson's property" east of town and chose that seventeen and three-quarters acre tract on April 21, 1873. Subscriptions began coming in, and the University of Oregon was officially on its way.

The plan for financing devised by the committees called for a $30,000 bond issue by the county court plus $20,000 in private subscriptions in Eugene City. But the panic of '73 was on, cash was scarce, crop prices down, and times just plain hard. Loud protests sounded out when tax time rolled around. Then outside interests came up with the idea of calling the location bill unconstitutional because "all State institutions were to be located in Salem." The committees brought forth their strongest talking points: increased population, greater income for both town and county, higher standards and morals, the bringing of wealthy families and influential interests to the community; greater value of farm lands. In spite of all this evidence, opposing elements obtained a revocation of the bond issue, and only private subscriptions saved the University.

These subscription agreements carried promises of labor and farm products, as well as cash, and this early dilemma was only one of many which faced a plucky and determined citizenry with a pet scheme in its breast pocket. Cash came in varying amounts, a few cents to perhaps $500 which was a round sum in those days in a tiny community of 1100 souls. Of the 200 families listed in that year in Eugene City, it has been said on authority that 140 names were on the subscription list; church groups gave suppers, and there were strawberry festivals to raise money.

In an early July paper of 1873 we read:

"Stores closed early and people came to own in large numbers to attend the celebration. A procession from the courthouse headed by a brass band marched to the University grounds east of town where ample shade had been provided. The usual exercises of July Fourth were followed by an excellent dinner provided by the ladies of Eugene. A number of toasts were proposed and responded to, and a ball in the evening was largely attended. Entire proceeds of the day were given to the University.

"E. J. McClanahan is the one who erected the tall

flag pole on the University grounds from which the flag floated yesterday."

Another item read like this: "Land For Sale—To the highest bidder: 320 acres of land six miles southeast of Eugene, also 1100 acres at $6 per acre one-half mile east of Spencer, and 722 acres at $5 per acre two miles southeast of Spencer, $6000 of the proceeds to go to endow the University of Oregon and given by Thomas Judkins."

Even so, there was barely enough cash to pay for the building materials and some day labor, and the board was having a truly bad spell.

But up went that first building, planned by W. W. Piper of Portland, to be an impressive edifice of three towering stories topped by a mansard roof, in the architectural style of the period. It was 122 feet long and 57 feet wide, and at each end was a winding, narrow stairway, leading to the top floor which housed a chapel 78 feet by 50 feet, with a small stage 39 feet by 12 feet. There were classrooms on the second floor, and offices for the faculty on the first floor. There were tremendously durable walls of concrete-covered brick three feet through.

A wonderful groundbreaking ceremony on May 7, 1873, was cause for great celebration in the little town, and all its citizens and most of their families turned out in the best dolman, most frivolous bustle and shiniest silk hat to see that first magic shovelful of dirt turned, and to help lay the cornerstone of a great University.

By fall there it stood, full three stories high on the highest rise of the bare tract—and badly minus a roof. Once more, money had run out; once more the town dug into its pockets and came up with enough to buy tin roofing for a hollow shell. It seemed the end, but Governor Grover proved a friend in need when he recommended to the legislature of that fall an extension of time, which was granted to the extent of two years.

Other institutions and counties have evinced great jealousy toward the University and Eugene since the very first, and we have already seen one example at work. The second major one occurred in the legislature of 1874 when Christian College at Monmouth, headed by Mr. T. F. Campbell (father of P. L. Campbell), put on a campaign to have the University relocated as well as reorganized. The plan called for a college of literature and arts, a normal college, law college; for free tuition, and for a board of curators assisted

"BEAUX OF THE 1900S" UNIVERSITY OF OREGON

GLAMOUR GIRLS OF AN EARLIER DAY

UNIVERSITY OF OREGON ABOUT 1886

Original Deady Hall on the right, Villard Hall on the left, and the fancy trapping of the time much in evidence.

Photo courtesy of the Univerity of Oregon

UNIVERSITY OF OREGON, CLASS OF 1896, WHO CHOSE THE UNIVERSITY COLORS, YELLOW AND GREEN, DR. CONDON IN THE CENTER.

DEADY HALL, FIRST UNIVERSITY OF OREGON BUILDING,
BEGUN IN 1873, COMPLETED IN 1877

by a board of visitors to run the whole. The move seems to have gained little support.

With time again on the wing and a vast deal of unfinished business, the committees sent flying squadrons of solicitors into the field in March of 1875 with $16,000 as the goal.

What might have happened to the University of Oregon without wheat no one knows. When only about one-third the needed cash was received from this drive, the solicitors called for wheat, and about $6,000 worth came in, valued at 90 cents per bushel. The constant drive of the weary promoters was for cash—scarcely ever was there enough of the precious commodity to pay for more than a small portion of the materials and labor. Judge Walton, as the man who faced workmen and creditors on pay day, was the one who frequently had to jaunt to the nearby farms and wheedle chickens, a pig or a calf, a box of apples or other fruit or perhaps a few more sacks of wheat from the long-suffering friends of the project. One anecdote tells us that he rambled out one fine day and led in a heifer so part of the workmen need not go home unpaid. Most of the produce thus garnered he took to the store of T. G. Hendricks where it was sold for a profit thus benefiting both merchant and University—and wearing out a great deal of good shoe leather and energy for the go-between, we suspect.

Judge Walton was possessed of complete determination, faith in the future of the school, tireless energy, and an optimistic viewpoint which helped many others to see a bright side to what seemed a losing battle. And Mr. Hendricks brought to the whole problem a businesslike, logical approach. Possessed of good judgment and a sound, shrewd business head, his advice was invaluable, and his enthusiasm and determination great assets to the project. It has been said by many authorities that W. J. J. Scott was the man who spent more of his own time and money toward the University than any other person.

A discouraged populace could scarcely believe that the lower floor of Deady Hall was actually completed by the following spring, when another blow fell in the resignation of two of the professors. Almost immediately afterward, the unpaid mechanics filed a lien on the building for the $5,000 debt still remaining of the previous $16,000. Once more benefactors arose in the persons of Mr. Scott and James Holt—two of the men who had maintained unswerving faith from the first and from their pockets came the final, clinching contribution.

On July 26, four years after that first small meeting, the building was declared ready for use, accepted by the regents, and the town celebrated quietly in its heart the completion of another difficult step in its progress toward a bright future. Almost every nearby business man was on the honor roll of those who made sacrifices—along with their entire families.

Now the regents met and elected the first faculty: Mr. John W. Johnson as the first president, and Dr. Thomas W. Condon, Mr. Mark Bailey, Mrs. Mary Spiller and Miss Mary Stone as the first professors and instructors. Entrance requirements, courses and rules were set up. The faculty assembled in September. The young school children of Eugene had contributed money for glass to fill in the empty window frames, and through the great west door to Deady Hall beneath the memorial glass inscribed with their names, 177 students of the University of Oregon entered that year.

Of what stuff was this first faculty made, that it could steer a frail educational craft through its very maiden voyage among the always-present reefs of financial troubles, jealousies, policy-forming, and political pressure? Let us see.

John W. Johnson, born March 22, 1836, in Missouri, had had typical frontier experiences. He had driven an ox team over the great plains to Oregon when he was a boy of thirteen, coming with his parents. Failing to get the education he craved in the raw and sparsely settled valley he went back to Yale in 1862 and entered there after his trip across the Isthmus as a young man of twenty-six. He must have become attached to the open spaces out here, for he returned to Oregon Territory to take up, first mining, then teaching. He held a reputation as a disciplinarian, and became principal of the only fully developed high school in the state, Portland High School, where he first experimented in his always relentless driving toward the goal of fine grades and scholarship. Severe as a Roman senator himself, he had long been a Latin scholar and had acquired a Spartan hatred of all things lazy or shiftless. Not even his innate sense of humor—usually invisible—permitted much lapse from these standards, and his Baptist religion and Democratic political affiliations only intensified the stern die-hard quality of the man and scholar. A biting sarcasm was part of his teaching stock in trade, so that his scholarly students respected and admired him while the less facile ones shook quietly in their old-fashioned boots. Of sturdy stuff was he fashioned, and regardless of controversial feeling which raged over his head for many years after, his aims and ambitions for the young University were of the highest. His salary was $2,500 a year and his first home but a shack.

Dr. Thomas Condon, the next ranking faculty member, was the exact opposite in disposition. Irish-born in 1822, his was a quiet, delightful personality, outstanding for its gentleness, dignity, and scholarly attributes. Slight of build, almost delicate of feature, his direct gaze saw many things beyond the knowledge of the layman, yet retained its gentle twinkling over the problems of student and grown-up alike. He was loved by all who came in contact with him, for his kindness, modesty, deep and sincere religious faith and his own very great personal charm. Myriad speaking engagements carried him throughout the state and he soon became recognized as one of its intellectual leaders. A quietly dressed man in a frock-coated suit, a long gray beard falling over it, his eye-glasses in hand, he stood on hundreds of platforms to lead the thinking of mature people or to urge his students to acquire questioning minds. In appearance he has often been likened to a Druid.

Dr. Condon came to America when he was but eleven years old, to receive his education in New York—very largely through his own clear personal observations and human relations. Some routine education was acquired at Auburn Theological seminary and the Cazenovia institute and at forty-one years of age he was ordained as a Congregational minister. That same year he came to Oregon, serving in churches at Forest Grove, Albany and The Dalles.

Born, apparently, with an avid interest in science, he found the fossil beds of the rich John Day country a source of great fascination and started almost at once to acquire a collection of geological specimens. There he found the history of the continent's early ages written clearly, and interpreted them in many series of lectures of the most vivid quality and interest. World-famous geologists and paleontologists were his personal friends, and in the later years of his life, Dr. Condon's geological collection was known throughout the country as one of the finest in existence.

The theory of evolution was considered an almost shocking subject in those days, yet as a scientist he was frankly interested in its many phases; it is a happy commentary on his own character and the intelligence of others that it disturbed them not at all, or made him less popular.

When Dr. Condon died at the age of eighty-five years, he was still noted as a fine speaker and a great intellectual, and he was mourned through many states.

Of Professor Mark Bailey, we know a bit less. Born in Sterling, Mass., he was a tall dignified man who never sought the limelight for himself, yet seems to have left a vivid impression on his students. Perhaps that was because he taught both calculus and surveying! At any rate, he was a bearded, studious six-foot-three, the father of two sons, and lived, during his professorship, in a house where the Baptist Church now stands. A graduate of Brown University, he was a true conservative in religion, and much revered by his students.

Mrs. Mary Spiller was an instructor in the preparatory department of the university and came originally from Pacific College, while Miss Stone seems to have been in something of a secretarial position with a small bit of teaching on the side.

These, then, were the five who made up the original faculty. Two years later there came another, from Mercersburg College, Pa., who was a tutor in Greek and modern languages. His name was John W. Straub. And until his death he was one of the University's outstanding personalities. Having tremendous vigor and a quick mind he took hold at once and made himself very much a part of the new, young campus. He helped students obtain jobs and find places to live, spoke at rallies and went to parties; in every way he began preparing himself for the later important roles he played in University history. This man with the merry twinkle or the stern iron-gray stare, the quick step and the equally quick wit later became dean of the college of liberal arts, then dean of men.

In that particular period, local option was the law in Oregon and Eugene was dry. It was one of the stock jokes for students to write Hornbrook, Cal., and have great kegs of beer shipped to Eugene addressed to John W. Straub, Dean of Men, University of Oregon. He came early and stayed late, this alert and friendly young man who was to become known as "Daddy Straub" to later generations of college students coming and going beneath the great fir trees in the shadow of the Pioneer.

Equipment was quite a problem for the new school, and when the 1876 legislature appropriated $10,000 for two years' equipment needs, it was Judge Matthew Deady who wrote the bill. Physical needs only were to be purchased, and the first improvements were a well and sewer, more teaching rooms, completion of the assembly hall to seat 600, and the seven-foot high Kentucky board fence, which old pictures show surrounding the entire campus tract. Some physics needs were purchased in the East, also a piano, and a portable telescope. Salaries could not be made up out of this sum, and deficits were frequent so that numerous times in those first trying years the Eugene (and nearby) businessman had to raid his own till, or often his family savings banks to pay instructors.

By 1881 the institution had an annual income of $13,000 which looked huge in those days, but no sooner had such a modest degree of prosperity fallen into the lap of higher education than old debts began to rear their ugly heads. Certain merchants began to remember things owing them. Once again newspapers carried appeals for funds, churches worked, and individuals scraped the very bottom layer of an already splintered barrel. Even the faculty dug up contributions from various places.

Most happily for the future of the school, the dire situation came to the notice of Mr. Henry Villard, railroad and financial tycoon of the state and a great believer in higher education. He at once wrote Judge Deady, took up the approximately $10,000 in debt, visited the University campus and became very much impressed with its promises of growth and future greatness. He donated, a short time later, funds for a library, chemical and laboratory supplies, five scholarships, and the salary of an English professor. His next and perhaps greatest gift was $50,000 in Northern Pacific bonds, and this began a long series of private donations to further higher education.

The Villard endowment now brought in $3,000 annually, a state appropriation brought $5,000, the land fund income had mounted to better than $6,000, and fees were totaling $4,900 so that more than $18,000 was coming into the so-far scanty coffers. From this important turning point the income never went below $20,000 which seems a pittance now but was far from the proverbial "hay" in those days. It enabled the board to gather together an adequate faculty, and a wonderful period of peace and prosperity cast its rosy glow over the University.

Congestion followed as a natural sequence, and in 1885 the legislature authorized construction of a second and similar building of two stories, to cost $30,000 and to be named fittingly, Villard Hall. So a decade had passed, and there they stood, staunch as their namesakes, firm upon their barren hill, with only the waving prairie grasses to give them ornament until the little trees painstakingly planted by the senior class of 1883 should grow up.

They did grow up, along with scores of others planted by succeeding classes, and there they stand today sheltering the old campus quadrangle—stately firs and elms, cedars and beeches. Boston ivy brought from the East waves slim green tendrils over all the old buildings when spring comes on, and walls of shimmering scarlet and crimson glow where the autumn sun and crisp frosty air touch them.

Soon now there came a men's dormitory (Friendly Hall and named for Hon. S. H. Friendly) an astronomical observatory atop Skinner's butte (later torn down as a nuisance and because it was thought to be a demoralizing influence), and the first gymnasium. The remodeling of formal educational standards into a pattern practicable for a frontier community caused many a faculty headache, and the school was starting plenty of growing pains.

The first entrance requirements encompassed not much more than the three R's, a little Latin and a bit of Greek, but almost immediately the curricula began to change and requirements were boosted continually. Composition and speaking were held to be very important and flowing penmanship along with flowery language were the ne plus ultra. Everyone made great speeches with gestures by Del Sarte and the graduate with the most overpowering voice and delivery was usually voted the lad or lass most likely to succeed.

The still-existing Failing Beekman oratorical contest originated during this verbal period. An ornate 1890 graduation program shows a numbing total of nine orations in the morning and six for the afternoon. Fifteen members in all—and their grade average was 92.76!

Rules were indeed rules in those dear old days. No student was permitted to enter a saloon or brewery, nor to drink intoxicating liquors while in attendance at the University unless under doctor's prescription. No tobacco in any form was allowed on the campus, nor could the students leave town without permission of the president. Forbidden utterly were skating rinks, public dances, concealed weapons, profanity and indecent language. Not a man's world, certainly.

In those early years many unusual things happened to the graduating classes: the class of 1892 had not one girl, and only eight men. Another class was the first to wear uniform hats; then came the first class to wear cap and gown, the boys and girls of 1896. All in all '96 seems to have been quite a group—several of its stalwarts were on the first football team the University ever knew; and later, class members left a trust fund of $3,000 which was to be used as a loan fund, the principal to be left for 100 years, intact.

Not only were they active, but they were sturdy. Every member attended a twenty-fifth anniversary party held in the same spot in the garden of the old F. M. Wilkins home where the original class day party had been held. And when fifty years had rolled around since graduation day, age had treated them kindly; all of the women were living except one, and all other class members save two were present.

2. Administrative Changes—Campus Personalities
The Century Turns—A Student Body Organizes
Earliest Athletics

From the rules laid down for students, it is easy to see that the board of regents mixed its activities right into campus life, and expected obedience. Judge Deady, as president of the board, was fortunately its guiding factor in those earliest years and the marked prestige of his federal judgeship proved a wonderful thing. Of him, one author has written: "Not a man of especially popular qualities, he owed his influence largely to a definite assertion of his principles as he saw them and to his own industry in pursuing them. He was a loyal supporter of the University and wielded an active hand in the whole framework of the state for more than forty years."

Second in command was the faculty, and many neat entries in the minutes are Dean Straub's precise handwriting—in which he declares that "Mr. Blank, having been seen three times entering a saloon, has had his name stricken from the student lists." Whispering in class called down quick wrath from professors, church socials were suspect, and theaters were strictly taboo. There were no dormitories at first, and fraternities of course were unheard of; there were only such rooming places as Underwood's "Castle" located near Fifth street on the east side of Willamette, Grandma Fitch's home, or the Croner residence—both downtown. Many students were fortunate in finding rooms among the private homes in town, and scarcely a one but housed some embryo lawyer, doctor or teacher, treating them as members of the family in order to contribute that much more toward University progress. There was no "hello dance", no underclass mix, no Junior week-end.

There was, however, one thrilling, stimulating, social event at the beginning of each year. A "walk-around", it was called. And it was exactly that and little more—the evening was spent, literally, in walking in a circle around the hall with your partner and conversing sedately. The fluttering girls donned their wide skirts, high collars and ruffles, preened their fluffy bangs and waterfalls of curls, delicately touched their glowing faces with rice powder and stepped forth as pertly as they could in their snug bodices. The men in turn chose single breasted long coats, knotted big flat ties or narrow strings about their wing collars, gave the mustache a twirl, plastered the hair down, took a round-crowned hat from a peg in the corner and went forth to conquer or be conquered.

What mud they must have encountered with nothing but narrow board walks to take them to and from the "campus"! What weather and wind and rain they must have ploughed through! How cold the buildings must have been in the light of dim coal-oil lamps! In one college publication we read, "Give us a boat, give us a boat—if you can't give us a boat give us a sidewalk!"

All other social needs, save private entertaining, were met by organization of two literary societies, Laureans for the men and Eutaxians for the women. Both of these were formed in 1876, both were empowered to hold property, and both were assigned special meeting places. Fridays were the big days and the entire college year worked into a frenzy of excitement as the two annual joint meetings approached, and debates were held. On these special dates the coed of olden days took her best silks and laces out, and added a bustle just to be doubly glamorous; her escort appeared in a form-fitting dress suit, perhaps, with a bleakly-starched white shirt below the white organdy tie. His trousers were painfully tight, his shoes were buttoned, but his voice was full and vigorous, his delivery eloquent and his manners impeccable.

Even before the first graduating class had left old Deady Hall behind, the first baseball club was forming; in an exchange game with the Albany school both alcohol and brawling became mixed with the innings, and the club was short-lived.

The June of 1878 saw the first commencement exercises on the University of Oregon campus. Five sons and daughters of prominent families, who were later to make important places for themselves in the state, held those first five ornate diplomas: Robert S. Bean, later to study law and serve well and honorably on the supreme court bench of Oregon for many years; Nellie A. Condon, daughter of Dr. Thomas Condon, who lived in Eugene all her life and in later years wrote under the name of Ellen Condon McCornack (Mrs. H. F.), a vital and important volume on the life and works of the great geologist; Matthew S. Wallis; George S. Washburne, who was admitted to the Oregon bar in 1879 after his graduation, and later served in the Lane county court as county judge; fifth member of the class was John C. Whiteaker, son of Governor Whiteaker.

In 1883, Arthur Veazie and F. K. Masters attempted to form an athletic club but the conservative faculty proved violently allergic to such pastimes, and barred all boxing gloves from the gymnasium. Next came a band, with public concerts, then a college paper, and at long last a football team. Each struggled for a place in the faculty sun, and each finally survived. Things were happening fast in the old quadrangle now.

Town and gown were on the friendliest of terms, and from the very first year June commencement exercises were a magnet which drew all the best families. When the big day came, carriages and buggies were washed and polished, blooded horses were groomed to sleekness, and long before the appointed hour the "citizens in carriages" drew up beside the high board fence and tethered their four-footed transportation. Dusters were removed, hats adjusted, and whole families strolled together with groups of friends, up to Deady, and later to Villard, crowding in until even the deep window recesses were filled. While the lazy summer insects droned away outside, and little children nodded sleepily or protested their restraint in words more plain than the orators, the program went on and on. Duets and piano solos floated out into the shimmering air, gloved hands applauded daintily, and somehow after a while it was all over and another college year had ended. While congratulations went on and the elaborate baskets of flowers and the gifts were distributed so that each graduate had a share of the glory, smallfry tore off happily to chase butterflies or climb trees until they could be taken home to the festive dinner which always followed. It was all eagerly discussed for many days afterward.

When the University was nearing the end of twenty years of service to community and state, the Oregon and California railroad had come through Eugene, population had increased and isolation was lessened; news was getting around about some big institutions east of the Mississippi river, notably Cornell and the University of Chicago. Johnson had retired and the town and campus were eager to welcome as the new head, Dr. C. H. Chapman, who was an Easterner. Though he was the son of a farmer, his education was received at Johns Hopkins and he arrived on the campus with all the vigor of thirty-three years and a fixed determination to dovetail more closely together the interest of the University with the public school system of the state. Keenly desiring harmony, he proved a very fine speaker and succeeded in cementing relations with the high school principals, liberalizing the curriculum, broadening courses materially, and planning lecture and extension series. Shortly after his arrival, all preparatory courses were dropped from the curricula and commercial and engineering courses were added.

With this move, jealousies again sprang out like unleashed dogs and in Salem a "committee of 100" was organized to fight the expected legislative appropriations of 1895. The *Oregonian* accused the University administration of being wasteful and extravagant. Later, it is said, Harvey Scott, who had written the scathing articles, and Dr. Chapman came to an understanding, and for the greater part editor Scott was always a friend of the institution.

Governor Pennoyer, just before his retirement from office, appointed three new regents, all from Eugene, but newly-elected Governor Lord saw the fallacy in such a situation and fortunately changed the setup to one from Eugene and two from the state at large. Dr. Chapman and the University had now attained quite a strong position. The board of regents tacitly agreed to let him run the school and its employees, and he held a firm rein.

But when he released two old and dependable professors from active duty and put them on emeritus status, minus salary (Profs. Collier and Bailey) he led with his administrative chin. They were men respected and honored by all. In addition, President Chapman reduced salaries and with the money saved, engaged four new professors to replace the two discharged ones. Two of these four were Profs. F. G. Young and Edgar McClure, both of whom were to serve long and faithfully. The former was a Johns Hopkins man, and remained with the University until his retirement. This whole occurrence roiled otherwise peaceful waters, but subsided into progress before too long a time.

One fact Chapman could not escape however—his action had divided the campus sharply into two factions, and the townspeople were resentful of him. He seemed by now to delight in being annoying by mixing into local and political issues, into athletics, to the detriment of Oregon teams, and by assuming a querulous and rude attitude. Mrs. Chapman, who had earlier started a study club called the Fortnightly club, earliest of the many cultural clubs and still a most active one in the organizational life of the city, came in for a bitter share of protest. The *Guard* maintained neutrality for a time, but finally came out in the open to censure Chapman sharply.

That was all the state-wide papers opposed to University interests needed—in no time at all the battle was on and everyone waded in happily to have their say. With the trait common to so much of human nature, each enemy took a kick while the victim was supposedly down, and some hoped it would spell doom for the school. But a group of thirty-one prominent citizens and ten senior students petitioned the board to remove Dr. Chapman, and while these charges, along with some against certain faculty members, were dismissed as trivial, Chapman's days of real benefit to the institution were assuredly over.

The legislature of that year, 1895, placed the whole controversy with a committee of five for a decision, thanks to the friendly attitude of Governor Lord. This committee, which turned in a favorable report, thus assuring the continuation of all appropriations, was composed of C. W. Fulton, later a U. S. Senator, Bernard Daly, G. H. Hill, G. N. Williamson and B. B. Butt (Bull). Chapman was wise enough to resign at this stage.

The third man to enter the president's office was Dr. Frank Strong. Born in New York, he was a graduate of Yale, and a very genial but reserved and dignified gentleman.

The six-feet-five-inches of the man belied his peace-and-quiet-loving disposition, but offered a hint as to the ideas of efficiency he brought to the new task before him. Two of his chief interests were music and religion. Others were organizational excellence and a broadening scope of work and integration of courses. Early in his regime he established the graduate school as a main division, added a college of literature, one of science and the arts, a school of commerce and preparatory courses in law, journalism and teaching. A school of mines and mining came last, and all, plus the established schools of music, law and medicine, began to add up to quite an institution.

Turning his talents to the business end of the campus, Dr. Strong tended meticulously to scores of details hitherto neglected and it was under his guidance that the first full-time registrar appeared on the University campus, followed in short order by a full-time combined registrar and purchasing agent in the person of L. H. Johnson. Mr. Johnson served for many faithful years in that capacity, and is now living in Eugene.

An excellent speaker, Dr. Strong carried the University to its statewide public and encouraged his professors to do likewise. During all this activity, he felt keenly the campus division dating from the previous regime. Shockingly small growth had blessed the University when the new century dawned—only 225 students were enrolled after a twenty-year struggle. But with Lawrence T. Harris, R. A. Booth and W. A. Kuykendall as the Lane county representatives for the 1901 legislature, a requested $25,000 for a new building, and an increase of $17,000 in the continuing appropriation went through without a snag. Brighter days seemed ahead.

Dr. Strong's religious zeal made him place a high value on Y.W. and Y.M.C.A.'s and he instigated a drive for funds for a religious building on the campus, which would also serve as a student center. The fund was raised by Eugene people, students and faculty, but it roused another "anti" campaign among the busybody element whose members objected to the state furnishing light and heat to an organization closed to free-thinkers and non-Protestants. The building was abandoned, and Dr. Strong soon afterward decided to accept the chancellorship of Kansas university as a more suitable ground for his progressive ideas.

Having met with a marked degree of opposition from the more conservative regents, he left the campus rather disgruntled, and his parting shot was a tirade against the whole system delivered at the final student assembly. That he accomplished a great deal for the University can never be questioned. But for long years, wherever old timers gathered, the Chapman-Strong controversy raged on and on, shaking skeletons real or imagined from almost every faculty closet, rattling dry old bones of contention, and giving the critical something to chew over.

We can not bypass the origin of the University of Oregon's now-great medical school. In 1887, Dr. C. A. Strong, brother-in-law of Judge Deady, and eleven other prominent Portland doctors, petitioned the board of regents to start a medical department in Portland. The faculty was set at eight professors who were to be all-powerful in the outlining of courses, setting of rules and all other matters pertinent to the school. An approving board granted the petition, specifying first that no debts occurring in the new school be saddled on the University proper.

First Dean of the school was Dr. S. E. Josephi, while Dr. Strong was its secretary. From the little rude wooden building of two rooms at 23rd and Marshall streets in Portland has grown the great University of Oregon Medical school, a success from its earliest inception. Its graduates have won renown all over the world in research, in hospitals, in the armed services, and in private practice. The excellence of their basic and advanced training has been evidenced by their high standards of performance, scholarship in graduate schools elsewhere, and over-all intelligence. From the original investment of $1,000, borrowed from the First National bank of Portland on personal notes of its instructors, has grown the imposing group of buildings atop Marquam Hill. Because of the rivalry of the Willamette university medical school, from which Dr. Strong had withdrawn earlier, only 18 students made up the first entering group. But its growth was steady and marked, and in time the Willamette school was closed and absorbed by the University of Oregon Medical School, which has long since won its national, official rating as a "Class A" institution.

Law also had come into the picture by now, starting in 1885 under the tutelage of Richard N. Thornton, an Englishman who desired to lecture on subjects of law. Seven students made up the original class, and in the next eight years a total of seventy-two hopeful young barristers became bachelors of law and hung out their shingles. Among the instructors and lecturers were L. L. McArthur, Erasmus B. Shattuck, and Judge Deady.

The music school, opened the following year under the deanship of D. W. Coolidge, grew rather faster than the other two additions, having more than fifty students in two years. Many daughters of prominent Eugene families learned to take their musical bows there, and trill sweetly the sentimental songs of the times or play delicate airs on the family piano for all to enjoy.

As names make the news, names plus personalities make the background of a given situation. So, given the University, there came personalities like Prof. B. J. Hawthorne, and Dr. Luella Clay Carson, and no early chronicle could possibly be complete without them. Each came on the scene in the rather early 80's, when a lot of other things were happening to the campus.

Professor Hawthorne almost at once became known as "Buck" —just why, no history seems to say. But Buck he was and Buck he remained to his old students until the day he died. In his salad days he was graduated from Randolph-Macon college in Virginia, and probably no early-day professor on the campus had a more interesting history than he. Born in the South, he had entered the Confederate army as a boy of eighteen, and story had it that his first assignment was as a drummer boy. When the Civil war ended, he retired with the rank of colonel, having served on General Robert E. Lee's staff for an undetermined time. In the summer of 1898, he marched proudly down our Willamette street at the head of the G.A.R. column, carrying the stars and stripes as token of devotion for his son Wistar, fighting then in the Philippines, and later to lose his life there. A true Democrat, he was in sympathy with the rebel forces and faced a good deal of heartache during the early Eugene years because of it.

This war interval was followed by rather wide teaching experience, and he brought to the local campus a most kindly disposition, an eagle eye, and a very dry sense of humor to temper his academic and perhaps military dignity. When most men are ready to call it a day and relax from years of labor and study, "Buck" elected to study psychology, and he founded the first laboratory on the campus. Students loved him, and he gained a wide following in this newly opened field. Living until his death at the family home on north Lawrence street, he enjoyed a long life during which scores of former students came to renew old friendships and relate old anecdotes.

"Luella Clay" as she was usually known among the young ladies of the campus, came as a teacher of elocution and English composition, and very soon proved herself more than a master of both. A delicate little person of quiet charm and quieter wit, she was old school to the last flourish of the pen. Beneath her soft voice and prim mouth lay an iron-clad will—and one of the strongest personalities ever to grace the University campus. Her self-appointed task was to teach the young ladies social graces, proper morals, and graceful deportment on important occasions as well as in everyday life. When she became dean of women two years after her arrival, no college "lady" as she chose to call them, dared have badly prepared assignments, or to disobey the strict rules she made for social conduct.

Graduated from the old Portland Academy and St. Helen's Hall, she craved education and acquired it so long as she lived. Her father was Senator J. C. Carson, and it was said her ancestry could be traced back to George Washington—indeed in the long-featured face and general delineation of character one can almost see a resemblance. Undoubtedly repressed to a high degree, she became an extremist in manners and morals, and her detailed instructions to young ladies graduating were painfully comprehensive. They must learn the exact gesture with which to lay down their gloves, pick up a bouquet, or seat themselves; they must cross their ankles only, and never under any circumstances turn to look at a late-comer in any audience. They must never, no never, cheer, but could only clap hands. Her own manner of dress was daintily meticulous, her delicate hands always clad in long kid gloves for evening functions, and lovely gowns displayed her fondness for pretty clothing. Old friends said that she had endured a tragic love affair as a girl—true or false, she had a definite preference for the boys in her classes. Her late afternoon classes in rhetoric often found dusk falling, and one day her students risked the dignified wrath by each quietly lighting a candle, boys included. All came through unscathed.

Dr. Carson it was who conceived the idea of the annual Commencement Flower and Fern procession for alumni, seniors and undergraduates. First held near the original old buildings, where a singing group wound through the campus and deposited bouquets in the form of a large "O", the procession has maintained its place in campus traditions. Alumni now lead the way through the women's quadrangle on Sunday evening of Commencement Week, dividing ranks to accept the graduates in cap and gown into their number as they pass on toward the statue of the Pioneer Mother. There the beautiful, colorful bouquets are placed in tribute, and lovely voices ring out in songs of *alma mater,* as the assembled crowds watch quietly.

Dr. Carson resigned from the University deanship to become president of Mills College, leaving behind her hundreds of fond students who perhaps have a better understanding of her now than in former years. She died in California several years ago.

There were bright spots in those days, and one of the brightest of them all was S. H. Friendly, a town and campus personality, and later a regent. His was the enthusiasm never to be downed, his the cheer always to be counted on. "Sam", as many people knew and called him, was a small, quick-stepping man of much energy and one of Eugene's important and loved merchants. His store and that of F. B. Dunn stood eye to eye on Main street, crackling their taffetas and showing their passementerie trimmings in opposing windows. After his store, Mr. Friendly's interest was, first and last, in the welfare of the University. He gave of his wealth and his heart to his state regent's job. When town and students were low in spirit, it was Mr. Friendly who could always put the punch in a speech and leave them feeling that all was not lost.

One can see him yet, as the cheering, milling students lifted his stocky figure out of the Kincaid field mud and onto the platform. Never mind whether his speech was scheduled or not—someone always called "we want Sam Friendly!" So there he suddenly is, standing in the middle of the little platform, torrents of rain falling around him, hands thrust in long overcoat pockets, silhouetted against the sputtering flames of a half-burned rally bonfire. He begins to talk and everyone listens, "Boys and girls of the Uniwersity—" and soon his arms are gesturing and his coat tails flying, as he snatches the derby hat from his balding head, arms waving in the sodden air, he shouts heartily and happily, "Wictory must be ours!" The students fairly shout with him, and Oregon Spirit is on the move again.

To return for a moment to the opening year of the 1900's— the old more or less defunct athletic association gave way to a bona fide student association, with student taxes levied and athletic equipment purchased by means of entertainments and private donations. With the beginning of occasional team travel athletes themselves often times had to sign notes to pay their own expenses. R. S. Bryson ("Rock" to his friends both then and now) took over as athletic manager and not only paid the bills, but left a slight surplus.

On March 24th, 1894, the University of Oregon's first real football team played its first real game, and some names long familiar to student generations were in uniform that day: the late Dr. Clarence Keene of Silverton who always remained one of the University's staunchest and finest supporters; John Edmundson, a fine player and now deceased; Harry Templeton, now also deceased; and C. A. Wintermeier, Eugene attorney. The coach? Our own Cal Young, but in those days called "coacher", pioneer and the son of Walker Young of the wagon train of 1852, famous now in his own right as guiding spirit and authority on the Oregon Trail pageant. The final score was Oregon 44, Albany College 2. The *Reflector*, campus sheet of the day, said:

> Verily, we have met the enemy and they are ours. Much of the success of the game is due to Mr. C. M. Young, coacher of the U of O team. The crowd of spectators was very large. Not only were most of the sightseeing positions inside taken, but the fence, and even neighboring housetops were crowded. Mr. Mathews is the U. O. captain.
>
> The Albany eleven took possession of the field about 2:15 and limbered up till 2:40, when the U. of O. came on a sharp run from their dressing room. It was seen in an instant that the U. of O. had the advantage in weight; but could they, with their short practice, withstand the skill of their opponents? The game was called at 3:00. . . .
>
> Sweaters were laid aside and the two elevens quickly

lined up. The first play was through the center; the ball flew back. There was a crash and the referee called out a gain of five yards . . . the ball was finally sent through the center for a touchdown in just six minutes. The full back, Templeton, successfully kicked goal. . . .

The story ran on for another priceless column. A fine thing it was that a short time before that game the University color had been chosen—the yellow of the state flower, the Oregon grape. Later was added the green which makes such striking contrast in our athletic seasons.

The *Reflector,* original campus publication, was to give way before long to the *Oregon Weekly,* with the alert and driving C. N. (Pat) McArthur at the helm. An annual publication followed, edited by Allen H. Eaton and managed by E. N. Blythe.

Permanent "Christian Associations" appeared on the campus, sponsored by Willa Hanna (Beattie) for the women and Frederick S. Dunn for the men. Members met trains, assisted new students, conducted a book exchange and hunted down jobs for those who needed them. The present "Hello" book is probably descended from their original vest-pocket treasure of songs, game schedules and general information.

Track became an interest of men students the following year, second only to football. Under the able coaching of old "Dad" (W. O.) Trine the team won state championships four different years, going on to a northwest trophy in 1900 by defeating the University of Washington. Richard Shore Smith, already a great football player, rolled up 18 points for the home team to clinch a title. Homer Angell, Leslie Scott and Walter Whittlesey were names of the day important in organizing athletics.

Baseball rated very little, and came on the early day scene spasmodically.

But play-giving was no longer a shocking pastime and musical organizations sprang up eagerly. Things were looking up again, and into a pleasantly optimistic atmosphere stepped the fourth president of the University, and the man who was to serve longer than any other president to date.

But the Old Settler knew other things. It might well have been that he looked down and said to himself, it'd be mighty nice if I could give the home folks a little help about now—they deserve it. Move along, Old Pioneer.

And so he did. Through a few years more of hard and bitter times the rugged determination which first formed and nurtured a young University returned to stand beside its banners once more.

3. The Middle Years—Campbell Administration—Strife
A Victory Comes—A War Begins

As the first local educator to head the school, President Prince L. Campbell was rather the man of the hour. Eastern talent had not been as successful as wishful thinking had painted the picture. He was, to be sure, a Harvard graduate, and while his years there had given him wider opportunities in cultural matters, he had also taken social sciences, philosophy and English and had later worked his beat as a reporter for the *Kansas City Star,* so that he had a fairly realistic approach to life, for a time at least. Plus that was a background of religion, since he was descended from Thomas Campbell, founder of the Christian Church.

Missouri-born in the year 1861, he moved to Oregon with his parents and subsequently his father, Thomas N. Campbell, became president of the denominational school at Monmouth. After graduating from there and taking a turn at teaching, P. L. Campbell himself became president of Monmouth and remained for twelve years.

When he came on the University scene, he was undoubtedly aware that factions were many and old feuds still smouldering, but he seemed determined to see the school progress, so with a rare combination of tact, humor, human interest and self-sacrifice, he set calmly about his business. He built up self-confidence among students and faculty; quietly replaced the men whose terms expired, with others of more advanced training. The board of regents, headed at that time by Judge Robert S. Bean, were favorably impressed with his program and personality and gave him immeasurable help. They evinced confidence in his plans and supported them with fine spirit for a time.

Idealistic in the extreme, President Campbell refused to believe that others would ever stoop to take advantage of him; believing firmly in the right, he steadfastly refused to believe aught but good of those with whom he was forced to do business from opposite sides of the table. At no time, regardless of the provocation, did he stoop to the tactics employed by rival schools. He believed personal relations should be kept on a high plane, and that all people were sincere and honest. After he had been here for some time, there came to be a by-word abroad in town and on campus—"for the ultimate good of the University". Hundreds of times his listeners heard him point up a talk or a private conversation with the phrase.

Certainly no man before could have given more of himself than did Prince Campbell. Those who remember clearly his intent and handsome face, with the serious dark eyes shining from the depths of its pallor, can recall exactly how deep within him lay sincerity and good. It is a sad commentary that the very personal quality of his interest in friends and faculty forged a link in the ultimate breakdown of his prestige and, in time, of his health.

There came a time when he was surrounded by a small group of perhaps well-meaning friends, satellite in their quality of staying anxiously near the throne. Their influence for weal or woe is debatable. Whatever the answer to that may be, his policy soon became one of placation and while he kept some friends who might otherwise have become enemies of the University, he lost so much ground by his mild acceptance of a militantly organized foe that it took many years to overcome the infiltration.

Loyal as the town was to him as a friend, and admiring as it was of his endearing qualities and scholarly charm, it was deeply divided in opinion as to his effectiveness. Realistic thinkers realized only too well that a more aggressive policy must be adopted to overcome enormous advantages already gained by opponents of the University. They watched hard-won ground slipping from beneath the University with the wash of treacherous currents—yet they stood undivided in their affection and respect for a kind and deeply thoughtful gentleman who steadfastly refused to dip his own standard.

In 1923 President Campbell inaugurated a "gift campaign" to obtain funds for the University and to present its values throughout the state. The plan caught on, and was rolling full speed ahead the following spring. In failing health for some time and worn down by the rigors of his speaking engagements, he collapsed following a student assembly, was taken to the hospital never to be active again, and in August of 1925 he died.

While it is impossible to recount in detail all the University's fortunes—good and bad—of that period, it is necessary to recapitulate a little for an understanding of the situation.

Three years after Campbell's accession, the University began a long-overdue struggle for expansion. With increased enrollment new buildings were needed, and also more physical equipment.

The program was presented to the legislature and at once opposition rose and turned the session into a hotbed of trouble and antagonism. Dean Withycombe of the agricultural college, who later became Oregon's governor, was the rallying point and no weapons were barred in the long period of sharpshooting which followed.

With the then-Governor Chamberlain maintaining a middle-of-the-road policy, most of the University measures were passed in spite of the guerrilla warfare. Not a great while before this, however, Oregon voters—ever ready to try something strange and new—had passed a freak law known as the initiative and referendum, sponsored by Senator U'Ren. In brief, the measure as passed provided that any law enacted by the legislature could be referred to the people at a special, or the next general, election, providing a certain number of names were procured on duly prepared petitions. This law was as yet untried. Now was the time, antagonists said, to invoke its use.

The measure was hastily dragged out and happily dusted off. The required names were attached to petitions and the result was that all appropriations for the University of Oregon were held up until the next general election—as the bill specified. There the school sat, with no funds, no buildings, and deferred salaries; so the township once more tightened its belt and emptied its pockets. When the next legislature convened, University supporters forestalled any such move by quickly introducing a bill for "continuing" appropriations, and the bill passed readily. Art and politics are rather infrequent bedfellows, but this skillful bit of legislation was passed very largely through the work of Allen H. Eaton, University graduate of 1902 who was a "freshman" in the House of Representatives at that session. Owning a popular book and art store in Eugene, he yet had time enough to lend loyal support to his Alma Mater, and judgment enough to make his politics effective.

Governor Chamberlain very promptly vetoed this continuing appropriation of $125,000—some say because of his economy program, others say from the work of pressure groups. Perhaps only the governor himself knew why. At any rate, the measure was just as promptly passed over his veto.

No sooner had the gavel brought *sine die* adjournment to this session than Linn county and others of the organized opposition reached into their straw-filled hats and pulled out a second referendum. Leaders of this raiding party were named Eugene Palmer and Cyrus H. Walker. The latter, having a bit of fame as the first white male born in the Oregon country, should have known better.

By this time, even Senator U'Ren had begun to feel that he had a white bull by the tail in his casually-sponsored referendum measure, and feared public sentiment would oppose it if the anti-University movement went too far. As a result, his support was less than half-hearted; granges, meanwhile, had gone on record favoring the continuing appropriations. But Col. E. Hofer, Salem *Capitol-Journal* publisher, was still a fire-eating opponent and in his own sensational fashion, organized the Marion county opposition. In the flick of a pied line of type he produced 6,000 names on the referendum petitions, and they were carried to the secretary of state who declared two technical defects in them. In this, the circuit court concurred; but the supreme court reversed that decision and they were declared legal.

This was the blackest moment yet. The University of Oregon stood with her back to the wall, her very existence at stake, and Eugene stood beside her. The cards all seemed stacked against her, with an extra ace up every sleeve but her own.

Reeling a little from the blow, supporters began to gather their forces. To carry her battle flags to the voters, the University appointed a campaign committee headed by Clifton M. (Pat) McArthur, a graduate of 1901 and a most effective speaker. Campaigning with him were Allen Eaton, L. R. Alderman, son of a prominent farmer, Homer Angell and Dr. Homer I. Keeney—graduates all, and capable of a good battle in the interests of their *alma mater.* David Graham of Eugene was one of the staunchest workers.

Of the 140 newspapers in the state at that time, Hofer's alone was hostile to the cause. Portland's three largest papers, the *Oregonian, Journal* and *Telegram,* were all loyal University supporters as were the Portland chamber of commerce and board of trade. The state federation of labor and the women's clubs opposed the referendum. Campaign facts pointed out that appropriations for the University of Oregon were lower than any state in the Union. The entire issue came into almost national focus as an educational controversy.

Both sides campaigned heavily, and as the June election drew nearer and nearer feeling throughout the state was almost at Civil war pitch. Every able-bodied citizen of Eugene felt a personal responsibility for the election; so did faculty and students. They worked tirelessly up till the last hour, then sat back to wait. It was 1907.

No radio brought news in those days and throughout a long and nervewracking day the town and campus waited, weary and fearful. One must remember that the University was more than a school to those early Eugeneans—it was the future of their town, the future good of their children and grandchildren—the future they had sacrificed and saved and worked for. Anxious groups gathered in homes, little knots of worried men stood about the streets. Rumor came that all was lost.

It was near midnight of a despairing day when the University's victory was finally declared—won by a margin of only 3,500 votes out of 85,000 cast. But it was a great victory, and a soul-satisfying one to the town and her beloved campus, and Eugene gave out with a real celebration. That night a great horde of 3,000 grateful students and citizens, headed by the town's two or three automobiles, marched to old Kincaid field. When the cheering crowd of boys had gathered within the gates, the girls marched sedately through in a body, each carrying a gay lighted paper lantern, and took their places in the grandstand—as Dean Carson and decorum dictated. Roman candles, sky rockets and red and blue fireworks pierced the summer sky, there were speeches by President Campbell, by Eaton, and Alderman, and Steiwer, and Graham; there was a great bonfire and glad college songs ringing through the air. No doubt lovable little Sam Friendly waved his arms and cried, "Wictory is ours"! It was decided then and there that June 1 would become a future holiday for the campus, to commemorate a turning point in the history of the University.

Lessons could have been learned from those tallied reports, straws for future winds: The counties between Lane and Multnomah rolled up almost 10,000 majority against the University, with Marion, Linn and Benton as the leaders. It was Eastern and Southern Oregon, Portland and Multnomah county, and Eugene and Lane county, which saved a grim day. Commercial and manufacturing interests and labor unions stood up to be counted beside us; many farm interests voted against us.

Col. Hofer had not yet given up hope of upsetting the educational applecart, and decided to inject the question of course duplication into the next legislature. This possible pleasantry was well taken care of by Pat McArthur who by now had become speaker of the house and who personally introduced a bill providing for a board of higher curricula, the duty of which would be to pass on all matters of study courses—but not enforce their decisions.

Personnel of the board was thought to be impartial and fair-minded and its initial decisions seemed to bear out that feeling. Very soon after the board started functioning, however, University interests realized a different situation, as the first board decision resulted in awarding technical courses to O.A.C. The college had over a period of several years been expanding its educational and economic courses rather noticeably, and when University authorities questioned board members on this matter they tacitly admitted those courses belonged on the University campus—but allowed O.A.C. to continue the obvious duplications. It soon became plain to even casual observers that the board was neither so efficient and businesslike nor so impartial as had been at first supposed.

One more referendum popped up in 1911, born in Cottage Grove, as the result of a local grudge against the Lane county representatives who refused to vote for a bill creating Nesmith county from the southern part of Lane. Cottage Grove interests had designed this bill, and were not content to have the Lane county delegation remain merely neutral. So in retaliation they started the referendum but went further and hired one H. J. Parkinson to bring in 3,000 signatures at the price of three-and-one-half cents each. The whole thing was on a high plane, with hired canvassers, no holds barred, and few questions asked. Finally the University interests found it worthwhile to hire detectives and investigate.

As a result of this investigation, headlines of June 11 declared at least 4,000 of the names open forgeries and 9,000 of the 15,000 required, illegal and fraudulent. The petition scandals were the talk of the state all summer, and at the Salem trial Judge Galloway ruled them illegal. The case was then appealed, and thrown out; appealed once more and finally, for some reason, the court suddenly ruled that there were 7,600 legal names—enough to place the referendum measure on the fall ballot.

All this bickering caused the more radical element of the state, encouraged by the untiring efforts and clever political maneuverings of William Jasper Kerr, president of O.A.C., to start talking consolidation of the two schools in Corvallis. Having much more money to do with because of Federal appropriations to land-grant colleges, and not having referendums thrown at them every year or so, the college had very skillfully managed to build its physical plant up to a place where it could care for quick expansion. Dr. Kerr had been called to O.A.C. from Monmouth college in 1907, and prior to that from a Mormon birthplace and traditional training in Utah. In his heyday he was possessed of a most suave personality, backed by the aggressive drive of a locomotive, great organizational skill, political astuteness and an ambition to know influential people and political leaders. These attributes he kept working two shifts a day over a period of years, and with little active opposition from here he was rather successful in making people feel that the University of Oregon was of no special importance.

When the first consolidation move was proposed Campbell and Kerr staged a battle of wits, and Governor Oswald West decided that a unified board of control such as he had installed in the state departments would solve some of the problems. As prepared, this bill called for a common board of regents and a .6 mill tax to be divided three-sevenths for the University and four-sevenths for the college on the basis of their enrollment. People were weary of all the referendum business, so they voted a straight no ticket: no common board of regents, no millage for buildings, etc. About all the University had to cheer about was in still having its own identity.

By now the Oregon populace was evincing some embarrassment over very unfavorable publicity gained by such educational strife; it was likewise showing some irritation over having its accredited and established State University heckled year after year. President Campbell maintained his dignified silence, carefully laid plans for the next legislature, and all his bills passed: .3 mill tax, $190,000 for increased maintenance and extension from 1913-1915, and $175,000 for an administration building and improvements. Parkinson returned to the picture to try one more referendum but received short shrift from everyone he contacted. The old referendum bugaboo remained a spectre at the University's business table for many years, but was inactive for a period of time.

During all this storm, the board of higher curricula had been snoozing quietly in a corner, when its members suddenly heard a whisper suggesting it be abolished. Galvanized into quick action, the best thing at hand was the old duplication issue so they produced it. Important supporters of both schools went to the hearings, but Mr. Kerr had done his work quietly and well and at one fell swoop all civil, electrical, and chemical engineering courses remaining at the University were assigned to the college thus wiping out every technical course in the University's curricula. To quiet University protests, civil engineering was abolished at the college in Corvallis for three brief years but by 1917 was back as a fully established course.

Lane county, Eugene and the campus were bitter—and rightfully so, for a supposedly impartial curricula board had but shortly before allowed the agricultural school to continue her duplicating courses in education and economics which rightfully belonged to the state University. President Campbell came in for a vast amount of censure among alumni all over the state, and his peace-at-any-price tactics were held up to the sharpest questioning. Many University supporters were for the first time fully roused to a realization of what tactics had been employed and with what damaging results. So many times in human experience that type of action must be studied to be fully appreciated.

For publicity purposes, commerce, education, architecture and the graduate schools had been "awarded" the University but skillful wording of the proviso left all manner of loopholes. The way was open for indefinite expansion, and any amount of duplication of all these courses allowed them, and employing only reasonable caution Dr. Kerr and his cohorts started at once to make the most of their opportunities.

On the Oregon campus, authorities went about mending their battered fences as fast as possible. With a view to widening the scope and prestige of the business school, Hon. H. B. Miller of Portland was named head. He had but recently resigned as U. S. consul to Japan, and during his stay there had naturally become impressed with the huge opportunities for trade expansion. An elderly man of intelligence and charm, he did both students and faculty a great service during his term here. Another man who left his mark on the business school was D. Walter Morton, an accountant from Pennsylvania. The human dynamo type, he was a good speaker and outstanding at public relations. He did such a fine job and advanced the school so greatly that it was quite a match for the lost engineering.

In fact, the business school was so successful that a partial ad interim committee of the legislature, appointed to investigate how the various appropriated funds were being spent at both the University and O.A.C. made a startling attack. First berating fraternities and sororities at both schools, they went on to attack certain pamphlets dealing with the marketing of Oregon products, sent over the state by the business school at Mr. Miller's suggestion, then closed their report on Oregon by stating flatly, "We recommend that the issuing of bulletins on agricultural subjects by the University of Oregon be discontinued, also, that the department of commerce of the University be discontinued."

They further put the stamp of disapproval on any or all appropriations for the University, approved a new library for

O.A.C. and recommended removal of the Monmouth normal school to Portland. The report ended with this statement: "We find Oregon Agricultural College to be in most excellent condition and President Kerr one of the best organizers and most thoroughly efficient managers of an educational institution it has ever been our pleasure to meet."

Personnel of the committee was of much interest to all who had followed the play of the various referendum issues: Charles Childs, E. V. Littlefield, W. H. Strayer, W. W. Cardwell and George McBride.

It was Oregon's and Eugene's good fortune that the committee was so biased, or influenced, as to be unfair. The thinking business-men and the press of the state came to the University's rescue, and the education committee of the legislature was wise enough never to report the bill out of committee for action.

Though salaries at the University were not adequate because of a shortage of funds, the caliber and reputation of the school enabled it to procure and interest high class instructors. Thus Ellis F. Lawrence became dean of the school of architecture in 1914, and fine arts was headed by Allen Eaton. A. H. (Larry) Schroff, nationally known as an etcher, designer and maker of stained glass windows and as a painter, became an instructor in the art school, as did Roswell Dosch, member of an old Portland family who had become a well-known sculptor. Mrs. Schroff, an artist in her own right, also became an instructor.

Journalism had come to the campus way back in 1901—taught, surprisingly enough, by Luella Clay Carson—but had never attained importance. President Campbell had never lost his interest in the profession since those Kansas City *Star* days, and had moreover, been forced to recognize the necessity of good publicity and public relations throughout the heated years. So he brought down from the city editor's desk of the Seattle *Post-Intelligence* Eric W. Allen, of Wisconsin, and under his kindly, humorous and understanding mind and management, the resurrected school began to blossom. He was a practical dean, and every one of his students received the most practical training, from typesetting to editorial writing. During those years the famous John Henry Nash Press was established here, some special presses brought to the plant, and some of the finest examples of hand-printing in the entire country have gone out from there. A notable example was his wartime printing, on specially made paper, of the poem, "There'll Always Be An England."

Between Dean Allen, Prof. George Turnbull, who later became dean following Mr. Allen's death, and Prof. Colin Dyment, no journalism student of the earlier era ever went forth carelessly trained in either mechanics, standards or ethics.

The school of education reached its peak of development at this same period. In a new building of its own, and a University high school for practical application of class work, Dean Henry D. Sheldon was the presiding dean. On the faculty many years earlier, Dr. Sheldon had resigned to go to Pittsburgh in 1911, but was recalled to the Oregon deanship, where he remained until retirement. A further and most important upward step came with establishment of a course in educational psychology under Dr. B. W. DeBusk, already an eminent man in his field. Interest in the subject increased tremendously during his tenure on the campus, and his death was a cause of sincerest regret among all who had known his work.

Long, long ago the music school was organized under the able leadership of bald and merry Irving M. Glen, a rosy-cheeked early version of one of the seven dwarfs. He could sing like an angel on occasion, was a capable leader, and his glee and mandolin clubs truly gave when he waved his baton. Very bald, he wore a carefully waved toupee on all state occasions and looked much more like a well-fed cherub than a music professor. Starting from a few scattered majors back in the early days, the music school is now one of the University's largest and best known departments. With about 200 majors and a large building and larger annex of its own, the present school is a far cry from the days when the men's Dorm housed the young hopefuls, and strident soprano notes floated across the old quadrangle to drown out the booming economic pronouncements of Jimmy Gilbert!

The University of Oregon law school was originally started in Portland, with a very small appropriation. Soon there was marked local demand for law courses, so a chair of law was established on the campus in 1913, with Dean E. W. Hope as its head and guiding genius. Expanding very rapidly, the school soon evolved into a full three-year legal course, with a prerequisite of three years of liberal arts. Wayne L. Morse came here in 1928 as an instructor, was subsequently made dean, departed during the last war to serve on the War Labor Relations Board and is now serving his first term as Senator from Oregon.

The medical school was making strides all this time. By repeated effort, the board of regents had obtained a grant of

$10,000 for new, modern equipment and a like sum for maintenance. The initial course had been set at two years, and for the first time the school could be well staffed with full time professors. Dr. Kenneth A. J. MacKenzie, one of the best of Portland's many fine medicos, had succeeded Dr. Josephi as dean of the school, and it was very soon after this that the absorption of Willamette university medical school took place.

Impressed with the school's fine record, the O.W.R. and N. Railroad made deed of twenty-five acres of land on a rise above the Willamette river to the medical school in 1914, and close on the heels of this the legislature granted them $50,000, followed by another contribution of $25,000 from Portland. This marked the beginning of the University of Oregon Medical Center atop Marquam hill—that Center which has come to stand for excellence, efficiency, skill and good works among its colleagues.

These developments bring us to a crisis on the campus of a very different sort than any hitherto endured—the coming of war. The familiar mushrooming of every activity sped up the whole tempo of campus life, war activities took over, men departed, and women wept. Col. John Leader, late of the Royal Irish Rifles, and more recently invalided home from combat duty, arrived in Eugene in December of 1917 to command the R.O.T.C. unit and remained for two years, an integral part of the campus with his charming and beautiful wife and interesting family. He was a remarkable leader, and the atmosphere was electric with cooperation.

Wounded in the battle of the Somme, Col. Leader brought war and its needs and tragedies very close home to the small town of that era. Two thousand students and alumni were in the armed services and as time went on, thirty-nine gold stars grew on the huge service flag which hung in the Administration portico day and night during the war.

Following the war, there was the great rush back to education, with its tremendously increased enrollment, and during the five-year period from 1920-1925 the University received $1,200,000 in millage revenue, which produced a school of commerce building, a women's dormitory, a new heating plant, and funds to complete the Women's building as well as other expansions. It was a time of prosperity, and of virtual peace.

After the collapse of President Campbell, University affairs were conscientiously administered by a committee appointed by the regents: Dean Henry Sheldon, L. H. Johnson, comptroller, and Karl Onthank as executive secretary, but there were many intricate

situations developing all the while which required more knowledge-
able dealing, and at once the search for a new executive began.

4. Later Years—Greek Life—Hall Administration
Dr. Boyer Pinch-Hits—Chancellors Come and Go
Civil War—A Great School Sits Tight

Student life had by now become very much more complicated
and politically organized. Greek life at Oregon started in 1900 with
the installation of Sigma Nu fraternity; followed by Kappa Sigma
in 1904. Next on the scene was Gamma Phi Beta in 1908, Chi
Omega early in the spring of 1909, Kappa Alpha Theta in the fall
of that same year, while the very end of the year and the final year
of that decade found Beta Theta Pi, Delta Delta Delta sorority,
Alpha Tau Omega and Sigma Chi installed on the campus.

Now the Greek colony also includes Alpha Chi Omega, Alpha
Delta Pi, Alpha Gamma Delta, Alpha Omicron Pi, Alpha Phi,
Alpha Xi Delta, Delta Gamma, Delta Zeta, Kappa Kappa Gamma,
Pi Beta Phi, Sigma Kappa and Zeta Tau Alpha sororities, and Chi
Psi, Delta Tau Delta, Delta Upsilon, Lambda Chi Alpha, Phi Delta
Theta, Phi Gamma Delta, Phi Kappa Psi, Phi Sigma Kappa, Pi
Kappa Alpha, Pi Kappa Phi, Sigma Alpha Epsilon, Sigma Alpha
Mu, Sigma Phi Epsilon, Tau Kappa Epsilon and Theta Chi.

Not until 1915 were compulsory student activity fees required,
and they were later declared illegal. The state legislature answered
this problem a few years ago by voting a new fee system whereby
the many and varied activities were divided into two groups, one
to carry compulsory fees, the other optional fees. They are now paid
in full by most students as a matter of course.

The battle over Greek organizations on University campuses
is ever-present and will probably never be really settled. Greek
letter organizations have done much for their locales, and on the
Oregon campus they own many beautiful homes, impressive and
well-kept. Wherever several thousand people, young or old, are
gathered together and aiming toward the same goal, group life
springs up in some form. Group life is a natural, to be gregarious
is a saving human instinct, and should Greekdom disappear from
this or any other campus, something else less democratic would
soon appear to take its place.

The search for a new executive ended in Wisconsin, where,
at the University, the committee found Dr. Arnold Bennett Hall,
professor of political science. He reigned over the University's

destiny for six years—six difficult years. Born in Indiana in 1881, Dr. Hall was the son of a college professor and interested, as he grew up, in educational matters and political science, which was the major subject in which he received his degree from the University of Chicago. Before coming to Oregon he had been a professor at Northwestern for a few years.

It was virtually a matter of Hobson's choice with the selection committee, for after the long period during which the University was without a real head, administrative matters had gone badly in many respects and time was of the essence; Dr. Hall arrived on the campus with at least one factor against him. Yet his aggressive, forceful championing of the University's cause, combined with the numerous speaking engagements he filled, quickly made him a valuable asset. Most unimpressive in appearance, being short, stocky, and sparsely thatched with graying hair, he was possessed of a brilliant mind and persuasive personality.

Old-time Eugeneans can recall most vividly Mrs. Ella Haflinger, who operated Foley Springs resort up the McKenzie river, and still lives there. Loyal and honest, she was never known to pull her punches. After the first few weeks of hectic activity on the campus, Dr. Hall, much-pictured in the papers, of course, retreated to Foley for a breather. Arriving at the desk, he introduced himself to the inn hostess who looked him over coolly for a considerable number of seconds. Snorting slightly she cocked an eye at him and said, "So you're the little squirt that runs that University, are you?" It remained one of Dr. Hall's best jokes on himself.

No matter what else was brewing, one Hall eye and ear were always on the possibilities of research, and it was a happy circumstance for the University. As a direct result of his unflagging effort, he obtained research funds totalling $185,000 from the Rockefeller Foundation, and later a most influential figure working with him on this important project was Dr. Richard B. Dillehunt, then dean of the University Medical school, who also had contacts with the research staff of the Foundation.

Dr. Hall instigated a pension system for retiring professors who had been on definite tenure, and a novel and confusion-making system of letting the senior students rate their professors as to comparative teaching value. He had ideas, and the facts concerning those ideas; he gave a great deal of the spirit of the University to parents of its students as he went about the state, and a vast amount of valuable information to the taxpayers who supported the school.

He finally secured the services of Mr. Burt Brown Barker of Portland as vice-president of the University in charge of reorganizing the lagging gift campaign started by President Campbell. He inaugurated Mothers' day and Dads' day, thus introducing valuable parent contacts with the campus. By the Barker move, sufficient funds were raised to pay off accrued debts of the original gift campaign, and to erect the Murray Warner museum—which houses a collection of ancient and modern Oriental art objects, in this day quite priceless. While relinquishing a part of the old family-style hospitality, Dr. Hall put the University administration on a strictly business basis from front door to back. Finally, he persuaded the board of regents to purchase tracts of land leading up into Fairmount so that future expansion would be possible.

The final year and a half of the Hall administration was hectic in the extreme; higher education politics had been somnolent, but neither dead nor discouraged. Rather, forces opposing the University had moved underground, led by Hector Macpherson, former O.A.C. professor and currently a Linn county farmer. What they had devised dropped like a bombshell into the laps of the Lane county delegation to the 1929 legislature: a bill placing both major schools (minor ones likewise) under a common board of higher education with an over-all chancellor as the final authority, each school to have its own president. No hint of the plan had reached farther than the O.A.C. administration; the way had been paved and there was no opportunity for any effective counter moves by the Lane group.

President Kerr had, at this juncture, an unhappy session with the ways and means committee, members of which invited him to step into their parlor and explain the usages of a $290,000 continuing appropriation which the college was receiving for the biennium. With some variation, it had been receiving comparable sums for many years; while chicken disease, the cherry fly and similar ailments were costing the state from $10,000 to $30,000 each, every time the legislature met, the University had no continuing appropriations and was leading pretty much of a hand to mouth existence. Upon hearing Dr. Kerr's explanation, the ways and means committee favored a reapportionment of the millage tax on the basis of registration at the two schools. Only a small minority of the committee dissented.

Meanwhile, "rail-bird" rumor from the lobby indicated that many legislators had already been secretly pledged to vote for consolidation. On polling the house and senate personnel, Lane county members found such evidence to that effect. As a result, Senator John Bell of Lane, and Senator William Schulmerich of Washington gathered their respective delegations and worked together to prepare what they hoped would be the least harmful and most workable bill, providing for a common board to run all schools. After long conferences between Governor Isaac Lee Patterson, President Hall, President Kerr, Macpherson and the two sponsoring senators, the bill was somewhat modified, passed quickly by House and Senate and duly signed.

The Board of Higher Education thus established was to be made up of nine members who were to take over all former powers of the curricula board and the separate boards of regents, members to serve for terms of from two to nine years. Any one, two, or three members could be removed for cause after due notice and a public hearing. An executive secretary must be employed with offices in Salem. All institutional advertising and publicity must be fair and impartial and come directly from the new board. The group was to arrange an immediate and impartial survey of the schools, abolish all duplication of courses considered unnecessary, and be able to turn the wheels on its new setup by July 1, 1931.

Personnel of this first board was C. C. Colt of Portland (formerly a University regent), B. F. Irvine of Portland (former College regent), C. L. Starr (former Normal Schools regent), Albert Burch of Medford, Herman Oliver of John Day, E. C. Sammons of Portland, F. E. Callister of Albany, E. C. Pease of The Dalles and A. Watzek of Portland. Mr. Starr was elected the chairman, and almost at once moved toward having a highly technical and "experted" survey made by a group of ten men from over the country.

The net result of this survey was a 298-page report, which cost $30,000, dealing with every known facet of each school and concluding with a concise division of work. All ordinary (non-technical) courses were to be given in both schools the first two years so that transfer could be easily accomplished. After that, the University was to develop liberal arts and social sciences with the professions dependent on them, and the College was to have the technical schools and pure sciences. In other words, mathematics and the exact sciences were to go from this campus to Corvallis, and their school of commerce was to come to Oregon as a part of our own school of business administration.

Let us say here, parenthetically, that some time during the twenties, the agricultural college had made an attempt to have its name changed officially to Oregon State College. This could not in legality be done, since the word agriculture must be in the title of land-grant colleges, but the practice has become general, and henceforth the school was to be known as Oregon State College.

No hornets' nest broken open could have produced much more buzzing. The State College had been more than busy building up a department of business, noting that the University school was being most successful and producing excellent results. The University, having lost her engineering school, now saw the basic sciences being taken from her, when as a matter of record they are given in almost every State University in the country. The board was bombarded with troubles from both sides, and in May of 1931 the two presidents, assisted by numerous deans, presented their cases before the board. The official opinion of that body was handed down about July 1 and was mainly favorable to the University, but what happened in the next two weeks no one knows; the decisions were "reconsidered"—and left completely vague. Meanwhile, Dr. E. L. Lindsay of the University of Pittsburgh, had arrived in Salem as the paid executive secretary of the board.

Governor Julius Meier came on the scene now, and friction existed between him and the Patterson board appointees, who stood firmly together. The depression was biting at Oregon's resources, millage receipts were down because of decreased property valuations, Governor Meier had vetoed $500,000 of the annual appropriations, and the board was losing some prestige because of what was felt to be a vacillating attitude.

Far from it. In March of 1932 the board announced its plan for putting the state schools under one administrative head in an attempt to coordinate the entire system. Recommendations of the survey committee were followed as a whole: sciences at the College, liberal arts, etc., at the University, and in addition the board coolly abolished the school of journalism at the University and the school of mines at the College. The state press, however, made demands on board members for re-establishment of journalism at Oregon, which came about in May of that year (1932). By now the alumni of both schools were fully roused, insisting that individuality of both be maintained. So a decision was rendered, giving a president to each school, under the chancellor. Some of the newly powerful deans had stretched their authority too far and created severe friction, so to ease the troubled waters Presidents Hall and Kerr were given back a part of their major duties.

Hector Macpherson was discovering his idea as less ideal than

he had thought—he objected to the modifications of the original
bill, to the re-establishment of the presidents, to the survey report,
to Dr. Lindsay himself, and to political influence on the board.
The faculties of both schools were at swords' points. Part of the
state thought the common head idea a fine try at settling a most
difficult, fermenting problem; others thought it evasive and trouble-
making, as there was already known to be a concerted move on
foot by certain interests to place Dr. Kerr in the chancellor's seat.

All in all, the period added up to one of the most trying in
the whole fifty-year cycle of the University of Oregon, and indeed
of higher education itself.

It had been specifically agreed when the chancellor system was
proposed that neither of the two school presidents could be considered as a candidate for the post and both had definitely agreed
to resign. The committee had meanwhile recommended a salary
of $15,000 yearly, the title of chancellor, and the place of residence
as Corvallis. All during the summer of 1932 no action came about,
though the name of Dr. George W. Zook, president of the University
of Akron in Ohio was prominently mentioned, and he
visited Oregon for some time. It was after the resignation of Dr.
Arnold Bennett Hall, in August, that the blow fell: the Board of
Higher Education, by a vote of four to three, had named William
Jasper Kerr as chancellor of the state system of higher education.
Thus an agreement was nullified.

If one is to believe the comment, both individual and press,
it was then that the board reached its all-time low in prestige.
Those in sympathy with the struggles of the University against
odds and tactics trying in the extreme, felt that its cause had been
betrayed and its future hampered almost beyond endurance. Those
in sympathy with the college and its tactics realized that the situation was a little too obvious to be sound or helpful to them. Some
of those on the board realized the decision was both unfair and
unethical,—and probably even the most partisan of them doubted
the wisdom of such a move.

Dr. Kerr moved to Eugene almost at once and proceeded to
allot the various offices, central office of the board being moved from
its specified Salem location to Corvallis.

This new look was most unwelcome in many quarters, and
reading over the mass of editorial comment, pro and con, one
wonders if even the University's bitterest critics believed deeply in
its wisdom.

Soon events shaped about which proved the beginning of the

end for Dr. Kerr's wide influence over the state, and in the board of higher education. One of his earliest moves after taking up residence in Eugene was to request the resignation of Mrs. Hazel Prutsman Schwering, dean of women, and her assistant, Mrs. Alice Macduff. As Miss Prutsman, the new dean had arrived on the campus soon after President Hall's inauguration. Young, well-dressed, of attractive and gracious personality, and a quiet speaker of considerable ability, she had very soon gained the support of various mothers' clubs throughout the state and had made a place for herself among the students. The ill-timed and unexplained attack of the new chancellor roused the University of Oregon Mothers' club in no small way, and under the leadership of Mrs. Arthur M. Dibble of Portland, president of that large group, Dr. Kerr stood "on the carpet" and lost a major battle.

At almost this same juncture, one E. P. Jackson, building and grounds superintendent at the College, came under sudden observation for certain alleged irregularities, and a special audit of the College accounts was ordered. Developments proved that board members had had no access to the books; Dr. Kerr disclaimed any knowledge, and the whole affair was whitewashed as much as possible. Governor Meier asked for the resignation of C. L. Starr, chairman of the board, who had refused its members access to the audit books, and Starr complied within a few days. Meanwhile, Mr. E. C. Sammons of Portland and Mr. Albert Burch of Medford had resigned as board members following Dr. Kerr's appointment as chancellor, each giving the press of business as his reason, but each admittedly feeling that no harmony could come to higher education in Oregon under the existing conditions. It was not to be many moons later before Mr. C. C. Colt of Portland, Mr. F. E. Callister of Albany, and Mr. Herman Oliver of John Day would also resign, leaving the board disorganized, to say the least.

Arnold Bennett Hall, during the last months of his regime, faced poor morale among his faculty, lowered registration, slashed budgets and a very questionable future—black clouds hung low over the University's fortunes. His health was failing, he was deeply humiliated over events which had preceded his resignation, but he made an almost heroic effort to build up student and faculty confidence in themselves. Late in that fall of 1932, he went with his family to Washington, D. C., where he had been engaged to head the political science division of Brookings Institution, and there he died in 1935, his life probably shortened and without doubt greatly saddened by the many developments of his stay in the West. Dr. Hall had visioned originally "a University as a source of pride to

the state and of inspiration to the sons and daughters of Oregon,"
to quote his own words. By his aggressive manner of carrying the
school to its supporters and helping them to see its strong points
and battle for its weaknesses he had made big strides for the University and brought many friends to its banner. By his ineptitude
in handling political situations and the many personalities therein,
he had lost some ground. But he went down to the defeat of his
resignation without complaint, and without a bitter word—perhaps
even without a backward look.

One last big storm to rage over higher education in Oregon
was brewing in the winds of Benton and Marion counties at this
juncture. A group named the Marion County Tax Conservation
League was furnishing the wind tunnels, and when the storm finally
emerged it bore the title "Zorn-Macpherson bill"—a cyclonic little
idea for moving the University of Oregon to the State College
campus. Its authors were our old friend, Henry Zorn, president of
the league, and a Willard H. Stevens of Gervais, its secretary, with
the durable Hector Macpherson as a collaborator. It was cunningly
timed with Dr. Kerr's hand at the state controls. Actual sponsors
were said to be a group of business men who refused to identify
themselves with the damaging and costly movement, but the known
sponsors admitted they had $5,000 to spend on its first promotion.

As a solace to Eugene, the Ashland, Monmouth and LaGrande
normal schools were to be placed here and called Oregon State
Teachers college, the Corvallis institution was to be Oregon State
University, and the University law school was to be moved to
Salem. The fat was in the fire.

Editorial proofs show that actual first mention of such a move
came in the Corvallis *Gazette-Times,* edited then by Mr. Claude
Ingalls, when he wrote on April 20, 1931: (Referring to the attempt
to cut costs and course duplication suggested in the Federal survey):

> "The Eugene *Guard* propagandist says that $500,000 a
> year can be saved by moving the school of commerce and
> industrial journalism to Eugene. We know how to make
> a bigger saving than that—move the whole darn University
> to Corvallis. The state college has the plant to care for
> most of it, as all a university needs is recitation rooms."

Later in the frenzied discussions occasioned by the same

survey, Dr. Kerr wrote in a reply to questions from the
board of education: "The college concludes that the University of Oregon school of business administration can be
lifted bodily from that campus to be merged with the
school of commerce at the College with a minimum of
disturbance as compared with the disastrous effects of a
move to transfer all commerce to the University."

Black despair was no stranger to the University and Eugene.
Storms and troubles aplenty had rolled over town and campus since
that first summer of 1872. But this was the blackest hour of them
all. Fury, consternation and fear mingled in the hearts of campus
and townspeople. Talk was of nothing else. Finally it was sheer
fury that rose to the top;—and the Old Settler tightened up his
rawhide belt, squared his burdened shoulders and pulled down his
hat, better to breast the storm and determine its direction. We'll
weather it, he thought, tired-like. Seems like there's no end to what
a body can do if they have to. We'll be safe in camp when the
wagons are counted.—Tired-like.

The effect of that bill on loyal University of Oregon supporters, not to mention those connected with the smaller schools,
was dynamic. Sides were sharply drawn overnight, ammunition was
collected by both sides and everything in the state, practically, was
adjusted to point toward the fall election. Another fateful November seemed to be approaching for the University and Eugene. At
that time there were 2,700 students on the campus here and 2,900
in Corvallis.

The board of education at once stamped the bill as unwise;
under an editorial headed "the Governor Spikes a Gun" Governor
Julius Meier's reasons for opposing the bill were set forth: destruction of $5,000,000 security on property bonds held by Oregonians,
destruction of the normal school investments, the necessity of
$3,000,000 in new buildings in Corvallis, well over a million in
fraternity house values in Eugene sacrificed. And lastly, but most
importantly, the fact that such a move would abrogate the solemn
pact made between state, Eugene and Lane county when the University bill read "permanently located" if the initial funds were
subscribed.

Before summer waned, the battle grew hot. Petitions were cir-
culated by a Sam Slocum and a Cyril Brownell, ex-president of

the O.S.C. alumni group, and by July 4 they claimed a total of 20,000 names to place the referendum issue on the fall ballot. Meanwhile, many state college alumni had refused to identify themselves with the bill, and were out of sympathy with the whole unsavory mess; things were not going so well as Messrs. Zorn and Macpherson had hoped. Suddenly, just before midnight of Independence day, there was a great "theft" from the Portland office safe where the petitions had been placed. The night watchman told a fearsome tale of having been bound, gagged and held at revolver-point while the papers were filched. Later he admitted it was a hoax, that the safe had been left open, and the papers had departed under quite peaceful circumstances. His testimony, according to newspapers of the day, pointed to Brownell and two other men.

There were hearings, and accusations on both sides, and a trial of sorts. O.S.C. sympathizers said University forces had stolen the petitions so the measure could not be voted on; University supporters said the bill's sponsors had cooked up such a scheme to rally weakening support. Someone, of course, knew the truth, but it seems never to have been straightened out or explained to anyone's satisfaction. The fact remains that planes were hired to pass new petitions out over the state, names were garnered to the merry jingle of fifteen cents per signature, net gain to the circulators, and when the deadline of midnight, July 7, rolled round, twenty specially engaged deputies checking names in the Portland office announced that enough of them were valid to assure the "grab-bill" as it was called, a place on the fall ballot.

The University at once engaged the services of some of its most prominent supporters to head a School Tax Saving association formed to fight the school-moving bill: Mr. Amadee Smith of Portland as chairman, Mr. Lawrence T. Harris as Eugene representative, Mr. Hugh Brady as LaGrande representative, Mr. John Fuller as Ashland representative, and Mr. F. H. Young of Portland as manager. Working hand in hand with these men were members of the Eugene University Affairs committee, composed of Lynn S. McCready as chairman, J. W. McArthur, W. M. Tugman, Lawrence T. Harris, T. O. Russell, A. F. Sether, H. L. Edmunds, E. R. Bryson, J. H. Koke, W. H. Jewett, A. C. Dixon, Carl Washburne, Tom Sheridan, Fred Fisk, Richard Shore Smith, Alexander Brown. All these men worked almost full time against the "raiding" bill as it was sometimes known, and formed flying squadrons which covered the entire state with a series of speeches, conferences, and general meetings which kept accurate knowledge of the bill and its damaging purposes before the citizens as a whole. Cartoons filled the papers, accusations were hurled about, literature filled the mails, editorials filled the state newspapers—mostly against the bill. It was another bitter period.

But the Old Pioneer must have looked down about then and said it's time those young folks began to get some sense and quit tampering with a good school—seems like they could remember it was put there to stay forever. We worked mighty hard to get it going. Looks like they can do the rest.

And so when the smoke of battle was all cleared away, 292,486 people had voted against moving the University of Oregon, and only 47,275 were in favor of it. The obnoxious bill had caused terrific expense, trouble, and loss of time and money to countless businesses and individuals, not to mention the deep and lasting animosities caused between the schools and their supporters, the towns, and the alumni.

The University during this biennium had lost, as we have seen, almost half a million dollars income from decreased property valuation and decreased enrollment, while the state legislature further complicated a discouraging picture by snipping another half-million from the millage tax income and transferring it to the general state fund. Salaries had to be greatly reduced, and repairs to the physical plant delayed. While declaring against any partiality toward the college in Corvallis, Chancellor Kerr's first budget presentation denied his statement and so antagonized the local faculty that its members prepared an alternate one for board approval. So keen was feeling by now that the American Association of University Professors was requested to investigate the Oregon problems and recommend some answer to the snarl.

Their decision was to place presidents at each school who would absorb some of the chancellor's duties, as originally planned. As a result of this, Dr. C. Valentine Boyer, acting president since 1934, was named president of the University of Oregon. A Princeton graduate, Dr. Boyer had come to Eugene from the University of Illinois in 1925, had been a well-known and popular member of the liberal arts faculty during all that period, and in the 1932 shake-up, had become inter-institutional dean of arts and letters.

Dr. Boyer, always a modest and rather retiring figure among the faculty group, undertook his new duties with a good deal of hesitancy. He felt a certain lack of knowledge as to the general campus predicament, many of his interests lay in other directions, and he had no wish whatever to cope with the difficult personalities which always arise in such a picture. But with the definite knowledge that he would be better able to handle the reins than would some of the older-tenure members, he courageously took over for a time the heavy administrative duties. That he suffered keenly over the problems and worked conscientiously toward their solution no one who judged him impartially could doubt. But with health failing, and problems growing rather than decreasing, he was more than happy to hand over the reins, in two years, to the capable and vigorous hands of a new president.

In the elapsed interim, Chancellor Kerr had apparently seen the handwriting on the wall, and had announced his willingness to retire when a qualified successor could be found, but not until the following spring did this materialize. A selection committee of the education board put in a busy few months, and in the summer announced choice of Dr. Frederick M. Hunter, chancellor of the University of Denver, as their selection for the chancellorship of the Oregon system. He arrived in Eugene in the fall of 1935, assumed his duties with very little fanfare, and took up his residence—with Mrs. Hunter and their two sons, Arthur and Maurice—in the newly acquired chancellor's residence atop Fairmount Heights.

This beautifully located home, incidentally, was presented to the Board of Higher Education by Campbell Church, stepson of President P. L. Campbell, who lived in Eugene for many years, and was most prominently identified with the University, civic, and social affairs in Eugene. Having amassed a fortune, Mr. Church through his family interests and loyalties, chose to invest large sums in financing sororities and fraternities which wished to build their own homes, and as a result many handsome homes appeared on the Oregon campus long before the enrollment seemed to justify them. His investments were almost 100 per cent successful, however, as almost no house was ever turned back to him for lack of ability to pay off in the stiff terms he specified.

The chancellor's home itself occupies the most sightly spot in Eugene, standing on top of one of the dozens of hill sites surrounding the town. Gnarled old oaks and stately, sighing fir trees surround the house, gardens, tennis courts and swimming pool, and from inside the spacious and comfortable rooms the view sweeps out to the west, and to the north and south for endless miles.

Chancellor Hunter's first move was an attempt to heal deep

CLOSE TO THE WILLOWS AT MCCLANAHAN'S BOATHOUSE, 1899

University of Oregon

UNIVERSITY OF OREGON, DEADY AND VILLARD HALLS,
LOOKING SOUTH

wounds of former battles, and to encourage the various state schools to work in accord rather than in such disharmony. His modern executive council was composed of heads of the various units, and the council met just prior to each Board of Education meeting. There was also an inter-institutional curriculum committee of nine which considered all plans for new courses or all decisions to abandon old ones.

Depression got in its worst licks in 1933-34, when registration was down from its 1930-31 all-time high of 3,358 to 2,386. By the end of the 30's registrants had climbed back up to better than 3,600, so the downward trend was safely passed. Millage cuts were restored, further appropriations ultimately made, and the Federal government spread its huge funds to cover much campus construction in the period from 1933 to 1939. Thus we gained a new library, infirmary, physical education building for men, humanities building and a new grandstand on the athletic field, all to the proud jingle of about $1,212,000. That sum was substantially bolstered by student fees.

In 1937 Dr. Boyer asked to be relieved of his presidential task, and was returned to his deanship, to be followed by the seventh president of the University of Oregon. Eugene later added Dr. Boyer's name to its honored list of "first citizens."

5. *President Donald Milton Erb—President Harry K. Newburn*
"The New Look" of 1948—Chancellor Paul C. Packer
Personality Sketches—The Future

Dr. Donald Milton Erb, formerly acting dean of the department of economics at Stanford University, and now the new president of Oregon, walked into his office on March 1 of 1938 and took up his new duties without fanfare or ceremonials of any kind. He asked for the next year's budget estimates and went to work.

Nothing could have presaged more accurately his course of action for the future; nothing could have served as a more revealing index of his essential characteristics.

President Erb of the University wanted a businesslike, efficient, well-run organization. He wanted to know what was happening and why, and what would comprise the choicest and finest plans for the future. He wanted to know what the students and parents and taxpayers were getting for their money. Donald Erb, the man, disliked show, never talked until he knew his facts, loved to have the other man's viewpoint, and found much of his greatest happiness in accomplishing things he felt important to his job—whatever it might be.

He was no stranger to the campus, having been a professor of economics for six years prior to 1933 when he had gone to Stanford. Consequently he was able to take over the reins with comparative ease and devote his time from the first to vital University affairs. His first official meeting with the Board of Higher Education occurred in just one week after his arrival and upon his presentation of the next year's budget, the board at once found a thorough-going businessman who was straightforward, honest and withal tactful and easy to work with. From that time on the University had a real head, after years of difficulty.

Dr. Erb was born in New York state on August 3, 1900, the son of Dr. and Mrs. John Lawrence Erb. His early education was in the public and preparatory schools of that state, and for his first college work he went to the University of Illinois, graduating in 1922. He served there as a professor until 1929 when he journeyed back to Harvard for a Ph.D. It was immediately following this that he came to Oregon for the first time.

He was chosen by the board after a country-wide search, and at thirty-seven years of age he came as one of the youngest educational executives in the country. With a cultural background (his father being an organist-composer-director-author in the East) he had been rather interested in a business career, but found later, as he once said to a California newsman, that "to stimulate the intellect of promising young men and women to the point where it becomes a permanent and consuming passion to achieve a clear and unafraid analysis of the problems they see around them constitutes for me the greatest opportunity in the world for achievement." His arrival at Oregon opened the most important epoch of growth and prestige the school has ever known. The Coos Bay *Times* wrote of his presidency, "Who knows—he may become the Hutchins of the West." And well he would have, had he lived to complete his career.

Commencement of that year marked his only inaugural ceremony, and his charge to the graduating class his first public appearance. His own character index lies in the advice given them:

"Be intolerant of superficiality, false analysis, evasion, and confusion of issues. Be tolerant in viewpoint regardless of religion, race, politics, economic status or education. By the force of your leadership and the consistency of your

example help return a sane morality to the world. . . .
You have an opportunity to shop in an emporium of
ready-made opinion. Classify these things as to their
relative importance and true significance, and synthesize
them into your considered personal philosophy. . . . May
you find, as the years pass by, that your learning and our
teaching have combined to establish in you the elements
of a rich, happy and complete life."

"Don", as almost everyone called him, was certainly the best
proponent of his theory that versatility and intellectual liveliness
did not end with college—he believed in athletics and all manner
of extra-curricular activities provided they were kept in proper
proportion in life, loved good music and played the piano a bit for
his own fun, gave deep devotion to his family no matter how long
and arduous his working hours, loved fishing and golf, was an unusually fine speaker with his deep voice and clear-cut enunciation;
and his economics students at Stanford named him their "best Good
Joe"—a college accolade in anybody's league. He always carried his
full share of the load over the roughest trails, were they mountain
trails or educational battles. He believed the goal of education to
be wisdom measured in useful living, not in dollars made or dollars
piled up. People were deeply attracted to him by his fine sense of
humor, his frankness and his modest yet self-assured personality;
he loved a lively fireside discussion more than a platform.

Probably Dr. Erb's greatest accomplishment in the five short
years he was to stay, was in his relations with the Board of Higher
Education. He took into all those long and trying sessions such
honesty and frankness, such sincerity of purpose and friendliness,
that even the bitter moments left no sting. More than ever before,
the board dealings rose above personal animosities and held to the
essentialities of each decision. His greatest battle was for the return
of upper division sciences to the University curricula, and when
the cards seemed hopelessly stacked against him he still would not
compromise. When the crisis was reached, he made this final presentation: "Gentlemen, either a thing is right or it is wrong. All
the weight of educational evidence shows that a great liberal University cannot be without the sciences, so that, as I see it, the question is not to restore a portion of the sciences, or try to work out
some expedient balance, but whether we shall recognize a principle
which has everywhere been found correct. There I must take my
stand." He won his battle, by the weight of facts, reason, and

courageous honesty. A university has a right to ask such things of its leader, and fortunate is the school which finds a great man to answer. Eugene named Dr. Erb her First Citizen in 1941.

His great plans for the post-war University were never to be. On December 23, 1943, worn out from months of strenuous traveling and heavy problems, he died of pneumonia, to leave behind him only the impress of an indestructible personality. One tribute sums up what he had meant to higher education in Oregon: "He brought youth, vigor, courage, scholarship and good judgment to a difficult task. His success was unqualified. His death is a bitter loss."

Now the beautiful Erb Memorial Union building is rising in the heart of the campus. Though it can never take his place in the hearts of those who loved him, it will epitomize much that he aspired to and believed in for his student body. It looks toward the future, as he did; it promises bigger and finer things for Oregon as he visioned. It will stand as the visible monument to his spirit, and to the deep affection all Oregon felt for him.

Second chancellor of the state system of higher education was Dr. Frederick M. Hunter, who came here directly from the chancellorship of the University of Denver in the fall of 1935.

Just preceding his seven-year tenure there he had served for eleven years as superintendent of the city schools of Oakland, California, had held the same position in Lincoln, Nebraska, and had also been principal and professor of the University of Nebraska school of agriculture, in 1911-12. Add to that several summer professorships in various universities from east to west, work with city chambers of commerce, and some experience in a variety of businesses and authorship of many educational articles, and we discover a man of unusually broad training.

Dr. Hunter was born in Missouri in 1879, received his earlier education in Kansas, and was graduated from the University of Nebraska in 1905. Education was his path from that time on, and during the course of his studies he received several honorary degrees. Having covered the country in his activities, he was well-qualified to take over a difficult and highly demanding role in the Oregon system. He saw, sensed and studied the entire situation, and at once began to make it his first task to overcome much of the trouble he found. It was not an easy one, and suspicions of favoritism between the two major schools were often prevalent. The fact that both his sons, Arthur and Maurice, chose to go to the University no doubt added fuel to fire.

But Chancellor and Mrs. Hunter went quietly about making friends, and accomplishing as many of his educational aims as possible. A deep thinking man, Dr. Hunter's already fine speaking ability increased steadily during his tenure of office and he carried many of higher education's problems to the state at large in a most convincing manner. The younger son, Maurice, lost his life in the Pacific theater of operations during the last war, and with retirement age at hand, Dr. Hunter asked to be relieved of his heavy and often troublesome duties. At their home in Eugene, the Hunters are finding joy in their freedom and among the many Oregon friends they have made since 1935.

The next man to take over the chancellor's desk was Dr. Paul C. Packer, who arrived in September, 1946.

During the last war, Dr. Packer was addressed as Lieutenant-Colonel, having held an important post in the Education and Information Division of the U. S. Army. One of his most important jobs was to establish branches of the Armed Forces Institute in Alaska, India, China and England; another was to organize educational programs for our troops on the European theater. In this capacity, Dr. Packer served for three years.

The newest chancellor is another midwestern-bred educator. Born in Iowa in 1886, he received his B.A. degree from the state university in 1918, went on to the University of Michigan for his master's, and completed his doctorate in 1923 at Columbia university. For ten years he taught and served as principal of the public and experimental schools in Iowa, then became acting director of educational research for the Detroit public schools, and spent a period of three years as a lecturer. For a score of years, Dr. Packer travelled widely on educational matters, going to various countries.

In 1923, he was called back to Iowa to serve as dean of the college of education—and it was there the Oregon Board of Higher Education selection committee found him and contacted him for the job in Oregon.

With Mrs. Packer, he assumed his new station promptly and settled down to enjoy his experiences. Not only does he bring wide educational background to his new status, but an easy and friendly personality have helped him fit into the Oregon picture with unusual comfort in the two years since his arrival. With a practical head and a fine sense of humor, he possesses marked excellence as a speaker, and is making friends for the entire educational system wherever he appears.

The blow of President Erb's death was a numbing one to the

campus and town. Yet events shape themselves about in spite of sorrow or trouble, and a large student body carries forward under its own momentum even with the heart gone from its administration.

Problems must be met and policies properly carried out, so very soon an administrative committee named Orlando John Hollis from the school of law to serve as acting president of the University until a permanent choice could be made. He served for two years.

Meanwhile, an industrious committee from the board of higher education was busy looking over a field of possible candidates, with ample time to conduct interviews and choose their man. As a result another young educator of wide background and interests was chosen, and on January 16, 1945, he took over the helm.

This eighth president of the University of Oregon is Dr. Harry K. Newburn, midwestern-bred and educated. With him came Mrs. Newburn and three children, Jacqueline, Robert Lee, and a very young Michael. They moved into the president's home on McMorran Drive during the summer, and very simply and unostentatiously began the business of adopting their large faculty family and attempting to discover the myriad facets of life at Oregon, along with its problems.

President Newburn was just thirty-nine, having Cuba, Illinois, as his birthplace, and January 1, 1906, as the date. Following his earlier education in the public and high schools, he was graduated from the Western Teachers' College of Macomb, Illinois, in 1928, and later took his master's and doctor's degrees at the University of Iowa, finishing in '33. Five years' work in the Illinois public schools as teacher and athletic coach was interspersed, and still later he pursued the educational pattern by serving as high school principal and superintendent of schools in various Iowa towns. Immediately following his Ph.D. degree he was made full time principal of the university high school of Iowa university. In 1941, Dr. Newburn became associate dean of the College of Liberal Arts at Iowa University, and that same fall he was promoted to the deanship, which position he held when elected to the presidency of Oregon.

Many phases of education and teaching have come under his notice, and he carried on several special studies under the Carnegie Foundation. Teacher-selection was one of the most important of these. Later he travelled to England where he studied English secondary schools, and the teacher-training programs of Great Britain. From all this it becomes evident that the University's new president had a rather wider approach to certain types of problems than any man preceding him, and his personal educational and professorial training had brought experience which was to prove highly valuable in future work.

President Newburn brought to his new position another welcome portion of youthful enthusiasm and the will to get things done. Tall, of impressive build and stature, he carries with him on all occasions a hearty and likeable informality evidenced both in his mannerisms and the quality of his fine speaking voice. He is thoroughly approachable, thoroughly enjoyable. People over the state always listen attentively to what he has to say, and so do his student body and faculty; the football team always likes to have him along on the plane, or train, or sitting on the bench. He is that sort of a person. A clever raconteur, he is equally at home with young Michael on his Sunday morning walk around the neighborhood, or on a speaking tour. His home life is his greatest hobby.

6. *Some Personality Sketches*

The campus role would be woefully incomplete without Dr. James H. Gilbert, just recently retired and until then Dean of the College of Liberal Arts and head of the Department of Economics. But to thousands of students who have taken econ, or heard about it, he was that puzzling professor, "Jimmy Gilbert". The hard taskmaster, who made shy girl students quake in their buttoned shoes or saddle oxfords, the man who shouted and waved his arms and made you forget the answers even if you knew them. The man with the great convictions of right and wrong, with the high scholastic standards, with the keen understanding and appreciation for athletics—the man who taught you things that stuck, but who loved to flunk you in an exam, if you weren't sound.

Though born in Tennessee, in 1877, Dr. Gilbert was no soft-voiced Southerner, for he came out to Oregon when eight years old and was graduated from the University in 1903, later receiving his Ph.D. at Columbia university in 1907 and being elected to Phi Beta Kappa along the line. Following that he worked at real estate, insurance, and as a clerk in the First National bank before joining the Oregon faculty in 1907. In 1925 he was made Dean of the College of Literature, Science and the Arts, and in 1932, became Dean of Social Science, which was his title for ten years. At that time he was advanced to Dean of the College of Liberal Arts which position he filled until his retirement last year. He was also head of the Department of Economics from 1920 until his retirement.

"Jimmy" has cast a tall shadow at Oregon since 1908. His is a traditional figure, and myriad students remember him. No single man, alumnus or otherwise, has stood by more faithfully during all sorts of troublesome times. Completely factual, he has been an active and lively participant in every phase of campus development, and as a private citizen of the commonwealth. Now he and Mrs. Gilbert are enjoying life on a small acreage north of the Willamette river, and he has ample space for those long hikes he always took, rain or shine.

One of Oregon's "greats" in the faculty roster was Dr. Orin F. Stafford, who came to the campus in 1900 as a chemistry instructor.

Having been born in Ohio in 1873, he had spent many years where grew no such quantities of trees as we of the Northwest take for granted. And as he stayed here year after year he became fascinated by the immense piles of sawdust lying about in apparent waste. To see was to think with Dr. Stafford—and to think was to solve. He carried on research for four years, and from those idle sawdust heaps came the perfected Stafford process for production of wood alcohol and high grade charcoal from wood waste. Later on he did extensive work on producing sugar from wood waste.

Dr. Stafford was one of the most scholarly and dignified of the University's many brilliant professors. His demeanor was always quiet and friendly, and his ability as a teacher of the intricacies of chemistry seems to have been equally notable. Few students ever left his classes without carrying away the basic principles he taught so meticulously—or without a deep impression of the teacher himself, with his fine-drawn patience and kindness.

Orin Stafford's greatest contribution to science was destined to be concerned with war. There again, something at hand which was unusually excellent appealed to his trained eye—he realized the value of McKenzie river water and its great adaptability to special processes, and when he heard governmental lament that such a vital research tool as "heavy water" was lacking, he brought in 5,000 gallons of McKenzie water, electrolyzed it down to 50 gallons, and sent it to Washington. At the time of his death in 1941, he had just completed the first unit of work on a great governmental experiment for national defense.

Dr. Stafford was a Fellow in the American Association for the Advancement of Science, and had been retired for age by the Board just two months prior to his death.

There are those who become great by training man's brain, and again there are those who train man's muscle, and teach muscle and brain to work in harmony for the achievement of excellence and fame. There was such a one at Oregon.

The *Daily Emerald* of 1904 carried this notice: "The Athletic Committee of the associated students of the University of Oregon today signed a contract with 'Bill' Hayward, the athletic trainer, to keep him at the University during the entire school term for the next two years. He will devote his entire time to athletics, keeping the men in condition for the various contests. He is considered one of the best trainers in the country. Both Notre Dame and the University of Wisconsin wanted him this year and offered splendid inducements. . . ."

So it was that William Louis Hayward, traditional figure without whose picture no University history would be complete, came to the campus. He had come north from his coaching job at the University of California and spent each summer coaching Pacific University and Albany College, and each year they beat Oregon so badly that Virgil Earl, athletic manager at that time, decided the only thing to do was to hire the man and see what he could do for University athletics. In the meantime Bill had hooked onto one of the huge redsides abounding in the McKenzie river in those years, and signed on gladly with such good fishing close by. And here he gladly stayed for forty-four years. He was perhaps the only campus instructor who ever achieved international fame.

Bill Hayward was no ordinary trainer and coach. Born in Detroit of French-Canadian parentage, he inherited an extremely rugged body and a love of the outdoors. Spending all his younger years in and near Toronto, he became a "six-sport" athlete, excelling in track, rowing and lacrosse as his summer sports, and wrestling, boxing and ice hockey in the winter. Of all these, his first love was track and when at eighteen years he decided to see the world a lot of his travelling was done via the various county and state fairs where foot-racing was the great sport. The days were rough and ready, and stories have been told of how Bill ended some of his races with a horse and buggy waiting to make good his escape. Races in those days were over any road open enough to run on, and many a winner was badly beaten up by his opponents when the race was over.

Before coming to Oregon, Bill had coached at both Princeton and Annapolis, and sometime later had traveled with Gentleman Jim Corbett prior to the Corbett-Sullivan fight. He had already established a national reputation, and was just next-door to being a human dynamo. So when he arrived on campus no one thought it extraordinary that he should be assigned to coach all sports, teach all gym classes for both men and women, and act as athletic director. There were about 300 students. His schedule was full, but not too full for him to coach Olympic teams in the off seasons, and in the on seasons he gave the University eleven Northwest track and field championships in twelve years. He became more and more famous for his ability to develop latent talent, get the utmost out of his athletes, or pull a seemingly hopeless meet into the win column. His strategy was clever, his methods fair, and his influence on the young athletes such that their affection for him was lifelong. He could always dream up some special brace, or splint or cast to help his boys over tough spots, and after worrying an idea around from all angles, he would pick up his old hat and make a trip to the town blacksmith shop. There he and the grimy but helpful friend at the forge would work with pencil, and tongs, and red hot iron, until they fashioned exactly what Bill wanted, and he would go exultantly back to his lame-duck athlete and make him more comfortable, or perhaps even able to play a game.

As coach of the six Olympic teams from 1927 to 1933, he won international repute for himself as well as for Oregon athletics, and his Olympic greats from this campus included Dan Kelly, Walter McClure, Martin Hawkins, Ken Bartlett, Art Tuck, Ralph Spearow, Ralph Hill, George Varoff and Les Steers.

When "Colonel Bill" had been here thirty years, alumni, students, and men of the town gave him a great celebration banquet, and his old athletes came from far places to pay him tribute. And when he had been here forty-four years, the Homecoming slogan was "Win For Bill"—for the great and kindly heart was giving way. His boys did win for him, and the whole theme was a Hayward Week-end.

The flashing trout, the cinder track, his McKenzie river home were to know him no more. He died on December 14, 1947, but the spirit of the bronzed, erect man who came to Oregon to fish and stayed by her side for almost half a century will always hover about Hayward field and Oregon's athletic destinies.

If one single impulse (short of self-survival) pulls American men, women and children together as a magnet, it must be baseball.

And in that field, too, Eugene and the University have their big-leaguer.

He is Joe Gordon, "the greatest second baseman in history", and pride of the Cleveland Indians. Also recently of the New York Yankees, he is one of those great sportsmen who come on the American scene once in a blue moon to give the poor boy hope and entertain the rich boy. When he was a little shaver, Joe pretty much had to shift for himself, and this state of affairs existed for eight years or more. During that time he supported himself entirely, and learned to be mighty proficient at all sorts of sports—especially baseball. Living in Portland, he earned enough money to start him in college, and came to the University. Here, he carried on with athletics and was outstanding in freshman sports. One fine spring day a Yankee talent scout from New York saw him in action on the campus baseball diamond and said, "how about coming with me?" Joe went, gladly—but he kept on studying during winters in Eugene, and was graduated with a bachelor of science degree. He had big years with the Yankees, and in 1948 had a prime season with the Cleveland club, ending with the world series.

Joe is married, has two children, built a home in Eugene, owns a sporting goods store, supports University athletics loyally, and does lots of nice things for deserving boys. Each year when he packs away his mitts and uniforms, he heads back to the Willamette valley like a homing pigeon—back to his deer, ducks, upland birds, and the fine hunting dogs he raises.

A younger faculty member who has made good in a big and unusual way is Dr. Lester F. Beck. A professor in the psychology department of the University, Dr. Beck was called to Washington, during the last World War to act as an educational specialist in the Army and Navy departments. He has long done research and has authored many scientific articles, but his most recent and greatest accomplishment to date is the perfecting of his film, "Human Growth". Interest in the correct type of sex education for the growing child came about as a natural result of Dr. Beck's work in psychology, and in developing the film and its narrative he did a masterly piece of work. Produced professionally, the film has been viewed by parent-teacher groups all over the country and has received their stamp of approval, as well as a governmental recommendation.

Dr. Beck was graduated from the University in 1930, and three years later received his doctor's degree from Brown University.

Dr. Warren D. Smith, now retired, has a national reputation as geologist and lecturer. During World War II he served in Washington as a government consultant in the Office of Strategic Services, Far East division, and did vast detailed work in coast line geological surveys of Japan prior to the start of the Pacific campaign. Dr. Smith for many years (1914 to 1948), was head of the University's Department of Geology and Geography. Prior to that he lived in the Philippines for a time, was an authority on geology there, and has written many books and articles. He probably ranks second to Dr. Thomas Condon in his geological knowledge of the country.

Dr. Chas. H. Secoy was probably the only Oregon man who worked at Columbia university on the atom bomb project and research, spending one year there. At the time he was called, he was working with Dr. Stafford, and was an assistant professor of chemistry.

A brilliant figure in the world of astronomy is Hugh J. Pruett, who is astronomer for the state system of higher education. A nationally known authority on his subject, Dr. Pruett lives on a picturesque hillside above Eugene, and there on summer nights is often host to interested friends whom he invites to star-gaze through his six telescopes.

Edgar Buchanan, a grand character actor, is Eugene's contribution to the gods of Hollywood. He was, perchance, the only man from hereabouts who got all tangled up in such bad grades that he stumbled into a great career. Edgar was a University student; he had planned to hang out a dentist's shingle one day. But the grades just wouldn't let him get by. So at his sister's suggestion he took a class in dramatic appreciation. The rest is history. And everyone enjoys it.

From the University medical school came the Matson brothers, Drs. Ralph and Ray (now deceased), who became nationally known figures in the fight against tuberculosis. A University graduate was Amos Burg, world-famous explorer, traveler and lecturer; Vivian Kellems, now head of Kellems Products, Inc., is known as "the woman who made a fortune out of a Chinese puzzle." She perfected a cable-grip used over half the world, dreamed up out of the principle of a puzzle. There were actors in the olden days—Clyde Fillmore, now in the movies, and handsome Jim Hammond and Catherine Cogswell Thorne. Congressmen Harris Ellsworth and Homer Angell and Senator Wayne Morse are all from the University, and very busy helping to look after Oregon's current problems in Washington, D. C.

Looking back over old *Oreganas,* one realizes how many dominant campus personalities have gone from the passing scene. Men like Herbert Crombie Howe, head of the English department from 1906 until a few short years ago, who was half poet, half tyrant in his classes, and whose tastes embraced Wordsworth and football with almost equal enthusiasm. And "Timmy" Cloran, the French professor with the Irish name, who always had a joke to crack and some fresh green vegetables to give his students and friends—and who sometimes staged a fit of temper in his classes. There was M. M. Douglass, head librarian, who was always called "Pussyfoot" because he took such good care of his job, and kept "piggers" out of the library stack rooms if he could; there was scholarly, dignified Dr. George Rebec, Dean of the Graduate School, whose cultural influence left wide mark on the campus; Dr. F. G. Young of the school of sociology, who came long before the turn of the century and remained until his retirement age, and Dean Colin Dyment, tight-lipped Scotchman who started in the journalism school and ended as Dean of the Liberal Arts college. The man who served as first Dean of the now-important School of Physical Education was John Bovard, and Virgil Earl, great football player in his undergraduate days was the first director of athletics and later dean of men. Karl Onthank, also a graduate, is still very much involved in being Dean of Personnel. And from early days there was Louis Johnson, first registrar and purchasing agent, who probably knew more of the inside workings of the University than any other one person. Now he is retired and enjoying life with a daily market basket over his arm instead of stacks of ledger books to balance.

We can still see "Molly" Perkins, red-haired English instructor, striding the golf course in her tweed skirts and shirtwaists; and lovable, frail Mary Watson Barnes in her Shakespeare classes. Mabel Holmes Parsons, now in Portland, left her definite mark and idealistic standards on many bumbling, incoherent poetry and literature students. And one of the merriest pictures of all is of Harriet Thompson, organizer of the women's athletic association, as she led her galloping girl charges through their workouts, swathed in yards and yards of black sateen bloomers and black cotton stockings.

It all has a nostalgic feeling. We pay them tribute of memory and thanks, these men and women who stood by Oregon's side for so many years, and left their shadows beneath the trees of the old campus.

The past is past, the future is here, and we find that the current personnel of the State Board of Higher Education numbers Edgar B. Smith as president, Dr. R. E. Kleinsorge as vice-president, C. D. Byrne as secretary, George F. Chambers, Mrs. E. B. Mac-Naughton, Phil Metschan, Leif S. Finseth, Henry F. Cabell, Herman D. Oliver, A. S. Grant and Chancellor Paul C. Packer. The board during 1947 lost three valuable members by death. Governor Earl Snell, who was killed in the crash of a private plane; Mrs. Beatrice Walton Sackett, and Willard Marks who had served on the board since 1933, and been its president since 1934.

Heads of various schools and departments are listed below. The College of Liberal Arts, which is the central and unifying core of the University, reaches into all branches of education and has eighteen separate departments. Eldon L. Johnson holds the deanship of this college, which has about three thousand majors.

Architecture and Allied Arts—Dean Sidney W. Little. This school is one of the largest of its kind in the country, carrying its own social and service organizations in addition to the Allied Arts League.

School of Business Administration—Dean Victor P. Morris. Has thirteen hundred major students.

School of Education—Dean Paul W. Jacobson. Will soon be on Senior standing (requiring two years previous work before entering). Will carry a special degree, M.S. and General Studies, for teachers.

School of Journalism—Dean C. F. Weigle.

School of Law—Dean Orlando John Hollis.

School of Music—Dean Theodore P. Kratt.

School of Physical Education and Health—Dean Ralph W. Leighton.

Department of Military Science and Tactics—Col. Frank Maerdian.

Department of Speech and Drama—Mrs. Ottilie T. Seybolt and Mr. Horace Robinson.

School of Medicine—Dr. David W. E. Baird.

School of Dentistry—Dr. Harold J. Noyes.

Department of Nursing—Henrietta Doltz, director.

Athletics has its own very important place in the scheme of things at Oregon, and Leo Harris is the present Athletic Director. It's big business now, and a fortune goes through the coffers each year. The football coach is "Jim" Aiken, as everyone knows him, and he is assisted by an able staff. Basketball draws great crowds also, and John Warren does the coaching there, while Don Kirsch is baseball coach. Howard Hobson, University graduate who had coached these sports for many years, has coached this season at Yale.

And then there is "Puddles" the white duck, a VIP on the campus. The Webfoot mascot, he is often the victim of a pre-game kidnapping, but usually returns in time for the bath and grooming which precede every game. In the summer he ambles sociably up and down fraternity row and around among the private homes, enjoying their lawn sprinklers, and their earwigs with abandon, and twirling his curly tail feathers in farewell when he is cooled and fed. A pampered and well-mannered rascal, Puddles is equally at home on the football field or in the basketball court; and equally at ease in his own white coat or in the rooter's cap and yellow and green necktie he sometimes effects.

Puddles feels that he and the boys have done very well during 1948. The football team has gone through the season unbeaten by any Pacific Coast Conference team for the first time in fifty years. They were eligible for a bid to the Rose Bowl, and the names of Van Brocklin, Garza, Wilkins, Eklund, Saunders, Chrobat, Meland, Doter, Bell, Stanton, Lewis, and all the rest will go down in Oregon's athletic annals. When the Rose Bowl bid passed them by, the great Cotton Bowl at Dallas, Texas, beckoned. Oregon has completed her greatest athletic season in history and will be facing a prosperous future. Puddles is very content.

And thus have seventy eventful years rolled away; it's another day, another age.

Class trees have grown tall and great; Villard Hall's vine-draped towers look down on things marvelous and new: a great highway stretching past the Condon Oaks and through the heart of a city; Quonset huts to house overgrown classes; a huge Memorial Union building which will house student activities for years to come and commemorate President Erb's great contributions to the University; a large new women's dormitory under construction; a new library wing. Soon there will be water in the "Old Mill-race" and canoe fetes again, with fine new seating facilities.

"Hello Lane" has stretched into miles of distance where students dash from class to class, busy and efficient in their skirts and sweaters, cords and rain jackets. No more bustles and peg-top trousers. No more derby hats and fancy hair dress.

The lovely, sightly parapets of the new library are courting places now instead of the halls of Deady and the old "Libe" stackrooms. Hordes of football men race through practice where a dozen used to go. Basketball has a huge court of its own. A student body which started with a few students from ten to twenty-three years old and no money has turned into a student body of more than 6,000 with a small fortune to handle each year.

The Old Settler murmurs, *well done, folks,* and heaves a weary sigh. It's good, he thinks, to shift the heavy part of the load to fresher oxen. It's good to know the roughest part of the trail is behind. Looks pretty clear ahead, he says to himself, though a body never knows from where he's standing, where the hardest bumps and the deepest ruts will come. Young shoulders for new tasks, but it's a mighty proud thing to drive along the beginnings of a long new trail.——The Old Pioneer stands staunchly on his rock, nor looks to right or left, but gazes straight to Johnson Hall and on beyond, into the unrecorded future of a bright horizon.

7. *Traditions*

As any institution grows, customs are inaugurated and enhanced until finally an aura of tradition surrounds the campus confines. Throughout their lives old grads, as well as outsiders who have come to know and love a school, have a wonderfully nostalgic feeling as they remember back through the years.

So when Oregon alumni gather in Timbuctoo or Tonopah, Peking or Paris, what happens? They talk eagerly about the time they sat on the ducking stool in the Kappa Sigma back yard and got three dunks in the Millrace; about the "Frosh-Sophomore" Mix which was always a "square mix", but never won by the "Frosh" without mighty fast footwork; about guarding the homecoming bonfire all night and how good the coffee and doughnuts brought by the co-eds tasted; about the times they built floats all night for the Canoe Fete. Then they remember the annual underclass tug-of-war which opened Junior Weekend festivities, and how icy the Millrace was if they were on the losing end of the rope.

And before very long, they're singing:

As I sit and dream at evening, of those days now past
and gone
And I think of all the old friends, whose memories to
me return
I can see them all in fancy, as they were in days of yore
And the sweetest dreams in all this world are dreams
of Oregon.
Oh those days at Oregon—they are the best of all
Dear old days at Oregon are past but oft recalled.
And when in fancy I return to those good times for
which I yearn
I'd like a shady place by the old Millrace at dear old
Oregon!

After that, its easy to remember how strange the little green "lids" felt when they paraded down town as brand new freshmen—and how important they felt when the traditional Junior "cords" could be worn; or the Senior Sombrero, carrying with it the importance of being a Senior Cop charged with responsibility for carrying on campus tradition and discipline. They eagerly dunked underclassmen in the Senior fountain for all sorts of misdemeanors like sitting on the Senior bench—set so temptingly close to the library steps beneath a sheltering fir; or smoking on campus, or treading on the sacred *Universitas Oregonensis* bronze seal in front of Villard Hall.

Junior Weekend was the real heyday for Senior Cops. Bright and early on Campus Day, which was Friday, they routed out the freshmen paint crew, marched them to the top of Skinner's Butte. There, under the potent influence of big hats and big paddles, the lowly "frosh" poured on buckets of lemon-yellow paint and by the simple expedient of scuttling busily around on the seats of their breeches they gave a shiny new paint job to the huge concrete "O". Marching back again, yellowed pants their badge of honor, they surrounded a big bonfire freshly kindled and tossed in the outworn green lids. Their first-year job was finished.

Junior Weekend is quite unforgettable; a time of fun and glamor. From the campus luncheon, served under towering trees to the accompaniment of music, the crowning of a queen and the "tapping" of new members by honor societies to the elaborate Junior Prom of Saturday night it is a magical whirl. When the heavy floods of 1941 tore out the Millrace intake, the traditional Canoe Fete became a float parade. But by the spring of 1950 there will be a Millrace again, with new landscaping, new concrete bleachers, a float-construction area, a launching basin and a take-out platform. Once more fantastic floats built 'round a special theme, and concocted with amazing skill and beauty, will glide down the stream with its underwater lighting and one of Oregon's most unique and appealing traditions will come to life.

An interesting tradition of a more serious sort was the annual Pledge Day ceremony of Homecoming. Inaugurated by the then-Governor, Oswald West, it gave opportunity for students, alumni and new residents of Oregon and Eugene to renew a pledge of loyalty to state, school and nation.

On February 20, 1918, the newly-activated University Battalion received the first official Oregon Flag, designed in the art school and constructed by a small group of coeds.

If some of these things have been forgotten or changed with time, others have come . . . the beautiful All-Campus Sing of Junior Weekend which has now become Mothers' Day on the campus; a special Dads' Day; the noise-parade of Homecoming, and its keen contest of greeting signs for returning alumni; Commencement, when Seniors toss pennies into the lap of the Pioneer Mother for good luck and happiness, and join in the Flower and Fern procession to bid farewell to Alma Mater. The "Hello Dance", no date, starts each freshman off; the Senior Ball ends campus social life, and in between are dozens of traditional honor awards and honor societies.

Howe Field, where baseball is king, is almost as traditional as Hayward Field's football history. Prof. Herbert Crombie Howe arrived at the Oregon campus many years ago, as an English professor. He mingled classical authors, poetry writing, and a virile concern with athletic events of all kinds into a varied and pleasant life which brought much benefit to the University. Champion of outdoor activities, he was the athlete's friend, and was Oregon's first representative in the Pacific Coast Conference where he served effectively for many years. "Prof." Howe could always be counted on as an active and outspoken champion of the University cause in the often-tricky conference meetings where each school had to hold its own, and Oregon was among the smallest. Part artist, part dreamer, and a good deal of a realist, he brought humor as well as sound practicality to an assignment he loved. Retiring from the Conference prior to his death, he was succeeded as University representative by Orlando J. Hollis.

Partly through the aid, support and encouragement of such men, the University of Oregon has built up one of the best balanced and complete sports programs in the entire Pacific Northwest if not in the country, with the more traditional sports including football, baseball, basketball and track, while the so-called minor sports embrace large groups of men who win laurels and renown in tennis, swimming, skiing and golf.

Traditional, perhaps, will be "Hobby" Hobson's "Tall Firs" basketball team of 1939, which won Oregon's first NCAA title, and whose bright stars were Laddie Gale, Slim Wintermute, Wally Johansen, John Dick and Bobby Anet.

Old customs, old songs, old traditions . . . what lovely, carefree things their memories bring back! Spring days when the willows were clothed in fresh green and the heady fragrance of balm trees along the river's edge was like wine in one's veins; an evening bonfire on a moonlit night, the crisp, smoky dusk of a football rally.

Float the songs from the Old Millrace
Songs of Our Oregon—

Chapter XIV

WAR CLOUDS

*"From the masthead he took the Stars and Stripes and,
landing, loosed the glorious banner to the breeze—"*

—Oregon Trail Pageant, 1926

I T WAS the dreariest day imaginable in Eugene.

Rain had fallen almost constantly the night before, bringing down the last few leaves and ruining the last few garden flowers. Trees stood stark against the lowering sky, newly handsome in their bareness. Mist and cloud fragments drifted about among the evergreen forests on circling hilltops.

Firesides were the most cheery spots in town, except that everywhere Sunday's papers were scattered about and people were reading a bit irately of the beating Tex Oliver's University of Oregon football team had taken 'way down at Texas University. A 71-7 beating, it had been. Well, that was that; and it wasn't even time for the good radio programs to start. That was about eleven o'clock.

Suddenly telephones began to ring: "Turn on your radio—it's bad news."

It was December 7, 1941.

Throughout that day and night, and for many days, Eugene with all the wide world, sat at her radios to hear the dreadful news and try to evaluate it in terms of the future years, and what they would bring to happy homes and nations. It was, in truth, the dreariest day imagination could conjure.

Like every other town in the nation, we sprang into action. We listened to the casualty reports, and to the stories which came out over our radios—oh! so gradually and so politically censored— telling at last how terrible the tragedy was and how complete the demolition. And all the time our minds geared to the things which would have to be done, the time that would have to be planned, the lives that would have to be changed. Before the stories were even half told, we had swung into Red Cross and all its volunteer services; into the searing routine of saying goodbye to sons and brothers and husbands; into the commonplace sight of great troop trains, of blackouts, and wailing sirens, and rationing and shipbuilding, and seeing our daughters go off in khaki and navy blue.

Suddenly flags waved everywhere, and the sound of our national anthem was almost the most important thing in the world. Overnight we became again one great whole, a nation undivided and indivisible, with a determination to survive and win.

Again men departed and women wept; again a huge service flag hung in the portico of Johnson hall and became a shrine as forty-seven of its deep blue stars changed to shining gold. Women took over the work of running the campus and its myriad activities. Under the heading "No Postage Required", page upon page of each Old Oregon brought letters from alumni and students serving on the far-flung battlefronts from Normandy to Okinawa; from Adak to Bataan. To read the records of Eugene's and Oregon's service men and women is to read a cross-section of the entire war, from enlisted personnel to top brass.

Eugene men have always been quick to rise to the defense of their homes, their country and their rights.

Eugene has always carried her share of the military load. In the days of the Rogue River Indian Wars, in 1855, the town and county boasted only a few hundred inhabitants, yet two full companies were mustered, and in addition, each man furnished his own horse, arms, and general equipment. Later, when the Civil War started, there were several volunteer regiments organized for Union forces, though none was ever called into active service, partly because of the still-present threat of war with the red men. When the year 1898 brought the Spanish-American war, two hundred or more men from Eugene and Lane county took up weapons and sailed away to make war on the aggressors in a land which seemed more remote than a star in those days of slow transportation. And it was our Company "C", Oregon National Guard that raised the first flag there! Many of these never returned, and when patriotic organizations sought some way to honor the men, they chose the courthouse corner, where an elaborate drinking fountain of marble was built. Names were inscribed on it, and remnants of the memorial still stand.

When World War I was touched off in 1917, almost overnight two artillery companies and a University ambulance company were formed and saw service, along with hundreds of others who went into the armed forces through other channels. More than 1600 went from the county. Long before Pearl Harbor, the Oregon National Guard unit from Eugene, with three hundred men, had been activated and was in training. Its members were the first entire unit to leave the town. Close on their heels went hundreds of men as volunteers or draftees, and throughout the long and bitter fighting they fulfilled their destinies with extreme courage, honor and fidelity. It has been said, though no figures have ever been computed to prove it, that Eugene service men and women won more major awards for valor and more citations than any other city of like population in the nation. It could well be so.

We end our resume of Eugene's war record with one of the light touches which were always cropping up among the gaily-dressed companies of early-day military. It was the summer of 1891.

It was time for the Second Regiment, Oregon National Guard, to go into its annual encampment of six days, and members sent out word that they would bivouac near the town which raised the most money for their entertainment and a general July Fourth celebration. Valley towns lunged into a campaign, and by raising $2,000, Eugene was awarded the coveted and gala encampment. Ten companies of infantry and cavalry, with five hundred men from the state normal school spread their tents on the old Blair farm west of town, and polished up their guns and buttons for a week's showing. Each night at seven o'clock there was a dress parade for all comers to see and admire, and after that there was platform drill, then dancing for the young belles. The Fourth of July itself was climactic; special trains ran into town from all over the valley, private homes were opened to accommodate all manner of visitors, and town housewives cooked up "eatables", the papers tell us, to care for thousands. The day was filled with baseball games between companies, "glassball shoots", and races between the various hose companies of town, attired in' full regalia. And the great and colorful finale was a "Grand Sham Battle on College Hill." It proved to be so frighteningly realistic to the onlookers that one terrified small fry ran screaming home to sob into his mother's aproned lap, "All the men are dead and now they're killing the women and children."

The situation wasn't quite that desperate, but the whole day was strenuous enough to send the town home in a state of collapse— to wait for another encampment.

Chapter XV

TALENT SHOW

"The new Eugene theater was opened for the first time November 17. The play was 'The Christian', an interesting but rather solemn illustration of the ups and downs of life by the Baker company of Portland. The house was well filled with an audience of as intelligent and refined people as can be found anywhere. Manager Cal M. Young had arranged everything in first class order. Just before the last act a defective pipe in the heating apparatus caused a fire to start in the woodwork of the basement. . . . The performance was good throughout and gave general satisfaction. . . . The next entertainment in the new theater will be 'Zaza', Nov. 23. . . . Manager Cal Young explained that in choosing ushers he had selected 'the nicest boys in town', all handsome looking. These were in uniform."

—Oregon State Journal, *1903*.

And that night Mike Gross played his "bull-fiddle" in the Svarverud Boys' Orchestra. Alf Dillard and Harry Devereaux were there. . . . When the fire started one lovely belle, hastily finding an exit, fell out into the deep alley mud in her new "opera cloak" and plumes. It was one of Eugene's biggest evenings.

ANY smaller city which is the home of its state University is apt to have a lively interest in arts of all kinds, and plenty of opportunity to indulge that interest. Eugene is no exception, save in one matter. Hundreds of people who never go near the campus carry on their own small pursuits in household arts, music, literary activities or a dozen other things.

Several workshop groups meet, also, to discuss and criticize their own various writings and push one step farther toward that always present goal—publication! Eugene and the University have produced an unusually large coterie of authors who have published, and many of them have been prolific, such as Edison Marshall, Ernest Haycox, and Nancy Wilson Ross, to mention some of the better-known and more contemporary authors. Add to these many more—Joaquin Miller, Poet of the Sierras, Maude Lischen Miller, Dr. Thomas W. Condon with his famous "Two Islands", and Mrs.

199

Ellen Condon McCornack from the olden days. Then from the next era Dr. Joseph F. Shafer, Dr. R. C. Clark, Dr. Howard Taylor, Allen H. Eaton, Sally Elliott Allen, Dr. Alfred Powers, Dr. A. L. Lomax, and so on down the lists to Clare Turlay Newberry, Ida Virginia Turney, Gischler and Hayden, Sophus Winther, and Opal Whitely, that strange character who supposedly wrote the "Story of Opal" when she was a small child, insisted that she was of royal East Indian blood, was clever enough to get the purported diary published by Atlantic Monthly and then disappeared from view.

Starting 'way back in the days of Joaquin Miller and Samuel Simpson, valley people seemed to have had a lot to say. In addition to the original works published by almost every major professor on the campus, there have been many fiction writers. Clara Cleaver later became a prolific fiction author publishing under the name of Kay Cleaver Strahan. On the long list are Robert Ormond Case and his sister, Victoria; Harrison R. Kincaid, Dean Collins, Stewart Holbrook, Alice Henson Ernst, Marion Lay Davis, and her husband, H. L. Davis; Ben Hur Lampman, Helen Hedrick, Vivian Bretherton, Walter Evans Kidd, Dr. Ernest G. Moll, who is known as the poet laureate of Australia; Pat Morrissette, Richard Neuberger, Margaret Thompson, Frances Fuller Victor, Nancy Wilson Ross, Edison Marshall, Harold B. Say. These are the names to be found in the University library list of our own authors. There, too, are Paul Tracy, Eleanor Allen, George Turnbull, Dr. Warren D. Smith, L. I. McArthur, Dr. H. D. Sheldon, Julia Burgess, Lucille Saunders McDonald, Margaret Skavlan and Nina Fedorava.

In the fields of art and music there are literally dozens of names well-known throughout the state and still farther: George P. Hopkins of the School of Music, who is a concert pianist of note and a composer; Mrs. Albert R. Sweetser, who throughout many years completed great numbers of water color studies of Oregon wild flowers; Dr. and Mrs. Alfred H. Schroff (who during their lives were better known by all their friends as Lucy and Larry), long guiding spirits in the art school. Larry was a prolific painter, working in both oils and water color for the hundreds of compositions of Oregon and California scenery which Eugene people have come to know, love, and collect. He was also an etcher of note, and helped design and execute the wonderful stained glass windows in old Trinity cathedral in Boston. Lucy was a water color artist and a professional photographer, but her finest works were the many miniatures she painted.

The W. F. G. Thachers (Jane and Goodwin) had real influence on the cultural life of the campus before their retirement this year. It was Goodwin who gave so many Eugene and University writers their initial training and interest in authorship, while he was short story instructor in the English department. And it was Jane who became a concert pianist of prominence, and interested numbers of music school students in following their careers. John Stark Evans, long a member of the music school faculty as an instructor in piano, was as active in town music circles as on the campus. He is now head of the School of Music at Lewis and Clark college in Portland. The Rex Underwoods (Aurora Potter) are figures long connected with the music school; as a violin instructor, Rex trained many students who went on to concert and orchestra careers, while Aurora was a concert pianist in her own right. During the last war, Rex designed and patented a device for mechanical manipulation of the fingers and hand, which found extensive use among the disabled veterans requiring educational therapy.

Many voice students have gone on to radio and movie careers, and at least one, Miss Marie Rongdahl, reached grand opera, to sparkle for a time. John Stehn, working diligently all the years since his graduation, has developed a University band which is one of the greatest moving spirits of the campus, and gives out with stirring music on all occasions. In their striking and well-tailored dark green and lemon yellow uniforms they cut a typical collegiate swath throughout the college year.

Eugene has likewise always been a great theater town and a great place for music lovers. From the days of Rhinehart's Hall and the old Lane Theater, down to the Eugene Theater (now the Heilig) good plays and musical comedies have found capacity houses to greet them, and in the old road show days Eugene was just the right length hop between San Francisco and Portland. About the end of the Gay Nineties, and until 1915 or a bit later, theater-going was a wonderful pastime, and for weeks after a "show" had been here people sang and played and whistled the bright tunes from ageless light operas, like *The Merry Widow, The Chocolate Soldier, Silver Slipper, The Red Mill, Chu Chin Chow* and *The Prince of Pilsen.* College boys and town characters alike shifted scenery, but the college boys were the stage door Johnnies, and some took their pretty girls to Otto's or the Varsity for a hot supper or an ice cream soda.

Roadshow days are past and gone, it seems; but the town is still show-minded, so that its two amateur theatrical groups flourish as the green bay tree. First of all came the University's Little

Theater, and then the town-sponsored Very Little Theater, lovingly known by its loyal members as the VLT.

Fergus Reddie, head of the University department of Speech and Drama, was the organizer and moving spirit of that first campus Little Theater group, then called Guild Hall. Its specialty at first was outdoor production, and in an amphitheatrical setting of great charm and natural beauty in The Braes, he staged some highly artistic and well-done dramas and plays. Following him into the picture somewhat later came Mrs. Ottilie T. Seybolt and Mr. Horace Robinson, both instructors at the present time, and under their intelligent and interested tutelage the originally small department has come into its own. Under Robinson, the students become expert technicians. They learn to take full advantage of the simple modern type of setting enhanced by novel and unusual lighting effects and the results are most impressive, particularly considering the very tiny space they have for stage effects and the closeness of a critical audience.

Mrs. Seybolt has proven herself a masterful coach. Under a watchful eye and a feeling for precision and good taste, the students develop unusual stage presence and proficiency in mastering long and difficult roles, so that the sum total of it all is artistry and excellence.

The Very Little Theater is something entirely different. Its workings amuse, stimulate and intrigue. Back in 1928 a small group of play-minded folks got together one Sunday evening to talk the whole thing over, and decided they could have a lot of fun play-acting. To think was to do with them, and they've been having fun ever since. Powered by the enthusiasm of Robert Earl (who now lives in Portland) and William Tugman, the original group grew and incorporated the following year with twelve members. They now have better than seventy-five paid-up members, with a few on the inactive list.

The original idea motivating the group was that it would be good for them and good for the town. They were right. They've had a lot of fun and plenty of work to keep them busy for twenty years, and the town has seen some remarkable results. Starting out in a little vacant store building on East 13th street, where they put up benches for seats and improvised a stage, the VLT finally landed, a few years ago, in an accessible but old and dilapidated building on the county fair grounds. Here they worked out their problems and their future, giving six or seven performances every season which played to capacity houses, often for a full week's run. Men and women who had never acted before went for the business wholeheartedly; everybody studied and worked together; their scenic effects and stage settings became famous, and were always so designed as to take full advantage of modern theater trends. As time went on they tackled larger and more difficult productions. Their roles were letter-perfect and such incidents as always mark "home-talent" efforts only frequent enough to keep them all intrigued and on their toes. *Entr'act* coffee is always a feature, and sociability at its best. They do their own costuming, make-up, stage managing and ticket sales.

By 1948 they had laid themselves a nest egg of $7,500 plus contributions of $2,500, and now a full half-block tract on 24th and Hilyard streets bears a signboard which reads "Future Home of the Very Little Theater." The new theater will be built soon, will seat about three hundred, will have a flexible stage and an outdoor stage as well, and will be in the informal and intimate manner which is its chief characteristic now.

VLT members keep up their social meetings regularly, meeting once a month. Each holiday season their own children contribute a Christmas program, so the future of Eugene's very worthwhile, very little, theater seems assured.

A grand outlet for male music lovers is the Eugene Gleemen, a group of men who organized under the leadership of John Stark Evans, then a piano instructor in the University School of Music. One of those men seemingly capable of extracting the utmost in music and cooperation from a chorus, he gathered together a half-hundred or so business men including merchants, salesmen, bankers, plumbers, gas station attendants, clerks, and coupon-clippers, welded them into a going concern which produced real music of a thrilling quality and real popular appeal. In great demand all over the state and for radio programs, they give their two annual home concerts for the benefit of some chosen and worthy philanthropy. They sing for the fun of singing, and have a rollicking good time doing it, as most of their concerts prove. A Women's Choral Club was organized a few years ago along the same lines, and while it is a partially new venture it is filling a similar need and purpose.

The Civic *a cappella* Choir is still newer, having been organized three years ago. It is the type of singing which appeals to the owner of a "small" but true voice, and likewise a type which has tremendous appeal to almost all audiences. The first such choir was organized at Eugene High school and was in popular demand. The

University has a very excellent symphony orchestra, and the Eugene high school's orchestra is a more than creditable organization. There is an ambitious Junior Symphony orchestra and a Junior Symphonette, Byron Miller directing, which are delightful and entertaining.

Largest and most important of all the local music-sponsoring groups is the Civic Music Association, which brings to Eugene each year a full program of the finest artists on tour in the fields of music, the dance and stage arts. It is supported entirely by local subscription, season tickets being sold each fall. A thoroughly democratic proposition, there are no reserved seats, and it is a matter of first come first served.

An artist of many years ago in Eugene, who followed through from the simple sketching of grade and high school days, where she received her first training under local teachers, to the advanced and difficult techniques of portraiture was Leone Kays, who later married and painted under the brush name of Leonebel Jacobs. At the peak of her artistic career she executed portraits of many nationally and internationally known figures, working in New York City, Washington, D. C., and even as far afield as the imperial palace in Peking. There she was commissioned to do official portraits of the Chinese ruling family. Among her best known subjects were President and Mrs. Calvin Coolidge, and it was the beautiful and remarkably true-to-life Jacobs portrait which the president's wife chose to be hung in the White House. The artist later wrote interestingly and most entertainingly of many of the notables who sat for her during that period. Mrs. Jacobs maintains her residence in the East, as she has for many years.

Miss Maude Kerns is another well-known painter of Eugene. She was graduated from the University of Oregon in 1899, later attending the Mark Hopkins Art institute of San Francisco, and Columbia university. She received her diploma in fine arts from the Modern Academy of Paris in 1913. Since then she has exhibited with certain foundations in numerous galleries in the East and in invitational art exhibitions. Miss Kerns was an instructor in painting in the University for more than twenty years, retiring last year. She has done work in both landscaping and portraiture, using both oils and water color as her mediums. This year she has had canvasses shown in Europe.

Painting in oils was the thing C. J. Fulton has always wanted to do—even when he was selling suits and socks to his friends and acquaintances over the counter of a men's clothing store. So he started dabbling, and kept right at it whenever he could get time. Some of it was pretty bad at first, and no one knew it better than he. But he dabbled some more, and still some more; and all of a sudden it was much better. His color and line and composition were beginning to smooth out and subject matter to come to life. All that was a good many years ago, and since then he has painted prodigiously, turning out some canvasses of true beauty, especially among his snow scenes. His works have been shown several times here and elsewhere.

One of the most interesting hand craftsmen in town is Frank W. Bonson, artist in copper and brass. He is a man who has literally hammered and pounded out his own career. A good many years ago, Mr. Bonson was in the heating plant business in Eugene, and there he had to do a good deal of pounding around, but the mediums were not at all to his liking. It seemed a dull business, at best. War came in 1941, and he went to Hawaii for civilian service in battleship repair. His tour there ended, he and Mrs. Bonson did two years' service in the Kaiser shipyards in Vancouver. Still the sound of hammers and the feel of metal was in him. When at last he could return home and settle down to enjoy peace, he had time to let a creative mind wander over the possibilities. Almost faster than his hammer blows, he was in business in a tiny shop on Willamette street near 15th; he assembled his copper and brass and tin and iron, his blowtorches and hammers and sand bags, his vises and shaping tools—and ideas. Soon hand-crafted objects were appearing in the windows, and before very long stores in Washington, D. C., Reno, Seattle and San Francisco heard about them and began to buy.

Production of any purely creative work is slow; in metal craft it is both slow and bulky, painstaking and often stubborn. One son, Frank, is Mr. Bonson's only co-workman and he divides his time between the shop, a home, and studying for his college degree. While there is no retail selling here, the shop does special order work, and the Bonsons consider that at last they have found the thing they like to do.

In 1930, in a tiny shop among the tall firs and oaks of College Crest, the Gray Gypsy Craftsmen came to life. They were Art Clough and Ross McClure, and they had ideas about a good many things, chiefly about wood carving and how it could best be done, and in general about what real craftsmanship should be. Art Clough had lived up at Rainbow on the McKenzie river, looking out on the huge cedars and firs and pines of the upper river country. Studying them, he remembered snatches of an old Japanese wood carving method he had read of long before, known as the "sugi" method. Its name was derived from the giant cedar used mainly for that purpose. Clough's father had been a designer and builder.

So he came to Eugene, and no one suspected that the hurried, busy, half-dreaming little man was in all reality an artist. He found a small home out in The Braes, with a pocket-size garage, and began to assemble his tools. A most unimpressive lot they were, too, resembling screw drivers and ice picks with strangely shaped heads. That was about all, save for work benches, a torch, a lot of stiff wire brushes and some wood stains. Then the search for wood was on, weirdly shaped or grained chunks and strips, and he haunted the mills and forests and roadsides for them. Flat slabs would do if they were thick enough—but they must come from the *down* side of a sloping tree where added weight and pressure would have made a closer and more unusual grain. Construction started. First a sketched design suggested by the wood-grain itself, perhaps of flying birds, or forest trees, or a human or animal figure; then the carving itself; then the torch, carefully burning the entire surface—this was delicate and exacting business. And last, the artist took his stiff wire implements and brushed out the char, throwing figures and design into relief and giving a variety of depth not obtainable in any other two-dimensional craft. Sometimes he used a sand-blasting method further to perfect and blend his design. After that the wood was rubbed down and often stained in dark tones, or soft blues or greens, or grays.

One of the most important works Clough and McClure ever did was a huge panel depicting the mythical and fabulous Paul Bunyan and his blue ox Babe, which was purchased by a Minnesota lumber company for its display room. They executed scores of fireplace screens, or over-mantel panels depicting hobbies or particular scenes for their patrons, and made numbers of large plaques designed around real or mythical characters of the McKenzie river, or of the nearby mountain scenes. When war came these artists were absorbed into the Vocational school, but they did original creative work long to be remembered by artists and hobbyists.

The State University's School of Architecture and Allied Arts is unique in that all of the eight curricula embraced there are under one head, with complete correlation and integration among and between the different fields of study.

This plan is a pet of Sidney Wahl Little's, Dean of the school since 1945. Under such integration, each student, no matter what his field, has a first year in basic design, after which he may choose the particular path down which his professional, or non-professional, interests will take him. This basic year is taught cooperatively by the members of the school faculty.

"This year in basic design is so important," Dean Little said, "that we wish every student in the University might have it. As groundwork for our courses it is vital." That basic course, which is open to non-majors, has at present three hundred and fifty students enrolled.

The school has come along rapidly since its beginning in 1914 under Dean Lawrence. By 1928 it was staffed by thirteen and its students numbered 259. Ten years later its staff numbered sixteen-plus, its students 302. This year's staff stands at twenty-four plus and students at 760. Even now, applications are being received for 1950, and at this time more than forty students are signed in the School of Liberal Arts, waiting for the time when the art classes will have room for them. New students this year alone number more than the total enrollment ten years ago, and in this year of 1948 the building floor space has been increased by 12,000 square feet.

The curricula here cover: architecture (design option, and structural option), interior design, landscape architecture, drawing and painting, sculpture, art education, general art. The school has a large reference library in connection with the University library, but quite its own and housed within the Art building, where two librarians are in charge. There are 50,000 art slides, University owned, for the use of the Art school; and it has a gallery of its own, formal, and used by traveling exhibitions. This is a gallery accepted by the Metropolitan Museum and the Modern Museum of Art, and by San Francisco and Seattle museums, so that exhibits may be exchanged.

It has its own art exhibit, too—a working exhibit for study. This is one of the five dreams Dean Little has, and one already coming true. There is a fund for the purchase of pictures chosen, not for their intrinsic value, nor even for historical values, but from the standpoint of their worth for study in the evolution of painting techniques. Dean Little took from a case two such pictures.

"These are both done by Hayter. He taught Picasso some of his technical skill. The thing is not the subject matter, but the study of changes going on in art."

Another fund was more easily explained. It is a fund which will go toward development of a typically Oregon architecture.

"This school should be a repository for things historical in Oregon architecture," the Dean said. "And another thing I hope to get under way, with the generous help of those interested, is a building up of an insurance fund for the purchase of Oregon historical drawings—sort of Oregon-iana of reproductions of the originals we can't procure. These would be for staff research." Then there is the fund for scholarships for students in the school of Architecture and Allied Arts; and the one for the purchase of "working drawings", not only of Oregon architectural designs, but of those from other parts of the country which are worthy of saving and study. All fine dreams! Talking to Dean Little one somehow feels they will all come true.

Figures and funds and dreams are impressive, but not lovelier than the things the school is accomplishing. One may enter the Art building where pillars are lined by outdoor foliage and colorful art design, and pass along halls where open doors reveal studies in basic design, ceramics, canvasses in oils and boards in water-colors, jewelry design and creation, and looms filled with bright yarns and softly colored ones, where someone is tying intricate threads to mazes of color.

"You mean you do that and retain your sanity?" I asked. She admitted that sometimes she threatened to blow up. The plaid that she would create with yarns of green and chartreuse and blue would be fair cause! The jewelry design, of silver, copper, aluminum, is as intriguing. At this time there are no classes in gem cutting, but the theory is taught, with the thought that in the near future such work will be made available.

Under general art, which is really applied design, come, besides weaving and jewelry, classes in painting, ceramics, and sculpture. There is a full course in ceramics, with not only the study of design, but casting, and every sort of apparatus for glazing. The course in sculpture here is one of the few given by a state school, and one of few under the supervision of a School of Architecture.

Topside, there is the School of Architecture with its rows of high tables and high stools, where broad north windows bring in the whole green world toward the Coburg hills. This school covers structural, landscape and interior design, and is the only one in the country having high enough requirements to turn out a finished architect, which it does in one additional year of study.

There is a course in the history of art and architecture, with two full-time instructors; there is a course in Oriental art. There are advanced degrees to be battled for, even that of Master of Fine

"THE PIONEER"   UNIVERSITY OF OREGON

F. M. WILKINS HOME, NORTHEAST CORNER OF CHARNELTON
& 9TH AVENUE (BROADWAY), CA. 1920
Photographer: E. F. Martin

Arts. There is an auxiliary course in museum technique, training in cataloguing, shipping, arrangement and scheduling of showings.

"All these courses are integrated so that students may collaborate; may work together," Dean Little said. "And we feel that our staff members are equipped to serve a student in not only his own specialty, but in others that touch him and his chosen field."

In a category—and class—by itself, is the Oregon Trail Pageant. It is presented every three years by the city of Eugene, in commemoration of the great overland immigrations whose pioneers settled Oregon and gave her statehood, and a future.

The pageant was produced originally as "Trail to Rail", and was the fitting climax to completion of the Natron cut-off, Southern Pacific's new and shorter scenic route to California via Odell Lake on the Willamette Pass. The year was 1926, and a great statewide celebration had been planned by Eugene which, by building of the new route, had become the most important division point in Western Oregon. There were to be two parades; one depicting transportation of the olden eras, and the other a civic parade showing all types of modern progress; there would be a queen and princesses from all the towns around, and amusements and a carnival and all the trappings of today's celebrations. But best of all, there was to be a great pageant, given both nights on Hayward Field, depicting the origin and growth of Oregon from prehistoric times to the present day. W. F. G. Thacher, professor of English on the campus, short story writer and poet-at-heart, was commissioned to write the script. The cast would include some 2,500 people; their services would be voluntary, and the entire project would be a dyed-in-the-wool, homespun, colossal, amateur to the last word. It would be called "Klatawa", Chinook term meaning "going far away."

It *was* a great pageant. It was done with great taste, great beauty and great enthusiasm. It was so successful that the citizenry vowed then and there to make it a triennial event and such it has been since that time, except for once during World War II.

Director that first year, as she has been since, was Mrs. Doris Smith of Portland, and the general manager was Mr. J. Roy Raley of Pendleton. Many hundreds of prominent Eugene names were associated with its inception. Superb weather made August 19 and 20 memorable to an eager town. In a vast setting of wooden hills covered with real fir trees cut from the forests, and a great replica

of the Three Sisters as its background, the pageant unfolded its
dramatic story of man's yearning to find new frontiers. A brilliantly
moonlit sky was star-strewn. Hark, what words are those? "I am
Klatawa; Hear me, oh people!—Earth-freed at last, Heaven assailing,

>Breasting the wind-tides,
>Exploring the cloudy continents
>Venturing ever further into the vapoury spaciousness,
>There comes the new day
>The next cycle,
>The pioneers of the air,
>Following a star-blazed trail
>To the last ethereal frontier."

And as the last words died away, the great mountains parted,
a huge locomotive rolled onto the stage; from overhead a plane
dipped terrifyingly low over the scene, and the red and black-clad
drum and bugle corps struck up its most inspiring and martial
rhythm. It was in all fact a climax never to be forgotten by the
masses who saw it, and they rose to their feet and cheered.

That was the start of the Oregon Trail Pageant, as it will
always be known. Now it is run by a board of elders, some of whom
have served for each of the six celebrations. Beloved Cal Young is
the moving spirit of its pioneer aspects, and anything he and
"Dorrie" Smith say is pretty apt to be the law. Hordes of people
work on the scenery, makeup and rehearsals. Parents by the hundreds wait for their youngsters night after night while the dance
routines are readied, and make the many costume changes required
by dancing groups. Everyone donates the time and energy uncom-
plainingly and with a single-minded purpose. A special orchestra
practices long hours.

The Vigilantes were the original fun organization for men of
the community, and are in charge of official hospitality headquarters for visitors; then came the Whiskilantes who manage the old-
fashioned whisker contest and exact fines from the unwhiskered at
their daily kangaroo courts; the Brigadiers, colorfully dressed, are
official and dapper escorts for Susannah, Queen of the Trail, and
her princesses. Many ladies and children dress in old costumes in
the weeks preceding the pageant, and for the celebration every store
window and home displays its choicest relics of the bygone days.
There is a pioneer village and a big barbecue following the pioneer
parade; and there is Potlatch Gulch for night fun, a luncheon and
style show featuring elaborate and beautiful clothing from earliest
days down to the present time. A Queen's ball ends the three days

of strenuous celebrating, the hundreds of visitors leave for home, and all Eugene digs in for some well-deserved rest.

But during those three days and night events go off with clock-like precision. Last year the second show was deluged with such rain that the great dirt-covered ramps became perilously slippery, and the flimsy cotton clothing of the women and dancers was cold and sodden. But the huge oxen brought their covered wagons down onto the stage, bawling with fright though they were and shaking their ox-bowed heads in protest; and the pony express rider galloped down at breakneck and dangerous speed. Come rain, come hail, come thunder, that show goes on, to the last cue.

And the Old Pioneer likes it. Seems like the folks down there are sort of keeping him company. It's right nice, now—them not forgetting.

Chapter XVI

ECONOMICS

Growing pains started 'way back in the little cabin beside Skinner's Butte.

They grew and grew, and now the town finds its arteries and feeder veins stirring in far sections; east to the upper McKenzie, Mohawk and Willamette river towns and down through the painful congestions of Springfield's rapidly expanding area; west through the Coast Range where Route F will bring Florence and the other coast towns to within a sixty mile radius; north to Junction City and wide over the prairie lands; south to Cottage Grove and on to the first rise of the Siskiyous.

That lone general store, where the Old Settler traded what he had for what the owner could offer, has expanded into more than six hundred separate business classifications each with its many retail stores. And each separate kind is maintained, serviced and equipped by still other types of business.

That first country doctor with the few simple remedies in his little black satchel, his faithful horse and his own kindly conscience to guide him, has grown into a hundred trained men with the finest equipment available always close at hand.

The newcomer and the oldtimer alike sit by and quietly try to figure out what is happening to "This Place."

EUGENE is more than the population figures, the annual statistics, the tabulated columns in bulky reports. Eugene is a living, growing community, and like all growing things, Eugene works hard for a living. There are hundreds of separate ways, of course, by which the people of Eugene and Lane County earn their livelihoods by subjects, each in its proper turn. We'll take agriculture first, then discuss Eugene as a sportsman's and fisherman's paradise. Then we'll tell the story of transport—the roads, stage lines, railroads and the modern airlines. But lumber and logging, which have really put Engene on the industrial map, come in, too. We'll leave that for the last section.

Of Cabbages and Kings

Joe Myers untied his boat from an alder tree, pushed it from the bank of the millrace and stepped in—a trifle shakily, because he was not a young man—and let himself down upon the wide seat. Oars in hand, he pushed off. There was barely room in the heavy boat for his load and he kicked aside the two gunny sacks of corn and the box of summer gravensteins, fixing to brace his feet for the pull downstream.

He sniffed the morning. The sun had swept away the first fall shroud of fog from the coast and blue sky was everywhere. Joe, his back a little weary from the three hours of gathering and washing vegetables fresh from the ground, stretched himself and let the boat drift slowly, for the pull back home when his load had been sold would be a tiring one; and today it would be warm in spite of the overhanging shade of occasional alders and willows and balms. Three great yellow pumpkins, the first of a fine season, rolled gently with the motion of the boat.

By the first slow bend, cows fed under a maple tree, belly deep in sweetbrier. The grass where they'd nibbled through the summer was sparse now, so that the University campus across the end of Eleventh street looked green and fine in contrast. There was the sound of a mower cutting the high dry grass down by the college track, and as Joe watched, seven little girls rode tricycles up the board walk to the oak trees and settled themselves with picnic baskets. Out of sight of Villard hall now, Joe had to pull oars to cover the smooth pond by the tannery, but after that the boat rode faster. Current was swift just above the "tail-gate" and he ducked his head and guided his cargo through the swift, narrow passage. Then the stream flowed ahead of him, clean and sparkling in the sun, or dark where the trees hung low.

It was a market day for Joe, in a good growing season. When he had tied up at the Eighth street fording he would sell his great white ears of sweet corn for fifteen cents a dozen, and they were worth every cent of it, being sixteen good inches long if they were a foot. Sweet as honey, too. And not a sign of a worm. Corn and potatoes, Joe thought, letting himself drift close to the willow at McClanahan's boathouse, were best for his river bottom land. Not that he couldn't raise peas and beans and all the spring crops, but they took more time, and Joe was wise enough to know that sometimes the high waters hurt them. With potatoes eighty-five cents a sack, and as long as your hand, a fellow didn't have to worry too much. Joe took off his hat and wiped his forehead, pushing back the white hair that somehow ran right on down into his white beard. He could see the cattails thick ahead, and he steered his sure way to the pebbled beach at the Eighth street fording.

This was Eugene's first, and most unique "farmer's market." Leaving Joe to row back home as best he could, let's go to the next market place. Stalls, they were, along the park area west of Hitching Post Square and the jail, and only four blocks down Eighth street from Joe's boat landing. Farmers came there on market days with the fine fruit and vegetable products of fine land, and gleaned their then good prices.

After awhile someone said there ought to be an uptown market with shelter from the rain and sun, where farmers could sell, and Eugene could buy, in comfort. The park stalls were only hunks of old lumber, but somehow the County was paid several thousand dollars for them—five thousand, the story goes—and the farmer's cooperative market visioned for the corner of Ninth street and Charnelton. That move was the first swing of business so far west into residential property, and it marked a new era. Old Joe Myers would have no more need to guide his boat the length of the mill-race, nor even to fish for chubs along its bank.

For most early settlers wheat was the "one best crop because it was exportable, exchangeable, and transportable and finally because it resisted well the long dry summers of the Willamette Valley."

Authorities on the subject say that moldered granite cannot be beaten as a strength-giving soil for wheat, and the flat lands of the valley are composed in great proportion of this granite and silt.

So it was, in those early days, that almost all the settler had to do was sow his crop and wait for the sun, rain and wind to bring it to fruition. So it was that by 1884, nearly every acre of the three hundred square miles of comparatively flat land was occupied by fine farms or herds of stock out to equally fine pasture. Nearly all of it was under fence, the farms varying from one hundred sixty to 1,200 acres, which explains why almost every old picture shows such amazing stretches of fence in a land which we think of as having been next door to a wilderness.

In addition to wheat, there were vast quantities of oats, barley and hay harvested each year, much of which was exported. When the first steamship company was organized for river shipping, the grain and other commodities went sailing off from Eugene City to Portland, on down the Columbia to sea and on across the ocean to the great markets of the world.

Mr. A. G. Walling, the author of *Illustrated History of Lane County,* would be surprised and no doubt delighted were he alive today to drive through the valley the greatness of which he believed in so deeply. 'Way back in 1884 he wrote: "valley population does not exceed 4,000 souls, and we do not think we err when we express the opinion that it is capable of sustaining fully ten times that number."

There had been little fruit in Oregon save that planted by the Hudson's Bay Company around Vancouver. Of those old trees, the story has been told that a young blade of the company, enjoying choice apples at a dinner party in London in 1824, tucked the seeds in his vest pocket and upon his arrival at the company base, planted them. What we do know is that Henderson Luelling, often called the "Johnny Appleseed" of Oregon, brought the first grafted fruit stock out to the West, after importing the tiny trees. Seven hundred of the precious sprouts he packed carefully in boxes in a covered wagon bed, and set out toward the Oregon country. During the long, hot trek across the plains he tended them with scarce and life-giving water, protected them from the heavy alkali dust and the blistering, trying suns of midday. Many pioneer families brought along seeds to plant in the new country, and whether they rode tucked into Ma's apron pocket along with the camphor bottle and the few priceless needles in their woolen cloth, or in the top drawer of the old commode, they were guarded carefully and put in the mellow ground with prayerful hopes.

And the land was good to them, for as the years sped on and the orchards grew luxuriant, 1,000 bushels of apples, plums, cherries and pears were harvested and part of them shipped—and all this on land which sold from five dollars to fifty dollars per acre. It was a far cry from the present day Eugene Fruit Growers, with its enormous business, but it marked the important beginning.

From the first, Eugene was very conscious of blooded stock both because of food and transportation. From then on down through the time of state and county fairs, and to the present with its large group of riders with their choice mounts, the stock business has been a constantly widening circle. All established transportation, before the railroads, was by stagecoach, and Eugene City was naturally the center of the valley wheel. It took fine and sturdy animals to carry passengers, mail, freight, and money over the terrific mountain passes and through the heavy mud and muck of pioneer roads. As a consequence, this immediate area has always produced blooded horses of many strains. The original ones were of medium size but of excellent blood lines which gave them fleetness and strength, while later on the Clydesdale, Belgian, and Percheron blood strains were introduced and developed.

Very definite economic angles followed the introduction of Merino, Berkshire, and later Angora, sheep. Mr. A. Cantrell's purchase of one pair of the latter for the then fabulous sum of $1,500 gave the valley its first angoras of royal Turkish ancestry and established one of its most prominent and lucrative pursuits. Eugene had a very early woolen mill, which is still one of the outstanding firms in the city, doing business near its original location.

Hogs were brought in as almost the first domestic animals, and through the years down to the present day have been an important commodity. Many of them are raised on stock farms near Eugene for sale to the various wholesale meat packers which have plants in the city. It seems doubtful, from their excellent quality, if they are descended from the old Hudson's Bay swine which had wild boar ancestry. Those razorbacks with their long snouts are said by old tales to have been able to reach the ninth row of potatoes through a tough rail fence.

Pioneers seem to have loved their growing things, and eagerly developed them into future businesses many of which are still very much with us. They were always on the lookout for new inventions which might lessen their labors or improve their crops, and many such an invention found its way to Oregon by the long sea route, carefully ordered many months before. Families were always on the watch, too, for untried crops which might do well in the valley. As for cash, they were poor in those days, but they had old-fashioned spunk and industry, and pride in their accomplishment.

We have from the pioneer, Cal Young, the story of Anderson Harlow, who rode all the way to Milwaukee and brought home on the back of his horse a load of small fruit trees and when the first frost came sat up all night to keep a fire going to save the precious trees. And then there was our own grandmother, Pamelia Ann, who carried her garden seeds in her apron pocket all the long miles from Missouri; from those seeds so carefully planted and tended through the dry summer months came one of the first gardens in the valley; the first bed of sweet williams, and hollyhocks, and a shower of pink blossoms on a hillside.

On January 1, 1882, the Lane County bank was opened by Messrs. Hovey, Humphrey and Co., changing hands, and disappearing ten years later. On Dec. 16, 1883, Messrs. T. G. Hendricks and S. B. Eakin opened their bank on the west side of Willamette street near Ninth, and near there it was to remain throughout the years

and become Eugene and Lane county's pioneer banking institution, owned for the most part by heirs of the family until 1947.
By now business in general was expanding.

Messrs. Cherry and Day opened a sizeable furniture factory
in the '70's on what is now Seventh street, and soon their business
grew, and became the first undertaking firm in the little town.

But the streets were still muddy and partly barren of trees or
grace and beauty. Daytimes, the men still wore their broad brimmed
hats on top of longish hair; and buckskin suits, soaked by the coast
rains, still shrivelled and shrunk before the open fires of the red
hot stoves. Daytime courting was pretty difficult. But night time—
ah, that was different. Then the young blade donned his long dress
coat of broadcloth with his tall beaver hat, and an ascot scarf,
beautifully tied.

When we glance back again we see the town in 1884.

William Skelton and Sons have built their woolen mill; there
is a Eugene City cider mill owned by W. H. Abrams which runs
fifty gallons per day; Joe Lane has converted old Lane's hall into
an opera house with a twenty-two by thirty-foot stage and a seating capacity of six hundred. Rhinehart's Hall is brand shiny new,
and the Home and Star hotels have come to town. There are six
churches, ten lodge organizations, one band and a choral society.

We read that a major interest was manufacturing within the
town in that year, and the Eugene City Flour Mill, established by
Hilyard Shaw in '55-'56 and bought by J. B. Underwood in '69 had
increased the power of crushing grain to three run of stones, ran
one hundred fifty barrels daily and had built a warehouse capable
of storing 450,000 bushels. It was powered by the millrace, then
as throughout its long years of service. One of the few pioneer businesses to come down through almost a century, and standing in its
original location, the mill was burned to the ground in 1946 by
tramps sleeping beneath its loading platforms, and has not been
rebuilt.

By 1884, too, there were several good sawmills out on the
banks of the Long Tom, that sluggish stream named after the man
whose legs were so long they dangled in the muddy bottom as he
tried to cross on muleback. The cut pine and fir were used in houses
and fences (and shades of our 1948 lumber prices!) sold for about
twelve dollars per thousand feet. There were mills in the Coast
Fork Valley also, and schools and churches, and nearly 3,000 souls.
Hay fever must have existed even in those robust days, since we
find that the mountain top lakes were considered quite fine resort

and health spots for the summer. The Siuslaw valley had some very fine family homes, such as could be built for $2,000 or $3,000 in that era. Land in and near Eugene sold for fifteen dollars to twenty dollars an acre—all you wanted. There was a big excelsior mill in Eugene where the sweet smelling balm trees from along the river's edge went in as logs and limbs, and came out as moist, white packing material with a good market value.

In 1876, at Philadelphia, Oregon was credited with the choicest and finest grains exhibited at the World Centennial. Lane County had no small part in this.

Six more years go by, and again we look over a shoulder to see what has happened. It is 1891.

There are 15,000 people in the county, and Eugene is described by one authority as "a city of fine homes, fresh paint, green lawns, beautiful gardens, tasteful architecture and handsome shrubs and imported trees. There are 5,000 people in town, and any class of building can be put up here for one-half the cost elsewhere. Thrift, good taste, and culture are evidenced on every side."

Both taxes and the general cost of living were low, there were water and light systems and the town was virtually out of debt. Eugene was shipping cereal, hops, fruit, vegetables, wool and minerals. New businesses included a packing company, a new tannery and another sash and door mill, a wagon and carriage factory. Two weekly and one daily papers kept the town well abreast of its most exciting news. Four fire companies kept the families with roofs over their heads, and a police force extended its welcome and protecting arm over highways and byways. Were you afflicted with a misery of any sort? Then drive to Foley or Belknap Springs for the waters—and never mind how bad the roads were. Did you have a fast horse to show off? Then hitch up the light buggy and hie to the race track for a swift spin around—and don't forget your veil and linen duster. Were you a young and ambitious business man? Then by all means join the Board of Trade with its one hundred ten members and pleasant meeting place, and remember it is affiliated with the State Chamber of Commerce.

It was the hey-day of the family. Family gatherings, family photographs, family picnics were the fashion. Mother did all the family sewing and most of the family work. In between her arduous duties of cooking a big meal for a big family and sometimes a work crew, and cleaning house and churning, she sandwiched in time for miles of fancy work on pillow cases that said "sweet dreams"; elaborate clothing for the children, lambrequins for the mantelpiece and fancy covers for the grand piano. The family had itself photographed collectively and individually against the most astonishing backgrounds of false oceans, mountains or trellises, accompanied by a strange assortment of animals, trees and other "props." Portable photograph studios came along, gripped their victims' heads in a new-fangled metal clamp guaranteed to keep them motionless, said "look at the birdie and smile" and charged father four dollars a dozen for the startling result. Sometimes these itinerant photographers were trying to make money enough to buy a buggy or cure a disease, and one admitted that she was trying to finance her own coffin.

There was a little leisure, perhaps. Small groups of ladies met in the afternoon to darn their family socks, or make tiny tucks and cotton lace for the long baby dresses. When the weather was fine they wheeled their babies out in wicker carriages with swinging umbrella tops and went to do their bits of trading. There was a drug store now with mirrors and shining big bottles of colored rock candy, and sweet-smelling creams to keep wrinkles away.

Now the new century is almost a decade gone. *Anybody's Magazine* says "Eugene Has Arrived." Building totals for 1909 mounted to over $1,000,000 and the same year the lumber output of Lane county was 200,000,000 board feet. There was a new Catholic Academy; Ax Billy's store was gracing Main street; the Elks and the Eagles had come to town; a new men's gymnasium was on the University campus.

In the Willamette river bottom to the east, George A. Dorris was soon to grow quantities of wonderful asparagus for local market and for shipping, and to start an orchard of Barcelona filberts to bear through long years. In the Willamette river bottom to the north, E. Terpening has netted sixty-five dollars per acre on his newly bearing walnut orchard, and more than sixty dollars on his cherries. F. B. Chase was growing vegetables commercially. M. H. Harlow planted one hundred and forty-five cherry trees which now brought him $1,000 or more yearly. E. F. Miller perfected the fine Miller sweet prunes and from his fifty-acre tract he always netted fifty dollars to two hundred dollars an acre. Just common soil made strawberries yield a net two hundred fifty dollars for each acre grown. Not a fortune, but with butter at twenty-five cents a pound, milk at seven cents a quart, and good wood for $4.50 a cord, one did very nicely, thank you, on prices such as those.

There was no need for our modern methods of crop rotation, then; soil was still rich with the wealth of the ages. There was very little wasteful soil erosion in the earlier years, because the prairie grasses still waved in lush gold and silvery beauty over fields and rolling hillsides. Came now the era when growth was just as verdant, but marketing vastly more simple, equipment more modern, and the dawn-to-dark labors of the farmer could be cut down by many hours. New crops were constantly being developed. More than two dozen farmers were trying the new idea of hop fields, roots of which had been shipped from England originally.

Time marches on rapidly, and it is 1940, or perhaps even 1945. Where the prairie grass waved like small windswept seas, other grasses grow now—grasses to furnish seed for other states and other lands and to bring one of our richest financial harvests and most important industries. There are also cabbage and spinach and pumpkin seed as top crops, and among the grasses ranking high in seed production are rye and vetch, all shipped out of the nearby farms in enormous quantities. Quite a small job, that—harvesting $50,000 worth of cabbage seed from one farm alone in one season.

Let's go back a moment to trace the growth of two pioneer industries in our town, and see what they have come to, up to date.

Eugene had her very early-day cannery, which fell on bad times somewhat later, and it was not until 1908, when the fruit and vegetable crops growing hereabouts were of established commercial value, that another canning project developed.

That year a group of eighty growers met and organized the Eugene Fruit Growers Association, capitalized at $5,000. Their sole possession, aside from the produce they planned to can, was a small warehouse, and the fixed determination to give each producer the maximum going price for his food items. This original plan has been steadily maintained by the cooperative farmers, and the organization has had steady and prolific growth. The large packing plant here is augmented by one up the valley, and each day of the growing season sees a steady stream of great trucks carrying fresh produce to the processing rooms. More than two thousand members now belong to the organization and its assets are valued at upwards of a million dollars.

It is the largest green bean cannery in the world, and the fancy packs bring fancy prices in markets which cover the world. Corn, beets, carrots, in all varieties and forms make up the next largest vegetable pack, along with tomatoes. By 1940 the payroll figures had climbed to half a million dollars annually, and the total pack added up to 42,000,000 pounds. More than forty varieties of vegetables and fruits are handled each year, including immense quantities of dried fruits and prime filberts and walnuts. Another way to visualize the scope of operation in the seemingly small plant is to note that in the same year (1940) the pack was 1,100,000 cases, valued at $3,000,000. For the current year of 1948, a $1,000,000 payroll will have packed over 1,100,000 cases. All-time high on gross sales occurred in 1947, when the output brought in $4,726,000. Some fruit crops were light this year, and labor differentials also cut down the pack. Some of the original board of directors included M. H. Harlow, Frank B. Chase, Jerry Beebe and Frank Harlow.

Wheels at the Fruit Growers begin turning in June when the first cherries ripen, and steadily pick up speed until August and September when the trucks of Blue Lake beans come rolling in. Then the plant runs full speed ahead and all the intricate machinery is whirling and cutting and trimming and boiling madly. Corn comes in, and with the fall trucks of rosy beets the season begins to taper off except for the latest fruit crops. Then labor shortages are no longer important; the crops are harvested and canned; and in carload lots they are on their way to feed a hungry world.

One of the really few pioneer firms still operating in Eugene is Chase Gardens, founded by Frank B. Chase in 1889.

Mr. Chase came to Oregon from central Kansas, where he had been engaged in raising white-faced Hereford cattle, because he heard this was a prime cattle-raising country. His original land purchase was sixty acres which had made up the southwest corner of the old Harlow donation claim, and since the cattle business seemed less successful than he had hoped, he planted a young orchard of prunes, cherries and apples on half of the tract. Even in Oregan rain and sunshine they had to reach maturity for either food or income, and meanwhile the good earth plus the wide open spaces between trees seemed to call for faster growing crops. That was when fine vegetables came into the Chase scheme of living— and there they stayed until World War II changed the major plan.

Frank Chase had a green thumb and a world of industry. His crops were prime, and he was in the vegetable business almost before he could catch a weary, sun-down breath. So in the big old ranch house northeast of Eugene, he spent winter evenings planning more and better vegetables, and spent summer evenings and mornings harvesting them. Ranged in fresh greenness and color in a wagon bed behind a pair of cayuse ponies, the food traveled to town to be sold from house to house—and invariably the wagon came home empty. By 1905 Mr. Chase built his first greenhouse; a small experimental building twenty by thirty feet, and there he grew special plants for the following season. This proved so worth-while that by 1910 all major construction was in glass.

The first outside market for produce was in Coos Bay, and followed directly on the heels of railroad development to the coast. Klamath Falls was the second outside market, and from that time on the Chase story has been one of expansion. There are now more than ten and one-half acres under steel-framed glass greenhouses, or about 450,000 square feet. Most of the greenhouses are fifty feet by three hundred and fifty to four hundred feet, but their newest range is for orchid growing, and the ideal size for these delicate plants is greenhouse space of about thirty feet by one hundred feet. Most of the houses are manufactured to their own specifications by an Oregon firm. Flower growing began in 1922.

As years went on, and four sons came into the firm, Mr. Chase retired from active work and management, but until a short time before his death in 1946, his chief joy was in taking groups of visitors or old friends on tours through the greenhouses and gardens. Before war caused the cessation of vegetable growing, it was a fascinating, or terrible, sight to walk into a greenhouse from which a half-acre of lush cucumbers hung from overhead frames— the reaction depending entirely on whether you could or could not eat cucumbers! And a half acre of pendant, ripe tomatoes looked wonderful. But it's a far lovelier sight now to come into an orchid house in full bloom, or to see the masses of gardenias and roses in bloom. The present store in town was built about 1925, at the same time that the sons Clarence, Elmo and Merle formed a partnership with their father.

The annual shipments now include three million roses, two million gardenias, half a million carnations and stephanotis, each, and one hundred fifty thousand Cattleya and cymbidium orchids, which go winging by plane or over rails to all parts of the country.

Lane county in its verdancy tops the world in amount of hops, lumber, filberts, and produce. Of later years, a new dark green plant which blooms in summer with a feathery lavender top is seen on all sides as one travels along the rivers and over the rich bottom lands. When early September comes, the whole world seems to smell tonic as the thousands of acres of mint are harvested and sent to great presses for extraction of the precious juice. Mint raisers have struck a bonanza while the price has been high during post-war scarcity, and many of the largest users in the nation send their buyers to the Willamette valley when the presses begin to roll.

In addition to the old familiar crops, Eugene and her immediately surrounding acreage of fine soil do a big business in commercially grown holly. From far and wide tulip fanciers send to the Conley Blossom farms for choice bulbs; spring in the valley and along the coast sees hundreds of fields snowy white with the fragrant Croft, or Easter, lily, showy dahlias are grown commercially, and the flower has come into its own as an economic angle of Eugene's varied existence.

Love of beauty and love of flowers came across the plains long ago. Grandmothers nursed their tiny gardens through the first hard years, and shared them with others. They sent 'way back East for more seeds, and even to farther places. And now, a hundred years later, Grandmother's garden is very much at home, and the valley bed blazes with color and beauty for a whole world.

Outdoor Heaven

Time was, as we have said, when the Old Settler could cast a fly on any river hereabouts and haul in a big fighting rainbow trout. No old-timer thinks of early fishing days along the McKenzie river without remembering the Seavey family—the father, Alexander, born to fish on the coast of Maine, and his sons, Tom, Will, Jess, John and James, born to fish in Oregon, as it turned out. In 1855 Alexander Seavey came to the banks of the McKenzie and cast an eye on the swift water, cast a line, and that was the end of the trail for the future Seaveys.

It had been a long trail. Mr. Seavey went aboard a sailing vessel, the *Challenge,* southward bound from the Maine coast, and when the ship burned at sea he drifted, with others, until their lifeboat found the coast of Brazil. There he waited a year for another sailing ship for San Francisco. It was a Scotch ship and after battling frightful storms made San Francisco in 173 days. Alexander dallied there to work on a pack train, and came to Josephine County in 1853. Southern Oregon mines held him until 1855, when he pulled out for Lane County. Three miles north of Springfield he came upon that McKenzie River.

Besides raising five sons, Tom, Will, James, Jess and John, who would all be famous as McKenzie fishermen of skill, Mr. Seavey raised hops—the first big yield in the county. He planted twenty-five acres to hops soon after taking his land, and was the county's principal hop grower throughout his life.

Those Seavey boys were mostly slim and wiry; red-bronzed from the sun on water, faces lined with the glare of the sun and the fun of fishing. And in the nineties when things were gay, they rowed out and caught one day a mess of rainbow trout to the number of several hundred—five hundred, the story goes—for a remarkable fish fry. The trout were not of the length we know now; fishermen then didn't take that size. The redsides, spread on long metal sheet stoves above underground fires, measured from twelve inches far upward, heads off. The "fry" was a breakfast on top of Skinner's butte meant to thrill a convention of editors from across the land. Business men as hosts were there to greet the special train and to guide, or help, guests along the steep trail that led straight up the front of the butte to the top of the hill.

It was an early summer morning, and the oak trees where Eugene Skinner had once stood were hung astonishingly with fresh-cut branches of ripe cherries. A wild bear cub was chained in the morning shade of the oaks, and the trout, sizzling above the ground fires, smelled of outdoor heaven. It was a sight to make news from coast to coast—and it did.

The Seaveys fished the lower river. Seavey's ferry was a popular spot for Eugene picnickers and their place across the river quite a sight, with its big hopyards, its barns and ranch house. Their boats were light skiffs, not the heavy, high-backed boats the upper river guides use now.

McKenzie river guides do an exciting business, and are unique in themselves. Their organization is close-knit; personal. Only once in a fishing moon does it admit a non-guide as an honorary member, and then choosily. At the little river town of Vida the association stages an annual ball, asking hundreds of guests.

Back in 1944 when the guides numbered but twenty-three, they took in eight honorary members, their first, chosen for "furthering good sportsmanship" on the river, and friendly aid to the guide organization. At one time out-of-town interests were buying up tracts of land along the McKenzie and posting no-trespass signs. Men who looked upon the stream as belonging to all sportsmen and beauty lovers were incensed; guides were hampered. Those areas where boats had been launched for their runs and landed when runs were completed, were being blocked off one by one. Something had to be done, and soon. There was one large purchase of land along Martin's Rapids, and there were small purchases of vital points, to the advantage of guides, picnickers and sportsmen.

Boats rent for eighteen dollars a day, guide service and all, and goodness knows the trip is worth it, even if a man never casts a line over the swirling water. McKenzie boats can't go upstream except for brief pulls back to likely pools. These brief pulls are strenuous, and in early season when the river is really on its way, even a husky Rube Montgomery gives the oars all he has. In late summer, when water is lower, a guide has to know every jut of rock and every riffle. September going through Martin's rapids is a five-minute whirl to remember, sounds, brilliant bank foliage, white water and all; and there are other rapids almost as wonderful, if not so noisy. Each has its charm.

The yearly guide boat parade is amazing. It happens on a day in early spring, the Sunday just before opening of trout season. A hundred boats, sometimes more, manned by expert guides and fishermen, run the wild, white water for a distance of fourteen miles, beginning at Blue River. The Cascade mountains loom in the east, purple and blue; willows are feathering out, light green, and Douglas firs stand dark along the hills. The sportsminded part of Eugene brings its picnic lunches and drives along the highway to follow the progress of the boats. And no doubt every smart old rainbow under his ledge of rock, or wide-eyed in his deep pool, warns his offspring of the next Sunday's troubles.

One could easily suspect that every rainbow in the McKenzie has been warned over and over, so wise are they. It is necessary for a man to love casting a fly to love a day on that river, for, due to a number of sad circumstances, such as short plantings and tourist "chummers" (who think it cricket to toss in a handful of salmon eggs in order to pull out a creel full of trout) have depleted the rainbow schools. The usual fisherman's day on the McKenzie is scenic and restful and thrilling, without being very productive of fish.

Sportsmen have come from all over the nation to the McKenzie. It was long a choice of Herbert Hoover's. The Izaak Walton League is seeing to it that planting and protection of stock will keep these friendly people coming. The thoughtless "chummers" and "hot-doggers" are not encouraged in these parts.

It has always been tough, that river, which is the fun of it. Even old hands have to know where to drop a fly. The famous and loved John Dose could usually snare a big one if he tried; he knew "where the big ones lays." But even John grew just a little weary of the trying at last, and used to pull his trailer off to the Umpqua or the Rogue for steelhead, coming back always to the McKenzie. Fish or no fish, he could tie his flies and watch the high, white water splash by.

It is quite impossible to go into all the corners of this outdoor heaven—lakes and coastal streams. But Eugene's other closest-by river is the Middle Fork of the Willamette, and it has its devotees. You might think, to hear them, that numbers of the McKenzie rainbow trout family had migrated cross-country to the Willamette. A man can run his own boat in that stream, but what present plans for the several dams for flood control will do to fishing there is a point yet to be cleared up, and we suspect not by the engineers, but by the whims of those nervous rainbow grandpas who tell their fingerlings the facts of life.

Roads A-Winding

One of the urges of pioneer life seems to have been to *go places*. It was acquired, very likely, in that three thousand mile "ride-and-tie" across the country, and young explorers who had traveled on foot, by ox-cart, on horseback, or on the springless seat of a bouncing wagon, kept right on through stagecoaches, river boats, steam cars and airplanes.

With the Willamette valley a quagmire where, it is said, "a horse could sink to his belly," earliest routes between homes and markets skirted the foothills of the Cascades on the east side of the river and the coast range on the west side, and were referred to as East and West Side Territorial Roads. The west one, through Dallas, was that route taken by Mr. Skinner; the east one ran by Brownsville. The two, converging at the Skinner ferry on the Willamette, formed what was called "the crossroads that made Eugene."

As early as 1852, five men from the McKenzie settlement tried to discover a means of getting through the mountains to Eastern Oregon. These were Thomas Cady, John Diamond, Jacob Spores, William Macy and a man named Louderback. They were unable to find a pass, but later in the same year two of them, John Diamond and W. H. Macy, covered the distance eastward as far as the high mountain they climbed and named Diamond's Peak.

It was not until 1861 or 1862 that Captain Felix Scott, who had arrived in Oregon with Skinner and Bristow, managed to drive a first band of cattle through, over what is now McKenzie Pass. He was aided by John Cogswell, another valley man filled with foresight and dreams for the new land, and by moneys from other settlers eager to see a wagon road that would open the Willamette valley to travel into eastern Oregon. These first roads were long in coming, muddy and bad even after they were given the name of roads; and many of them followed early Indian trails in order to avoid land that was low wet swale until summer, when it became dry cracked swale.

No matter how they crept along high ground, these roads that were hardly roads at all were forever being cut in two by rivers. Jacob Spores, from his place on the banks of the McKenzie, had begun at once to ferry foot passengers over by canoe, and after awhile was sparring quietly for ferry rights. Two other McKenzie settlers had the same notion, and were also maneuvering for ferrying privileges.

Authorities, scenting complications, ordered the three to join them to talk things over. Came the day, and the river was a torrent of roaring water, which Mr. Armitage and Mr. Stevens found it impossible to cross. The lucky Jake Spores argued in his own behalf, naturally, and so we are told that "Mr. Armitage built and turned over to Mr. Spores, a ferry across the McKenzie river"! Whether or not the story is true, there was, in 1850, a McKenzie ferry at a point near the present bridge on the Coburg road. With the Skinner ferry at Eugene in operation, Mr. Skinner presented a petition (at the request of twelve householders) for a road from Jacob Spores' place by way of the Skinner ferry to the Long Tom river, such road to intersect a road on the Long Tom leading from Marysville to Winchester. This road was the first one ordered, according to earliest records, and at the same term of the court supervisors were appointed for road districts.

Roads, roads, roads! The need for them fills the pages of those court records. The pages are written in what now appears to have been brown ink; some of them carefully written, some in hurried scrawls, a little hard to read. Names are not always spelled the same —Mulligan is sometimes Mulligin, Stevens is sometimes Stephens, the McKenzie is liable to be the McKinzie. But, rightly enough, Skinner is always and with no doubt, Skinner.

Eugene had her steamboat days; but she learned early that only in wet seasons was she the head of navigation on the Willamette. Until 1854 boats on the river were sidewheelers. The first stern wheeler to appear, the *Jennie Clark,* in 1855, is not on record as having reached Eugene. It took seasons of ample rain and melting snows in the mountains to bring any of the freight boats over the last of the riffles. At such wet times the Eugene paper would be apt to announce something like this: "A boat was up to this place on Wednesday and returned on Thursday loaded with hogs." In a few days the same paper might complain that "We have no boat at this place!" a wail that was often echoed.

The *James Clinton* made herself famous as the first steamer to go as far as Eugene. With its sloughs, its logs, mud flats, trees and rocks, the upper river was uncharted. The trip from Corvallis, a distance of fifty-three miles, required three days. A valley paper said: "They had a big celebration in Eugene, and they only got the boat there because Captain Cochran agreed to take her if the two towns would subscribe to a steamboat line he planned to build." Eugene subscribed. She put up $5,000. Those subscriptions were the beginning of the Peoples' Transportation Co.

January 1, 1862, the State Republican said: "The Steamer *Relief* arrived up-river from Portland on December 28, 1861 with Capt. J. W. Cochran. The following day it made the pioneer trip up to Springfield, returning the five miles in twenty-six minutes with thirteen tons of freight aboard."

In 1865 a new line was running the *Active*, the *Alert* and the *Echo* as far as Eugene. Boat fare to Portland was two dollars, meals included. The strangest of all the boats was one thought up by a genius at Corvallis who decided that steam was too expensive. He rigged a scow with a treadmill using cattle and hay for power, one supposes by the simple act of keeping hay just out of reach of the cattle. The "Hay Burner", as it was known, went aground in a slough, the animals ate the hay, and the skipper sold them then and there.

In 1867 a young lad of nineteen was a passenger on the *Enterprise*. He was going to business school in Portland, and he had walked from his home near the Coburg hills as far as Harrisburg to board the boat. The trip required three days from Harrisburg to Portland—an extra long time, he said, because men under contract to cut and pile wood along the route had failed to do so, and it was necessary to tie up while the crew went ashore and cut fuel for the day's run. Often the Captain had to back through the swift current, wheel turning fast to hold the *Enterprise* steady "It was a lonesome trip,"the boy wrote. "There weren't many passengers, and a cow bawled sadly all night long for her calf left at Harrisburg."

No matter how little the boats could travel the upper river, men kept on building them. In 1869 the steamer *Ann* made a risky trip up the Long Tom river. A Eugene paper commented: "The Long Tom people are so infatuated with the presence of a steamer on the placid waters of their quiet stream that they did not let the *Ann* leave, but tied her up permanently. They probably think that if a boat is a good thing they will keep this one while they have it.

Good idea! It might not be able to get back if it had been allowed to leave."

The *Active* and the *Albany* and the *Success* tried to go to Springfield but could not negotiate the riffles. The *Oregon State Journal* quipped: "It is certainly unfortunate to have the head of navigation so far up the river that boats cannot reach it. Rain enough for farmers don't do the steamboat men."

The Eugene city fathers and the riverboat men were slow to give up the dream of river navigation, so river traffic hung on in spite of the lack of water. Boat travel was pleasant, economical, often romantic and the town took one last optimistic try and built the *City of Eugene*. Somehow they felt that a boat, if it carried the right name, would be bound to be a success.

And then came that day in the gay nineties. The *City of Eugene* was fine and new and white, and on a bustling spring morning she lay alongside the dock, engines stoked, smoke easing skyward. Already the bridge approach was filled with people waiting to see the start. Among them were the parents of three small girls who were to present the flags to the new boat. These future belles of Eugene were not, however, as impressed as were their families, in fact they were scared half out of their wits, but this honor had been the means of getting new dresses, so they were determined to see the situation through. Standing on deck just below the pilot house, each girl clutched a flag—the Stars and Stripes, the Union Jack, and the Captain's emblem. They had been carefully instructed as to their part in the ceremony, but the blast of the whistle threw them into near panic, and one of them at least could scarcely see through her tears as she took what, she was sure, was her last look at her mother and father watching from the river's bank.

The *City of Eugene* backed slowly away from the dock into mid-stream, eased her way around and headed down river, banners flying, folks cheering, whistles tooting and the gold braid on the Captain's headgear reflecting the morning sun. Down stream she went, safely over the rapids, but at the bend in the river, just out of sight of her audience, she slid gently onto a gravel bar and there she stuck.

Special guests on board ate their picnic lunch, danced on deck, sang in the moonlight and somehow, under the cover of darkness, and with possibly a little help, the last river boat returned to the dock, the Captain's flag still flying but his pride trailing. And that was the end of steamboating for Eugene.

Stagecoaches were of course a standard, if not quite safe, mode of travel. Dashing off to an exciting start from in front of the St. Charles hotel, they were for many years making regular runs over both territorial roads. Records taken from an anniversary number of the *Register-Guard* give us a few interesting highlights on early stagecoaching from one of the original drivers. Headed "the Mail must go through" the story is told by Mr. McCracken, one of Eugene's pioneers in the freighting business. He said: "I began to drive as soon as I could climb to the seat of the stage (at the great age of sixteen)." For more than a dozen years he drove the rough mountain route from Grants Pass to Crescent City following what was later to be the Pacific highway, but he says "going over the mountains instead of through them."

The old stagecoach that Mr. McCracken drove is now one of the cherished possessions of the Oregon Trail Pageant Association. Those old stagecoaches! Intended to be pulled by four horses, they usually required six to take them through the mud of steep and narrow roads. Mail was carried in the front "boot" (under the driver's seat) while baggage was stored in the rear "boot" under a heavy cover of canvas. There were no doors, only heavy curtains buckled down to try and keep the snow and cold out, and the passengers safely in. The going was bad. At times the driver, with the help of "the shotgun man", had to break a path through the snow-drifts for the horses to follow, sometimes even having to leave the stage behind and ride on horseback with the mail.

In 1860 a positive necessity was felt for a route to other parts of the state, so the "Oregon Central Military Road Co." was organized with men of the town planning to finance it. Aside from the Old Settler himself the incorporators were J. H. McClung, J. B. Underwood, and A. W. Patterson. They voted thirty thousand dollars capital which later was raised to a hundred thousand. The land grant was completed in 1864 and work was begun on the first part from Eugene to Butte Disappointment, a distance of twenty miles. This was finished in the summer of 1865, as was also the part of the road from Butte Disappointment to Pine Openings in the Cascade mountains. Several of the ferries and bridges were completed that same year.

Other stage routes ran to the coast, one to the Siuslaw country and one to where the small seaside town of Newport hibernated through the long rainy winters, coming to life in the spring to plan and preen for the summer folks from the valley. Later, a railroad train eased its way a piece out west and on through the coast mountains over a dozen terrifying wooden trestles, finally landing passengers at Yaquina. Here a transfer was made to a two-decked ferry boat and passengers and wagons were carried across the bay to the dock at Newport where there was a thrilling welcome by a brass band, hotel owners, and wagon drivers who hauled freight over the hill to cottages and camp grounds at Nye Creek.

That ride in the Newport train in those red plush seated coaches, with swinging and swaying lamps overhead was a pleasant trip. With less than a hundred miles to cover, there was no great rush about it. On the way down the valley there were frequent stops to oblige hunters aboard who wanted to spend an hour or two stalking pheasants through the grain fields. The engineer would wait! Just so he reached Newport by six o'clock. It was nice going even when they didn't go.

Early in 1871, Ben Holliday sent a telegram to Mr. S. H. Friendly and Mr. Charles Lauer saying: "Eugene will have a railroad. We'll all want it when it comes! Who cares about expense?" and though there had been several companies formed, it was Ben Holliday who built the Oregon and California road. He got it as far as Harrisburg and then again sent word to Eugene:

"There are several reasons why I won't play with you if you won't raise forty thousand dollars toward this. I'll go through Springfield and I'll leave you out." That threat was enough for Eugene. She hustled the money (though it was never all paid) and she got her depot and her first train in 1871. In September of that year there had been a meeting at the courthouse for the purpose of planning the celebration for the arrival of that first train of cars, and when it chugged into the head of Willamette street that Sunday afternoon of October 8, 1871, the entire town was out to inaugurate service on the Oregon-California Railway.

The very name of the company was due to politically astute Senator James Nesmith. There had long been marked agitation on the part of a California company to obtain rights for a line through the Willamette valley to the Columbia river with Sacramento as its southern base. Citizens of Eugene and the other valley towns were naturally eager to see this great development come, bringing as it would tremendous outlet for heavy valley crops. Few questions were asked. The bill was before the State legislature, following much propaganda from its southern promoters, when Senator Nesmith realized what it might mean in the future. He went into action at once. When the bill was finally passed it stipulated that construction was to start in Portland and Sacramento simultane-

ously, that Oregon capital was to be responsible for the northern
end of the line building and that the road would be known as the
Oregon-California Railway. Now it is our Southern Pacific Line.

When this first railroad line had been built at the head of
Main street the city's influential men began to think of street
improvements, since, after all, there must be some way to reach
the line and the little station which would surely come. Soon the
city council voted to pave two blocks of the street and to put a
few lights along its distance. So the Maxim Gas Co. of San Francisco was queried as to the probable cost of installing suitable street
lamps for a "city", and by late fall they were authorized and soon
ready to give light and cheer to the dreary little street. The lamps
were of zinc or some such metal, nearly two feet high, shaped like
lanterns and having eight panes of glass. They were mounted on
posts, held coal oil lamps and, when the old lamplighter had passed
along the street at night, they cast a warm and welcoming glow
through storm and cold, but could never dim the beauty or bright-
ness of a harvest moon. When seven more of the really artistic
beacons had been added to various church corners the town seemed
quite bright and gay. A few of them still remain in private gardens
in Eugene, deeply prized by their owners.

By 1872, when trains were ready to begin the run to Salem,
the paper said: "Our city will now have to lay off its baby clothes
and put on big breeches" and sorrowfully, later in the year, it complained: "Oregon and California stages are no more! Passengers
and mail come from Creswell by cars. This is too strange after ten
years, but many things are giving way to progress. Horse power is
giving way to steam and the toot of the stage horn is now super-
seded by the shriek of the engine. SO MOTE IT BE."

The town again grew ambitious and by contagious enthusiasm
and optimsim (and another bond issue) decided to build the Oregon
Electric Railroad to accommodate increased travel to Portland.
This road was completed in 1912 and a fine station was built just
one block south of the Southern Pacific station. For a number of
years it was a successful passenger route, but eventually became a
freight road down the valley servicing towns between Eugene and
Portland.

The road to Coos Bay made a great stir when it was surveyed
in 1911. It was, according to the paper, to make Eugene "the second
city in Oregon".

In 1910, E. H. Harriman looked along Oregon's coast and
decided there should be a line to Coos Bay from inland markets,

and with little delay began work on it. He cut a tunnel half way through Hancock mountain, as well as completing some concrete piers for the first of the bridges across the Umpqua river. Business men in Eugene were losing sleep over this! A railroad from Drain to Coos Bay would leave them literally on the side lines! Working fast they made plans of their own and surveyed and began grading a line between Eugene and Veneta, not far to the west. They even named this road the "Western Pacific". At this stage in events they went to see Mr. Harriman and painted such a promising picture of the new railroad already begun that they persuaded him to buy them out, which he did, leaving his half-tunneled mountain and his concrete piers to fall, along with his own original plan.

Railroad-conscious Eugene left no stone unturned to lay ties in every direction. When the Southern Pacific planned to build its terminals and looked for a logical site, a group of Eugene's business men talked the situation over enviously. Their town would like a terminal, they said, and ought to have it. After some clever discussion this group paid two hundred and fifty thousand dollars for acreage a piece west and offered it to the railroad for one dollar. The Southern Pacific was delighted, Eugene was bonded to the amount paid, bonds to carry five and one-half percent interest and to mature in 1962-3.

The Southern Pacific Company yards—fifth in importance in the S. P.'s system on the coast—employ approximately 2,000 men and women with an annual payroll of over $5,000,000.

Our highways have kept pace with our railroads and the Old Settler and his folks are still going places. Now, in 1948, a fine network of modern highways offers easy access to Eugene from both north and south. U. S. 99 is the principal arterial route, while the Willamette Pass road has opened a new and scenic highway to California. Several fine roads serve Pacific coast cities and resorts, while Greyhound Bus Lines maintain a large and ever-busy terminal with a daily full schedule north and south.

Riding a Greyhound bus over fine roads, one is reminded of that mid-year stage driver, Earl McNutt. It was Earl who, with his brother Jack, later formed a team of road contractors undaunted by any mountain job.

Now we have attained the current height of transportation. To the north and west of Eugene lies her fine modern airport, able to handle the large planes of United Airlines, and also of West Coast lines. Ample expansion space will permit the field to handle largest planes of a future air age. The passenger terminal is known

among air travelers as one of the most distinctive on the trans-
continental route, and is an admirable example of the charm and
character which can be gained by use of variously treated native
woods. This field is known as Mahlon Sweet field, in honor of the
late citizen who promoted aviation 'way back in the days when
General "Hap" Arnold, his personal friend, was hopping around
the world in a tiny plane. Mr. Sweet was named Eugene's "First
Citizen" a few years ago.

Timber-r-r-r!

Our earliest lumber tycoon may be said to have been Hilyard
Shaw. At least he had things his own way, with no other sawmills
for forty miles around. He would look with astonishment upon our
present almost hundred wholesale lumber companies, and surely
he'd stutter, wondering how in t-t-tophet they c-c-could all live.
And it seems he might be justified, for already a number of
"quickie" companies, ballooned to out-size during the four or five
years just past, are taking the pin-prick that comes to most balloons.

The lumber life of Lane County would fill a book. But it
would be a book in which the heroine slept through the first
chapters, came awake just long enough to notice a few crises, then
drift comfortably off again. It is the same old book written across
the timbered face of America, except that its locale is further west
than Minnesota or Michigan. It has had the same cast of characters—the villain and the smart guy, and, thank goodness, the
decent hero.

We look back now through its pages seeing the minor crises
clearly. There were the land frauds of the early 1900's when lumber
companies bought up improperly "proved" claims. Those were
money making chapters! The accomplice was the easily purchased
little man who, having taken up land, supposedly lived upon his
acres the specified three years and then sold, for $2.50 an acre, to
the villain. Buyers were not always villains, because, in spots, the
little man really seemed to live up to the law. But in more spots
the big companies winked at the illegal proving, and gladly picked
up huge timber tracts at small prices. Oregon had her villains;
Lane County had hers. Land offices were definitely not beyond a
few sly winks. This is all a matter of record and has been written
many times and will be written many times again.

There were the chapters in which forest fires devoured the

trees. No bad men filled those pages with intent. They were exciting chapters, and sometimes terrible, as in the Tillamook burn and that near Bandon, where lives were lost. At those the heroine came out of her stupor to scream.

She rallied with such determination, if not with speed, that now, with her fingers crossed, she feels that the menace of fire has definitely decreased. To go into this chapter a bit, with its problem solution, there are now seventy lookout stations in the Willamette forest alone, and in the past summer seventy-seven men and boys received training in fire fighting at a school conducted in the Belknap Springs area. It is only a three-day school, but it trains guards in the fundamentals of locating, reaching and extinguishing forest blaze; it sends them hiking, with packs, distances of from two to fifteen miles into dense forest, and tells them that there they are on their own, each man alone. Yes, and women too, for during the war there were women lookouts, and one, Grace M. Harbick, still mans one of the most difficult of all stations, that at Castle Rick on the McKenzie; and glory to her!

College professors, high school students, and university students, some of them from far distant states, spend "fire season" doing their own cooking, hiking for water, waiting long days for supplies and mail. These things, along with the excitement of actual fire fighting when it comes, they take in stride, as patient as the pack mules that bring in their needs.

The summers now see planes trying out dropping of supplies to lookout stations, and surprisingly for so wild an area, bull's-eyes within a hundred yards have rated fifty percent.

Narrative pages ran unnoticed through this lumber account for long years, pages in which great timber interests cut wide swaths through forests as they rode up mountains and down, largely in out-of-the-way areas, bringing vast payrolls into happy, flourishing towns. Also there was the small mill man who, sighting trees ahead, hurried to whack them down, picked up his donkey engine and rushed toward the next hillside.

As a woman will, the heroine eyed the money-filled bags and decided to rouse herself. It is upon destroyers of her future lumber life that she now has her eye peeled, and some days there is a cold glint in that eye which tells them that she doesn't approve of all she sees.

What she sees is in effect this, and we quote: "Lane's logs top the world in quantity." This a newspaper headline. The gal can read, and some days she doesn't like what she reads. "Lane's saw-mills during 1947 cut 1,048,470,000 board feet of Douglas fir alone, more than was cut by any other county in the nation." We quote some more: "Lane County's 2½ million acres of Douglas fir timber support 218 sawmills, employing 7,200 men and women, with an annual payroll of $18,000,000. . . . There are 693,000 acres of Junior Forests, or second growth of under sawlog size from 10 to 90 years old in Lane County." That is an area of "Junior Forests" not showing up very large against the 2½ million ready to cut, and being cut.

Mr. Walling told the world in 1884 that Oregon timber was awaiting the cutting. "There are large tracts of timber lands that the lumberman has not yet invaded," was the way he put it. It has been invaded now, and great monetary wealth has come to the state, and particularly to Lane County through that invasion. The town that was once "Skinner's Mudhole" is the lumber center of the world. Down many of its tree-lined streets there is rejoicing over that fact; along others is the profound hope that some truly workable plan for saving timber for other years may be worked out. To get back to the book, the gal must stay awake to prevent being stripped.

Large lumber interests know that in order to continue to profit they must put back. Their problem is how best to do that. We asked a well informed lumber man about it.

"Something will be worked out," he told us. "The govern-ment's desire is for planting of greater areas, payment of higher wages, better equipment. But that same government never will say ahead what costs will be. Planting of large areas is rarely successful. Mortality of trees is almost 90 percent. Timber matures in approxi-mately an eighty-year cycle, and reforestation would better be car-ried on by leaving certain healthy trees at specified distances to re-seed the land. Maybe," he said sadly, "the pulp mills will save the day."

One can easily see that it is not as *Anybody's Magazine* promised all newcomers back in that yoo-hooing era: "Oregon timber lands reforest themselves without aid, and without expense to their owners. Within thirty years after the first cutting of timber the second growth is beginning to furnish telephone and telegraph poles and small sawlogs. The timber grows quite as fast as it is being cut off." With its advertising breath hot on the pretty neck of the heroine it continued: "It is now being cut as fast as facilities will permit, the total yearly output reading nearly one million feet per day, and putting into circulation among our people nearly $15,000 per day." Back in what the magazine said was sixty years after Mr. Skinner came here, which would be 1906, *Anybody's* was paying no mind to the stripping of the heroine, but only to the dollar that rolled into Eugene. But, naturally, that was a wasteful generation. This one, forced to foresightedness, will put money into the upkeep of the little doll with the sawdust heart.

Chapter XVII

"THIS PLACE"

"A boat was up to this place on Wednesday."
"There was no boat up to this place this week. What's the matter with our weather?"

EVEN if one memory could encompass it all, Main Street down the years would be a long, roundabout way. From the lean-to shop beneath the Skinners' roof it would lead past the Huddleston-Ankeny store by the ferry landing and end at modern shops catering to the whims and needs of hunters and fishermen, at markets that supply a trade population of 60,000 within a six-mile area. It would begin at the sawmill of Hilyard Shaw, touch at W. H. Abrams' Sash and Door Factory, Midgley's Planing Mill and the tall flour mills by the railroad track and lead to such lumber mills as the pioneer Booth Kelley one, Rosborough, Long Bell, Guistina, Fischer, Don-Bar, M. and M., and Associated and Springfield Plywood plants.

It would lead past Thomas Holland's small grocery to chain markets, past Killingsworth's Bakery to our wealth of choice modern bakeries, wholesale and retail; and it would pass the Hovey bank corner at Eighth and Willamette to do business in husky banks, one of them a pioneer as truly as the Hovey beginning institution. It would point the jewelry stores of Uncle Joe Luckey and Horace and Fred Crain, where a hundred clocks ticked all the while, to end in fine new-fangled silver stores where no clocks tick at all.

From Brumley's of 1853, Bristow and Hendricks, McClung and Johnson's and A. V. Peters it would pass such dry goods stores as F. B. Dunn's and S. H. Friendly's to those modern and pleasant shops which dress Eugene women smartly and know as well what a college girl will wear. And back along the way would be Hampton's and McMorran and Washburn's, not too long ago. At first the street would be plentifully dotted with brightly lighted saloons, but their doors would cease to swing, and would give way to a state liquor store.

There would be "Chinatown" on Willamette street and "Chinatown" on Ninth, and Sloan's and Luckey's Blacksmith Shops, with Chase's and Stewart's and Bang's Livery Stables where one could hire a cab on a rainy night. The cab would wear two lamps, to be lighted by frail sulphur matches in the wind. There would be drug stores like Osburn's, and Wilkins' (with a watering trough and pump out in front) and Linn's and Kuykendall's, selling medicines and exhibiting tall red and green bottles and giving helpful advice. And there would be many new drug stores selling many new things.

There would be Robinson and Church's Hardware and Page's Grocery, Reuf Robinson's candy shop and Poole's Ice Cream Parlors, and Preston's Harness Shop. There would be The Astor House and the Shadow House and the St. Charles; and at the other end of the street other and busier hotels and other and fancier ice creams.

Along the way would come the lamplighter to light his seventeen street lamps, and then the new Electric Light Company would flash on a gentle current to burn dimly indoors and spew and sputter in arc lights above street intersections. A blessed miracle! Neighbors would hurry out to thank Jim Robinson and John Church for the wonder of it. Then, first thing you knew, rows of electric bulbs would hang in draped lines above the lengthening street, block upon block, pretty as a picture. And then there would be electric street cars!

Soon a neon sign would show red and green, and another would flash in blue. They would spread and brighten until whole streets would come alive down the years.

For a whole day, June 26th, 1891, the new mule-drawn cars carried passengers free. Very little later Mr. Holden was tearing out several yards of track between a nearby farm and College Hill because owners of property failed to pay him what they had promised on lots sold along the way. Lots on College Hill were selling for $325.00.

Many people were objecting to the location of the cemetery so near the university campus. Others thought the site the finest to be had, and said the honored pioneer dead ought not to be buried in a canyon or on a mountain top.

Joe Myers said, "What's the matter with the people anyway? There are nineteen items on the last county list for paupers. More people are a good thing in a new country if they are the right kind. Too many who can't look after themselves are worse than none at all."

In 1892 a leper was discovered in the McKenzie valley, and hustled in the dark to a freighter at Seattle, bound for Hawaii.

1893 saw a telephone line completed, Eugene-Portland, with offices in the Osburn-DeLano Drug store.

The law said "the little launch *Merle S.* cannot carry passengers from Eugene to Fairmount without a license," the same as other boats. People said there would be six or seven boats running the river this winter and Eugene would be a great steamboat town. In 1894 O. W. R. Co. built the *City of Eugene* at Portland. It was planned to run it the *entire year*.

Eugene was making merry at the mountain springs. W. H. and James Hoffman and wives, Dr. D. A. Paine and family, W. H. Smith and wife, the Misses Nettie Stewart and Edythe Hoffman went in carriages, and the young men accompanying them, Walter Griffin, Darwin Yoran, Al Wertheimer and Dell Johnson, rode bicycles.

Another party went to the mountains: George A. Dorris and daughters Sue, Benetta and Cecile, Mr. Frank Matthews and Mrs. C. S. Williams.

Mrs. A. K. Patterson, Mrs. D. C. Thomas, Misses Kate and Angie Patterson, Messrs. Lester G. Hulin and A. L. Stewart left for a McKenzie Bridge outing.

And "the Misses Mary and Fanny Young, visiting in Prineville, drove there quite alone and successfully with team and carriage, though the carriage was overturned once or twice."

A man-about-town, drunk, the *Journal* raged, for about the thousandth time, proceeded to the "house" kept by Miss Nettie and Eva on 7th and Oak streets. Failing to gain entrance, he broke in and tore up the furniture until arrested by Gainey Mathews, the policeman, and was working out a one hundred dollar fine on the streets at two dollars a day. About this time a lady was arrested, then freed because the law said it would not look well for her to be repairing the streets.

And the Grand Presbyterian Assembly was coming to town. The reception committee was headed by J. H. McClung; finance, Mayor S. H. Friendly; entertainment, J. C. Goodale; conveyance, Eli Bangs. Eugene was truly tossing out its religious barriers. Music was in the hands of such popular soloists and musicians as L. G. Adair, Misses Alice Dorris and Mary McCornack, Prof. C. H. Jones and A. Brown.

On July 19th, 1894 the *Mazamas* organized atop Mt. Hood. Anyone at the summit on that day, with three dollars in pocket,

EUGENE AFTER A HUNDRED YEARS

was declared eligible for membership. After that, it would cost ten dollars and the scaling of a similarly high mountain. The *Mazama,* the strong ones explained, was Oregon's climbingest goat. Constable Dan Linton reported that young men were wheeling all about the town and country. Merriau's Park road often saw wheels. George Croner, H. S. and Arthur Flint, former university students, pedaling up from Portland, found seventy-five miles of mud to negotiate. One lady (not of Eugene, but London), set the pace for lady cyclists with 106 miles in eight hours and thirty-eight minutes, and was not weary at all upon arrival at her destination, said the *Journal.* She wore the latest garb for feminine cyclers; knickers of dark stockinette warm enough for no underdrawers, bodice and tunic of lighter gray. The national-minded Harrison Kincaid of the *Journal* told his town that France reported the invention of an electric phaeton, and in the East "was a new Society for the reclamation of husbands", their danger, "poker and the cocktail;" that Oregon hops were not selling at any price, that Oregon wheat had never been so cheap; that "wood will not get up to the usual $4.50 a cord this year", and that lumber formerly selling at ten dollars a thousand was down to $7.50, and that Eugene had "the best water system, the best light system, the best streets, biggest blocks, best business buildings, best schools, most churches and cleverest people of any equal-sized population in the country." But the Amazon, said the paper, ought to be drained.

L. G. Adair, who, between solos was the general passenger agent for the Southern Pacific, admitted that the train from Dunsmuir, due on Monday, reached Eugene on Thursday and that it had been en route from June 25 to July 19 from San Francisco to Dunsmuir because of strikes and burned-out bridges.

By this time the fine homes of H. E. Ankeny, Ira Campbell and the earliest home of George Miller stood on the East end of the butte. Following this East Eleventh St. and East Ninth street exhibited the fine homes of F. B. Dunn, E. C. Smith, H. B. Miller, Professor F. G. Young and others.

Lawrence T. Harris, class of '93, University of Oregon, was preparing to enter Ann Arbor, Mich., law school in that fall of '94; Frank A. Huffer, class of '86, was a successful corporation lawyer in Tacoma; E. H. Lauer had gone to Philadelphia to complete a course in pharmacy; and Casper W. Sharples, Class of '84, was proudly acclaimed "the most skillful physician and surgeon in Seattle." Judge R. S. Bean of the first University class ('78) was Chief Justice for the State of Oregon.

That first intercollegiate football game was fought one spring day on the field west of Villard Hall. The whole town watched from rail fence and carriages, then talked about it for days. The frogs sang along the Amazon in March as if it were April or May, and one man's fancy, turned to love at the age of 85, led his twenty-year-old bride before the justice of the peace, who is reputed to have declared them "wed in the uncertain but Holy bonds of matrimony." Less than a month later the papers announced "the aged but energetic groom is again a bachelor." And so spring passed into summer and winter came again.

In 1896 the steamer *Farallon* was running about every eight days out of Yaquina harbor to San Francisco. Eugeneans were making the round trip for eighteen dollars cabin passage, with a sixty-day time limit. Sheriff A. J. Johnson announced that several families from California, driven north by the drouth, were camping near Judkins Point while seeking Oregon lands for homes. The map of Glenwood made a sizeable advertisement in the *Journal*.

Will Hodes was the efficient foreman of Rescue Hose Company, and David Linn and Mable Straight were married in April at the home of Col. and Mrs. J. A. Straight. A few new names appeared in the guest list along with the old ones: Dr. and Mrs. C. E. Loomis, Dr. and Mrs. J. W. Harris, Mr. and Mrs. Huff, Mr. and Mrs. S. F. Kerns, Rev. and Mrs. Loveridge, Dr. Titus, Mrs. Watkins and daughter Flora, Miss Peggy Underwood and the young blades King Henderson, Warner Brown, George Yerington, Frank Wilkins, Walter Griffin.

A few years later, another crop of popular young bachelors was going to weddings but remaining free of strings—Orville Waller, John Hesse, Harry Powell, Harry Lumpkin, Creed Hammond, and Con Dillon, comprising the Bachelors Club, and Carl Washburne, Albert Applegate, John Finneran and a few college alumni.

Doc Davis plowed up his hops. "What's the use," he said, and to the devil with it. It cost five dollars with berth and meals to come from Portland on the O. R. and N. steamboat, $2.50 steerage. The University paid $2.50 a cord for body oak wood, and Lee M. Travis, young law student, won the local oratorical contest at Villard Hall, to represent the University in the state contest to be held in Portland. Lizzie Griffin, a freshman, was elected a delegate to that meeting.

K. K. Kubli, former student, from Jacksonville, Oregon, won

a silver pitcher worth $25 in a Boston Athletic Association meet for defeating Stephen B. Chase, world champion, in the 45-yard high hurdles. Time, six seconds. Kubli would graduate from Harvard in June.

In 1898 there was a call for volunteers and thirty-five signed up by noon that day. The week following the departure of the new company for Portland, a group of young ladies met in the park and conducted the ceremony of planting a beautiful blue spruce tree in memory of Company C. A telegram was sent to Portland to announce the honor to the new soldiers.

There was the excitement of gold at Myrtle Creek out in the southern part of the state, and offices were opened over the Lane County Bank prepared to place the stock on the market. And gold in Alaska was upsetting the peace of the valley. Mr. R. McMurphey, agent for the Southern Pacific, advertised: "Go to Alaska fields. First steamer for Nome City sails from Seattle."

"Horse racing loses none of its charm," the newspaper bragged now. "W. O. (Dad) Trine has been engaged and is now training horses for William Renshaw, Alton Hampton, Amos Wilkins, Dr. Harris and others." This same Dad Trine invented a famous horse liniment which he was to use most successfully later among the charleyhorses of his athletes at the University.

Men were taking on a new look which the *Journal* did not approve. "Is it becoming a fad to be whiskerless?" it wanted to know. "Some of the old residents have slashed off their old time face coverings and some of the younger ones, who for years carefully cultivated a pair of mustaches, have recently appeared with smooth faces. It may be comfort they are in quest of; but if facial improvement, some of them have made a sad mistake." Favorite barbers were C. Marks and Jerry Horn, that modest, likeable man-of-family.

On a bright spring day Pliny Snodgrass captured a forger in the front door of the First National Bank; and a tea store, no one knew whose or from where, opened its doors on east Ninth street to sell blue willow cups at five cents each and great, rare boxes of tea, and bowls to drink it from.

The turn of the century found Eugene no more extensive, but much more grown-up than Springfield is now. In spite of College Hill lots at bargain prices, the almost bare hill signified little more than a ghost-college burned to ashes. From that rise south, only the Lucas house (still marking the south end of Willamette Street) and the Farrington farm on the last steep hilltop, greeted the college hiker or the buckboard driver who dared the boulder filled dust and mud of the road to Spencer's butte. Blue of camas and yellow of buttercups, along with the jangle of cowbells, marked the Amazon-wet space between downtown and College Hill.

In the area west of the University campus, more camas and buttercups grew and more cows grazed. A dark red dot upon the slope above Fairmount was the modest new home of George Melvin Miller and his wife Lischen. Mrs. Miller's sister (Catherine Cogswell), a beautiful and rather remarkable person even by modern standards, lived close by in her tiny galleried bungalow. Cogswell, with her enormous gold hoop earrings and her dramatic voice was what Eugene thought of as "theater". Joaquin Miller sometimes dropped in from the blue to visit his brother's family in that Bohemian spot where genius burned and artistry toasted its toes by the open fire.

On around the slope toward the south, the Svaruverud home stood alone. From there to the campus lay acres of land sprinkled with salt box houses. There was no fashionable University Street; no Fairmount Boulevard.

Even the best of the early houses looked old-fashioned and knew it. They began gathering bay windows and trimming around them to hide their nice, straight lines; indoors things grew even worse. The "cozy corner" sneaked in where proper spindly-legged sofas had stood and the really quite good art of needle and oil brush gave way to hammer and saw and brass-tacked fringe. The cozy corner, of plush and velvet and felt, with Turkish-hung curtains, bore sofa pillows to warn the most daring of beaus. The Gibson Girl was here, and man hadn't a chance.

To keep her in ruffles, high collars, jeweled belts and parasols, father had better tend to his business, and tycoons spread offices and stores from Seventh street almost to Tenth and from Olive to Pearl. They grew, those tycoons, some more, some less, quietly. In 1904 a new mining baron, Mr. C. H. Parks, came to town, to build his handsome home where the Sigma Nu house now stands; the Chicago Potter Palmers astonished even the most enthusiastic citizens by settling down in the fine E. C. Smith home on east Ninth street, with a handsome male visitor and an English bulldog that had the town by its ears. The man, it was said, wore a corset.

Lillian Russell played in *Wildfire,* bosomy in Irish lace and a white satin automobile coat with panama hat trimmed in purple peonies. And one could buy calico for five cents a yard at Nicklin and Neal's, and Mr. Nicklin was sure that twelve yards of Suisine silk at 47½ cents a yard would make a dress. Straight-front corsets were the thing, and many morning gowns were of pongee. Ladies' hats, it was promised, would be enormous and trimmed with huge satin roses, uncurled ostrich, or morning glories, and collars must reach well up under the ears, featherboned. To hold the blouse down under the skirt, ladies were advised to use long, thick-headed black and white pins which came in cubes.

Grover Long had left his candy making at the Palace of Sweets and gone over to the O. J. Hull drugstore candy counter and soda bar. The town seems to have sprouted colonels: Col. Kelsey, Col. J. M. Williams, Col. J. M. Shelley, Col. S. P. Sladden. There was an immediate plan to put up buildings and sheds on the fairgrounds, that Huddleston land friends of a county fair had so long held an option for. At last the county had made its purchase. Still talking of "draining the Amazon."

Early in the century, Griffin Hardware and Chambers Hardware companies were doing rival business on Willamette street; later on Walter Griffin added Ray Babb, then made a partnership, and became the forerunner of Babb Hardware. Banks changed also. A Eugene Savings and Loan was headed by W. E. Brown, Dr. Paine, then W. W. Brown. Chambers and Bristow obtained the Hovey bank, which lasted briefly. L. H. Potter started a Merchants Bank—merged years later with the Savings and Loan to become a U. S. National under W. W. Calkins; then David Auld. H. L. Edmunds, as head, later guided its sale to Portland's U. S. National. G. C. Blohm is branch manager. H. B. Currie and C. D. Rorer had headed a Bank of Commerce. And always on Bristow's Corners stood the First National headed by Mr. Hendricks, P. E. Snodgrass, A. A. Rogers, Richard S. Smith and now, president under Transamerica, Lynn S. McCready.

There was a new hospital on College Hill in 1908, called "Mercy", with Dr. Wm. Kuykendall its head. Other medicos listed there were: W. O. Prosser, P. J. Bartle, B. F. Scaiefe, L. B. Bartle, George O. B. DeBar and L. E. McDougal. W. B. Dillard was school superintendent and E. U. Lee county clerk. G. D. Link was named president of the Eugene Merchant's Protective Association. Mrs. J. M. Pipes, superb violinist, was off to Europe, said the *Journal*, for continued study and her husband John M. Pipes would probably remain here at his law practice. Dr. F. M. Day was earning surgeon's laurels. "No need to make the trip here," wired the Mayo

Clinic to a prospective patient from Eugene. "Dr. Day can do whatever is required."

Mr. Alec Cockerline, for so many years a dynamo at the counters of the S. H. Friendly store, had his own place of business now, and would be glad to suggest a dress pattern becoming to its buyer's type, and Mr. Frank Wetherbee would come along as his partner to back the choice. Joe Kays had become a real undertaker following in the black-curtained hearse path of Day and Henderson. Uncle Billy and his fresh horseradish are again in town. The Fair board said "no" to the plan of the city engineer for improving the Amazon, declaring that there was no use until it could be done right. Inadequate for flood season. Costly.

Fred E. Potts was making the finest of cigars on Olive St. Fred Moullen, he of the strange foot, was kicking them silly on the football gridiron. Moon and Tingley had just received a shipment of trees, fruit and ornamental, for Fairmount.

The first electric lamp posts for cluster lights had been made at the Gross Brothers Foundry. Designed by Alvin Myers, they would be moulded at the rate of eight or ten a week. Home owners on east Eleventh street had offered to furnish the lights for that street, and, said the *Journal*, "they will make it a show place!"

A stray bullet from Hendricks Park crashed through a window of the fine Al Hampton home, and the park must be fenced.

A gentleman, filled with a bottle of toddy, told Justice Bryson that he had enough money to buy the whole town of Eugene. A pocket search revealed 98c and Justice Bryson gave the man five days for his presumption.

In 1912 at the Charity Club Ball, quote: "Devotees of the dance moved through the pompous figures of the stately grand march led by Mr. and Mrs. Dean Hayes."

Eight citizens owned Flanders 30 touring cars, $975 (Mozach). Fifteen citizens owned the Toy Tonneau at $1500. This was in 1912.

Scarcely a train arrived without several families from the midwest. (April.) And there is talk of doing something to what? Why, the Amazon. The PORTOLA Townsite Co. was incorporated by Earl Parsons, David Auld and Charles Hardy.

F. J. Berger was mayor. An ordinance was passed by the council that autos be slowed to fifteen miles an hour anywhere in town. There was serious talk about traffic, and vehicles passing from the rear were ordered to signal by bell or horn. There was talk and a plan for a $75,000 city hall.

It was just about this time that a thoroughly disgusted newspaper rose up to comment:

> In the old shack of a residence at the corner of 13th and Mill streets which should have been torn down fifteen or twenty years ago is conducted a junk shop. Ill-smelling hides and all kinds of trash are kept there much to the disgust and annoyance of the people residing in that vicinity.
>
> The old building, black with age, is in the center of the most fashionable residence district in the city and dwellings costing from $2500 to $6000 surround it on all sides. For several years past there has been a desire that the owner of the shack, a prominent resident of Eugene, should tear it down.
>
> There is talk of circulating a petition asking that the business be discontinued. It seems that civic pride would impel the owner to clear the lot of the eyesore and clean up the premises to give them a respectable appearance.

The same issue said: "Stephen Smeed, owner of the Hotel Smeed and well-known hop raiser of the McKenzie valley, today had on a pair of calfskin boots which he has worn every winter for twenty-two years. They are still in fairly good condition. They were made in the shop of L. O. Beckwith in this city, who was then in the boot and shoe business."

Turn the page, and you might as easily run across McMorran and Washburne's advertisement saying: "The backwardness of this season finds us with 100 men's and young men's suits too many, which we will sell at $11.85;" or you might read of the local suffrage groups rallying eagerly around a Miss Colby from England.

Later: Duck hunters were having fine sport at the duck preserves, but suffered from the cold. Mr. M. F. Griggs alone got twenty; with him were R. A. Booth, A. C. Dixon, Jay McCormick and Archie Morris.

Jim the shoe doctor would put on lost shoe buttons.

Lischen M. Miller, in her quaint bonnet with curls bobbing from beneath it, was Eugene's "Columyist" in those days, and her double-column spread called *Random Remarks on Timely Topics* carried all manner of serious, sprightly and educational matter. Concurrently, society pages named Arthur Frazer, son of the G. N. Frazers, as Eugene's favorite pianist, proved beyond doubt that whist and five hundred were the town's favorite pastimes, and proved too that elaborate dress and long guest lists characterized the social life of the town. Week-end columns told of beautiful gowns displayed at parties about town and small wonder, since the day's mode carried laces, draperies and fussiness to the extreme.

That was the hey-day of the town's two most stylish dressmakers—or modistes, if you will—Miss Maude Morris of the outwardly severe mein, and little Mrs. Etta Tobey who bobbed around town like a small cork on swift waters. Dark, French, and fiery, she peered through thick glasses to be sure the quality of her material was right, and she staged many a fit of temper over a bustline or skirt-drape gone wrong. Even as Miss Morris. But in between temper, partying and shopping, they turned out hundreds of gowns each year and the bride who wasn't dressed by one of the two was scarcely "in the book".

Mr. and Mrs. W. F. Osburn were hosts and owners of the Osburn Hotel, and there each year they presided at a large New Year's day at home, making use of their "Japanese Tea Room." Still in existence and now known vaguely as the Oriental room, it was actually a place of great novelty and charm at that time. Mrs. Osburn during extensive travels had collected much handsome furniture in teak and mahogany, and returning employed a University Japanese student to paint graceful and colorful wistaria vines and birds which covered the upper walls. Predominating colors were purple, gold and black, and throughout many years it served as the setting for Eugene's most elaborate affairs. To this day and forever, deserted and wornout as it is, it carries a nostalgic wistfulness for townsfolk and University alumni who knew it in the days when——.

It remained for the Osburn hotel to stage Eugene's first dinner dance, held on New Year's of 1915, and for that innovation a hundred couples made reservations for the nine-course dinner. Seven to ten were the hours, and no doubt Hendershott's orchestra furnished the music with Mike Gross sawing away happily at his bull-fiddle and "Babe" Hendershott singing *The Bubble Song* or other selections from *The Firefly*.

That same week the paper said "New Year's day is disastrous to hotels of the city. Beginning yesterday every traveling man left for Portland where the white lights burned brightly last nite. Hotel registers were blank today."

The Thursday Charity club was up to something besides charity when it gave a "violet luncheon" honoring Mrs. Lawrence T. Harris (Jennie Beattie) before her departure for Salem with the newly appointed supreme court judge. Every party was draped in yards of smilax in that era, every party had its flower "motif" and one which lacked hand-painted place cards was scarcely worth a hoot.

On the men's amusement side, an automatic baseball parlor opened up on Willamette street, and one can picture an early version of the modern pin-ball machine.

In business a brand new experiment was the shipping of dried Oregon grape root to eastern drug manufacturing companies for the making of a blood-purifying medicine and some 10,000 pounds made up the first shipment. Nothing happened, fortunately for the lovely Oregon wilds. A rather new attraction was Applegate's furniture store in what is now the Elks building. It was later to migrate south to the present Walling building and ultimately to disappear.

When the first World War broke in 1917, silver and gold seem to have gone down. Luckey's Jewelry store offered two pairs of solid gold hatpins for one dollar, a solid gold fifteen-inch chain with a solid gold pendant for one dollar, or one pair of sterling silver salt and pepper shakers for the same sum.

If you wanted to contribute to the *Morning Register's* tobacco fund for the boys overseas, two packs of Lucky Strikes would cost you twenty cents, or three packages of Bull Durham tobacco, fifteen cents.

Red Cross and other volunteer work were the rule, food conservation was a major issue, and everyone sold Liberty bonds. That is, almost everyone. For suddenly in the midst of it all the German Conversation club chose to hold a rally meeting and under the very noses of their town friends, stubbornly sang *Die Wacht Am Rhein* and lustily toasted Kaiser Wilhelm's birthday. It was a bit of a town scandal. Former friendships strained, creaked and rusted forever.

The old Country Club, where radio station KORE now is located, was the very center of social activity. Men and some of the sturdier women players puffed up *Dr. Painful,* assayed *Mossy Oaks,* worried over *Broken Back* and came whooping down *Homeward Bound* on a course that was all weeds, seldom mowed, always either drowning wet or powder dry, and furnished with sand and oil greens. But they had a wonderful time, and the little old club house was a haven of fun.

New names, new faces appeared at Eugene parties when Mr. and Mrs. Luke L. Goodrich had a big party at the club in 1917.

This was a typical guest list of the day: Dr. and Mrs. D. A. Paine, Mr. and Mrs. Elmer Paine, Mr. and Mrs. Dean Hayes, Mr. and Mrs. Harry Dunbar, Mr. and Mrs. W. B. Follett, Mr. and Mrs. Jack Pratt, Mr. and Mrs. Morris J. Duryea, Mr. and Mrs. Bruce Brundage, Mr. and Mrs. David Auld, Mr. and Mrs. H. C. Auld, Mr. and Mrs. Ralph Hamilton, Mr. and Mrs. Harry Hobbs, Mr. and Mrs. Earl Stanley Smith, Mr. and Mrs. Fred Smith, Mr. and Mrs. P. E. Snodgrass, Mr. and Mrs. C. A. Hardy, Mr. and Mrs. Richard Shore Smith, Mr. and Mrs. Herbert Roome, Mr. and Mrs. Graham Mitchell, Mr. and Mrs. John L. Harpham, Mr. and Mrs. Alexander Martin, Mr. and Mrs. Webster Kincaid, Dr. and Mrs. Seth Kerron, Mr. and Mrs. C. A. Burden, Dr. and Mrs. C. B. Willoughby, Mr. and Mrs. Frank Moore, Mr. and Mrs. Henry Tromp, Mr. and Mrs. L. R. Flint, Mr. and Mrs. Jesse Griffin, Miss Elma Hendricks, Miss Norma Hendricks, Mrs. Lillian Seaton, Messrs. Lloyd Magill, Jay Lewis, John Finneran, J. L. Hesse and Col. Creed C. Hammond.

Other new names in the town roster were the Clyde Seitz, E. R. Brysons, the B. L. Bogarts, Dr. and Mrs. G. S. Beardsley, the Schaefers families, the W. H. Abrams, the O. H. Fosters, and Mrs. Anderson, the J. W. Hobbs, the Claude Rorers, the Ralph and Seth Laraways, the A. F. Rapps, the Frank Jenkins, the Fred Stickels, the L. E. Beans, Dr. and Mrs. Waldo Adams, and Mr. and Mrs. Alton Hampton. Came, too, Mr. and Mrs. A. H. McDonald, Mr. and Mrs. W. W. Calkins, the George McMorrans, the Harry Holdens, the M. M. Tufts—all names in business and social annals, along with dozens of others, which made the sudden expansion and growth of prewar years turn Eugene into a much more varied and delightful place to live.

Before and since the Second World War broke, the same thing came about and now more new names and faces have come to take their place of importance in the town's development and growth. Somewhat of a medical center now, plans are in the making for finer facilities of the sort, and young medicos trained in up-to-the-minute postwar methods and knowledge are finding Eugene appealing. These names and development are for future chroniclers.

Almost came, too, a lace factory to produce Nottingham lace. Elaborate surveys were prepared, and a waiting world was to be ruffled in lace from Eugene's factory. But Henry Stevenson took his Zion City, Illinois, lacemakers and his beet-sugar manufacturing plans on farther, and the energetic Mormons decided to light elsewhere.

Eugene went to see Mary Pickford, Pola Negri, Charlie Chaplin and Bill Hart flicker on a wavery screen. A favorite pastime and major social outlet was the Assembly Club, organized on October 13, 1921, and still going merrily on its dancing way. Outgrowth of the Benedicts and Bachelor's clubs, it at once became the first such group of importance, and who knows but it may live to introduce its great-grandchildren to society when Eugene comes of real city age?

Eugene's altitude above the sea is four hundred and twenty-seven feet, but her head, along with her heart, has been in the clouds above that level for all of her hundred years. She has tried to build well. And for the most part she has succeeded. Her streets are not so wide as she could wish, but Boston has narrower; and if we widen them they will only be fuller of people and harder to cross.

Population has grown from one family to more than 37,000 persons. With that growth have come a number of heretofore alien problems. Since we are limited to the truth, our town has lately acquired its quota of delinquent adults. The actual fact is that in its hundred years never, until now, has Eugene worried too much about locking its many doors. The front door, yes, on occasion, but the back door almost never. And nothing happened. Piggy banks and pearls were there when the folks came home. Fur coats might air on the revolving clothesline, and air and air and air, even if a body forgot to carry them inside at dark. Morning, they'd still be airing. Back when Grandpa wore his black suit on a Sunday and Grandma defied the moths all the other days, a tramp from the railroad track hardly gave the Sunday suit a glance as he split up Grandpa's woodpile.

But things aren't just that-a-way nowadays. Grandpa doesn't wear a black suit. Grandma doesn't battle moths—much. The fur coat goes to storage. The piggy bank is unnoticed on the shelf. Knights of the road don't split wood. Pearls sometimes disappear. And doors had better be locked. The city management announces that certain lawless businesses have lately applied for housing in a town where even the law abiding can't always find a roof for its head. "This place", Judge Risdon would roar, "has come to a pretty how-de-do! It's one thing for a man to get a little drunk and have a little fun. It's another when he takes to stealing. Six months!" The oakwood hammer would bang on the little oak desk.

"Eight months!" A. C. Woodcock would shout, his face pink from the light shed by the Skinner stained glass window above his head. "Stealing we won't tolerate!" That's pure fantasy, because Mr. Woodcock was not a Judge.

"Ten months," Judge Skipworth would decide quietly, "and we'll build a jail to hold them all. Eugene's not used to crime!"

Rapid expansion in numbers and in area has brought other and more pleasant problems, costly as their solution is bound to be. There is the need for housing, not too different from that of other Pacific coast places to which people have been hurrying by the thousands since the war. But building permits in July, 1948, topped the million dollar mark, and only those of the previous March bettered them with an all-time high of $1,300,726.

The tax rate is high, and going higher, for there is need for many a project: a city hall, and for the county, a courthouse and jail; more power for homes and industries (with apologies to those early builders who prayed that their town might always be a "home and business town," and not an industrial city), and down to the simple need for a city dump and the basic necessity of added sewage facilities and a clean river. Headaches all. But curing a headache above the clouds is easier than curing one buried in the sand. The "doc" called in was a new City Manager, Mr. Seeger, and also to that end we have a county and a city planning commission. Lane County is the first in the country to try such an innovation, and we shall see what happens. On the esthetic side, we have a Century of Progress Fund; a plan begun five years ago by which gifts in any amount, large or counted in pennies, from any source, are welcomed and will be saved and budgeted toward parks and playgrounds for a finer city. The magic fund, unrelated to city business, caught on and has grown and will continue to grow.

And so we shall be zoned and parked and preened; our widened highways will lose their junk heaps and their ugly fringes even as they lose their precious trees. And we shall be grown up, come another generation.

Dawn had come with a flash of crimson above the purple hills, and as quickly faded. The distant valley lay in a cool mist of fog. The Old Settler brushed his hand across eyes that were dimmed, and there before him lay the city of reality. Its streets led far in every direction, off to the frame of hills; and down one that he remembered as Main street bright lights were burning against the waning night. Along others trees wove a dark pattern. Smoke rose from early firesides and from mills, and there was the hum of a city waking.

He allowed, the Old Settler, that a trek back to town might be worth while. It was better there now, with more folks for visiting; and on new fangled store counters there would be fancy calicos and silks and shoes, and new tools a man could use so the work wouldn't be so hard. Lights kind of cheerful, too—sort of beckoning you home again.

Don't know, he thought, as I like those doggoned engines on the track, and the sky full of flying things. Seems like the air won't be so sweet, and the trails won't be so quiet, with the leaves falling soft and the critters close by. It'll be wearying. Maybe Mary will like it though, the way we dreamed it. Well, better get moving along, Old Pioneer. There's lots to do yet.

But already he felt weary with the things he had done. So he turned his back on the lights of home, and went to sleep.

REFERENCE SOURCES

Walling, A. J. *History of Lane County.*
Sheldon, Dr. H. D. *History of the University of Oregon.*
State of Oregon. *Official Records.*
Gaston. *History of Oregon.*
Clark, R. C. *Willamette Valley.*
Wagner, Harr. *Joaquin Miller and his Other Self.*
Geer, Governor T. T. *Fifty Years in Oregon.*
Lockley, Fred. *Oregon's Yesterdays.*
Condon, Dr. Thomas. *The Two Islands.*
Corning. *Willamette Landings.*
Moores, C. B. "Oregon Pioneer Wa Wa", in his *Collected Speeches.*
Who's Who in Oregon.
Lane County, Oregon. City and County Records.
University of Oregon. University Records.
Kincaid, Harrison T. *Personal Memoirs of H. T. Kincaid.*
Wilkins, F. M. *The Story of my Father, Mitchell Wilkins.*
University of Oregon. Publications.

Newspaper files:
    Oregon State Journal—1864-1900.
    Oregon Emerald.
    Eugene Register-Guard.
    Old Oregon.
    Eugene Guard.
    Eugene Morning Register.

Periodicals:
    Anybody's Magazine.
    West Shore Magazine.

Bibliography of newspapers:
    Turnbull, George. *Newspapers in Oregon.*

Picture Credits:
    Carlisle and Co., San Francisco, Cal.
    University of Oregon, Oregon Room.
    Walling, A. J. *History of Lane County.*
        (Copies by Kendall-Ellis)

APPENDIX

Mayors of the City of Eugene

Name	Approximate term of office
J. B. Underwood	October, 1864–April, 1869
A. S. Patterson	April, 1869–April, 1873
Joel Ware	April, 1873–April, 1875
B. F. Dorris	April, 1875–1877
Geo. B. Dorris	April, 1877–April, 1879
B. F. Dorris	April, 1879–April, 1881
T. G. Hendricks	April, 1881–April, 1883
G. B. Dunn	1883–1885
(All Presidents of Council)	
F. B. Dunn (re-elected two terms)	April, 1885–1889
A. G. Hovey	April, 1889–April, 1891
J. W. McClung	April, 1891–April, 1893
S. H. Friendly	April, 1893–1895
J. D. Matlock	April, 1895–April, 1897
Wm. Kuykendall	April, 1897–April, 1899
T. W. Harris	April, 1899–April, 1901
G. R. Chrisman	April, 1901–1905
F. M. Wilkins	April, 1905–1907
J. D. Matlock	April, 1907–1910
F. J. Berger	April, 1910–1913
D. E. Yoran	April, 1913–April, 1915
W. A. Bell	April, 1915–April, 1917
C. O. Peterson	April, 1917–1923
E. B. Parks	May, 1923–December, 1925
E. U. Lee	December, 1925–January, 1927
A. L. Williamson	January, 1927–1929
H. E. Wilder	January, 1929–1931
Elisha Large	January, 1931–January, 1945
Earl L. McNutt	January, 1945–January, 1949
V. Edwin Johnson	January, 1949–January, 1953

BIOGRAPHIES

They never tell a tale in all its truth because biographers can only guess at what makes men do the things they do. The men who made the west had to believe that their task was worth the doing: they had to have faith in a government that didn't want the new land hitched to its kite-tail at all. Not every one of these men had physical strength. But all, from mountain man to statesman and professional man, had spirit. If they took time to dream at night by a log fire they pushed that dream toward realization when sun-up came; and the picture the mountain man saw in the coals of his oakwood fire were no less proud than the picture the educator saw, or the churchman. It was the vast canvas of a new country come to vivid life; of an America that would reach with strong arms across a continent.

Each must have had his own personal dream, besides. But it was the mass of individual effort and foresight and plan, of deprivation and labor, that made for us the one fine, enduring masterpiece.

These are Eugene's first: *The Old Settler,* founder of the town; *Judge Risdon,* the first house owner within the town; *Hilyard Shaw,* the first builder of house and mill, and the first to love our University campus site; *Charnel Mulligan,* one of the first to give of his land; *Dr. Patterson,* who made the first survey and plat of Eugene. Soon there were others, but these were the core. Farmer, carpenter, doctor, lawyer, miller—a slice of America strangely come together for the making of a new town!

Eugene Skinner was a young farmer in Essex County, New York. Born there in 1809, he was married in Illinois to Mary Cook, whose birthplace was also New York. The Old Settler was never physically strong but forever keen for any excitement that came along, and he thought that the rugged trip into the new West might bring him back to health.

When the Skinners had been married some seven years, their covered wagon joined others bound for California, and the first winter, that of 1845-46 they spent at Sutter's Fort, along with Elijah Bristow, Wesley Shannon, Mr. Dodson and Captain Felix Scott. In the spring they came together into the Oregon country, settling down gratefully near Dallas, in Polk County. But naturally the men could not be sure that they had found just the place above all other places in so great and empty a land, so they came up the valley to investigate. Sure enough, they found the hill where Mr. Bristow sat right down and planned to live his life, and they found the butte where the Old Settler began to dream of a town. Leaving his small new log cabin on the hill slope, he returned to Dallas and in the spring of 1847 brought his wife and baby daughter, Mary, to their new home. There the baby Leonora was born, the first white child in the land that was to be Eugene. Other children born to the Skinners were St. John, in 1851, Phoebe and Amalia.

Mr. Skinner did not see his town grow through many years. In the flood of 1862 he underwent wearing exposure in an attempt to save his cattle, and was ill during the next two years. The house in which he died still stands beside the highway northbound on Sixth street, at number 260. He did not build this house, but bought it from Mr. James McClaren. His

256

second home was a large log house on the southeast corner of Sixth and Lincoln, a house later boarded over. He is said to have built another just to the east, which he left for the McClaren house. Mr. Skinner was the first to be initiated into the Masonic lodge newly come to Eugene, and his death in 1864 was the first to occur in the ranks of the lodge. He was our first citizen, our first ferryman across the river; the "proprietor" of our town whose imagination, foresight and generosity put us forever in his debt.

Mary Skinner lived to see the town she had named take off its first baby clothes. She was a familiar figure to early Eugene, for she lived until 1881, then being Mrs. N. L. Packard.

Judge Risdon caused to be built the first house within Eugene's earliest corporate limits. Born in Fairfield County in Vermont in 1832, he entered the practice of law. The call of gold brought him to California in 1850 but did not hold him there for long, for in 1851 he came on to the Willamette valley, and finding Mary and Eugene Skinner in their cabin, decided to take land close by. He at once engaged Hilyard Shaw to build a house, and that house was the town's real beginning. It stood, Mr. Walling tells us, at a point where Pearl street was later cut through between Ninth and Tenth streets. A visitor, coming to Eugene by bus, is certain to step almost upon the homesite of the Risdons. In 1854 Judge Risdon bought from Eugene Skinner "lots 6 and 7 in block 18" for the sum of two hundred dollars, and there he built a house which backed onto the "slough" or millrace at Seventh street at about the present meeting of Seventh and the new highway that follows the line of the millrace.

Arrived here, Mr. Risdon was at once admitted to the practice of law within the county "as attorney and counsellor in courts of the Second Judicial District." He served in the Territorial legislature in 1851 and 1852, and was county judge. Judge Risdon's wife was Pauline Gertrude Wright, daughter of Ezekiel Wright. Their children were Ella Pauline and Augustus.

There is little factual data concerning *Hilyard Shaw*. Perhaps for that very reason his story interests us. He was in a very literal sense a builder, putting up the first house and erecting and operating, with William Smith, the first sawmill in Eugene. His own log cabin, one of so few, stood almost underneath the Condon Oaks that shade the north side of the University campus, facing northward from the spot where Villard Hall stands. It is said that Hilyard Shaw was "a lovable gentleman" and that he stuttered. One of his promises was when he d-d-d-d-died he would c-c-come b-b-b-back to haunt the shad-shad-shadows of those oak t-t-t-trees. Perhaps he has come back. If we look and listen and wait there we may add to our brief knowledge of Hilyard Shaw.

He made two additions to the early Eugene, giving land in 1856 east from the Mulligan addition, and in 1862 other land still eastward from this tract.

Imagination must fill the remainder of the pages of Hilyard Shaw's record. He died on September 6th, 1862, when he was sixty-two years old.

Dr. A. W. Patterson, born of Scotch parentage in 1814, had meant to practice medicine but when in 1852 he came to Oregon from his birthplace in Pennsylvania, he found pioneer families in astonishingly fine health but needing a surveyor; so he took up the surveyor's chain and began, at the request of Eugene Skinner, to mark off and plat the "Town of Eugene City." His wife was the daughter of Abram Olinger, who had come to Oregon by wagon with the Great Emigration of 1843. Dr. Patterson was in the office of the Surveyor General, located in Eugene; a member of the Territorial Legislature from Lane County, and while a Senator he was a very great power in the fight to build the State University in his town. He fought in the Indian ars in 1855 as a lieutenant, later as Surgeon, Medical Department of the Army. In later years he went back to the practice of medicine in Eugene, and was an extensive hop grower, operating a hopyard along the banks of the Willamette river.

Dr. Patterson served Eugene well as a school director, and as a county superintendent of schools for three terms. Later he was in the state senate for two terms. Although he lost his eyesight in the latter years of his life, he maintained a lively interest in all affairs of the town, and gave much financial aid to civic projects. .

Charnal Mulligan. The records call him variously Charnal Mulligan, Charnelton Mulligan and Charnal Milligin, but under any name he was one of Eugene's founders, coming to take up a donation land claim near Skinner's, and to turn a part of that land over to the town at the time of its second platting. All deeds of land within the early townsite still bear the names of Mulligan and Skinner, and it was they who, with their wives, gave land for use of the county with its hundred-foot-wide strip enclosing county buildings. It was for Mr. Mulligan that Charnelton street was named.

Cal Young: There is an interesting sidelight on Cal's parents which is worth repeating, though the story has often been told. Cal's father lived at Linnton, just outside of Portland, but raised wheat on his Willamette valley ranch, which he shipped by boat to England. The first boat stage was from Eugene to Portland and Astoria. Mrs. Young used to mount her pony, put one child in the side saddle with her and another on behind, take the saddle bags full of money and make the four or five day horseback trip from Linnton to Eugene to pay the shipper. Cal was one of thirteen children.

Born 1871 on parents' old donation land claim. Cal's parents crossed plains in '52 with Gillespie train and took up a claim two miles north of Eugene. Cal was born in their first log cabin. He was educated in Bogart district school and Bishop Scott Academy, Portland. He ran a meat market in Eugene for six years, then worked at Blue River Mines for a year and a half after which he managed the Heilig theater two years, then returned to farming on old place. There he raised hay, grain and beef until 1917 when he moved from his old house built in 1873 to a new one just east of that. He served on the school board, and was interested in all civic matters; one of main organizers of Oregon Trail pageant; very active in support of University. Baptist. Elks, Woodmen, Eugene Country club. He was named Eugene's First Citizen in 1937.

T. G. Hendricks crossed the plains from Illinois with his parents (Mr. and Mrs. James Hendricks) in 1848 at the age of ten. Was educated in district schools and at the Cascade academy. His business career started as a clerk in Bristow's store in 1858, which trade he followed until 1883 when with S. B. Eakin he founded the Hendricks-Eakin Bank, doing business on the west side of "Main Street" between Eighth and Ninth. He served as school superintendent, mayor, state senator, and as a member of the University Board of Regents for twenty-four years. Active promoter of many and varied business interests in Eugene. Member of I.O.O.F. Republican. He died in 1919.

S. B. Eakin was born in 1846, crossed the plains from Illinois with parents in 1866. Clerked in Peters and Parson's store for three years, then in Dunn's store. Elected sheriff in 1874 by one vote; re-elected two additional terms. State representative in '82; state senator in '88. Joined Mr. Hendricks in the bank in '84.

George B. Dorris was born in Nashville, Tenn., 1832. Worked at tinner's trade when young man, and later studied law in California after working-hours. Came to Eugene in 1865 and passed the state bar examinations. Practiced law for over fifty years, retiring in 1918. Served on city council, as mayor and as state legislator, representative and senator. Very active in University work and support. One of the oldest practicing attorneys in Eugene, active for many years. Republican, Mason.

Dr. T. W. Harris: Born in Indiana in 1849. Crossed plains in 1865. Educated in public schools, Albany College and Christ College at Monmouth. Graduated from Medical College of Ohio in 1872. Post-graduate degree, University of California. Came to Eugene in 1878; partnership with Dr. T. W. Shelton. Probably traveled more miles in horse and buggy than any other doctor in Oregon. Continued practice for thirty consecutive years with only one week's vacation. Served as mayor; very active in all civic and public works. Mason. Died 1925.

F. M. Wilkins: Native son, born in Clackamas county in 1848, and was brought to Lane county when two months old by his parents, Mr. and Mrs. M. Wilkins, when they took up donation land claim northeast of Eugene. Educated in district log school house and Bishop Scott Academy, later taking two year business course in Portland. Studied pharmacy and established own drug business in 1878 near what is now Smeed hotel. Later erected business block between Eighth and Ninth streets and carried on drug business there until retirement in 1899. Served on city council and later as mayor. One of the organizers of the first Eugene Water Company and city water works; responsible for first plantings of trees around early day schools and on streets while member of city school board. Chairman of Eugene Park board for more than thirty years; was responsible for city's obtaining Spencer's Butte as permanent park site for future development. Very active in organization and assistance to University as well as many other early day businesses. Oddfellows; Woodmen; Elks. Named Eugene's First Citizen in 1939. Died in 1941.

S. H. Friendly: Born in New York, and came to Lane county in 1865. Established first a grocery business, then a mercantile business, and dealt in wool, wheat and hops over a period of years. Served on the city council for two terms, and later became mayor. He was a Regent of the University for six years, and became one of the best known figures in Eugene, loved by all the students. Most active in support of all University affairs. Developed his first small mercantile firm into the pioneer S. H. Friendly Store, situated near where Hermanek's now is.

L. N. Roney: Born in Ohio in 1853, here is the man Eugene and the Willamette valley will always associate with building, and most especially with our covered bridges. He came to Oregon in '76 and in 1882 decided to settle down in Eugene. Here he immediately took up his business of building, and some monuments to the soundness and skill of his workmanship are the First National Bank building, Hoffman house and Willamette River bridge. He also built the original Eugene opera house, and their first churches for the Episcopalians, Methodists, and Christians. Numbers of the quaint, narrow old covered red bridges bore the name L. N. Roney and the date of construction. Mr. Roney served on the city council, was active in the Elks lodge, Eagles, held high degrees in Masonry, and was a Republican. He died in 1946.

Judge G. F. Skipworth: Born in Louisiana in 1873, son of Methodist minister. Came to Oregon following year, and his father was a circuit rider. Attended school at Santiam academy in Lebanon, and Methodist university in Portland. Studied law in brother's office, admitted to the bar in 1895. Was deputy district attorney four years, city attorney three years. Judge of circuit court from then to present time. University of Oregon Regent four years. Woodmen, Kiwanis, Mason.

Judge Lawrence T. Harris: Native son; born in Albany, Oregon, in 1873. Educated Eugene public schools, University of Oregon class of 1893. University of Michigan law degree 1896. Circuit judge in 1905, re-elected two terms. Elected to Supreme Court in 1914 and served until 1924. Practiced law in Eugene since then. Senior partner Harris, Bryson and Riddlesbarger. Republican. Rotary, Mason.

E. O. Potter: Native son, born 1860 in Lane county. Educated public school, University graduate with class of '87, University Law school '90. Returned to Eugene immediately to practice; elected county judge in 1896. Served on school board; state representative two terms.

Henry G. Hadley: Came to Eugene in 1851, when only one other white man was here and was the first justice of the peace in Lane county. One of the first county representatives in the legislature. Lived on donation claim until 1878. Made two trips across plains and on second trip brought back ten American mares and started stock raising near what is now Hadleyville.

L. Bilyeu: Born in Missouri in 1851, of French-Huguenot descent. Came to Oregon in 1862 with his parents. Educated at Pacific University, studied law under Judge Strahan. Admitted to bar in 1877 and started practice in Eugene in 1882. Elected to state legislature in '84, '86 and again in '96. Democrat. Very active in high-degree Masonry most of entire life.

Thomas Cady: Crossed plains to Oregon, 1847 with David Chamberlain, a Californian; settled in 1848 at West Point, north of later Coburg. Was

"secretary" at organization of Willamette Forks "Republican party" 1856.
Noted in minutes that the organization thought "slavery should be stoped
its spred."

John Diamond: Born Londonderry, Ireland, 1815. Took donation land
claim on which Coburg is located, 1847. Was thirty-two at time and a
bachelor. Found and climbed and named Diamond's peak when he and
William Macy were seeking route south through mountains.

Lester Hulin: Born Saratoga County, New York, 1823. Made exploring
expedition with Fremont and Col. Ebert 1845. Left St. Jo 1847, came by
southern route to Oregon, took up claim on Long Tom river. Only whites
here when he came were Skinners. Fought in Cayuse war. Went to California for gold, tried to come home by boat and was stranded in calm for
sixteen days and grounded on bar at mouth of Rogue river. Hulin, Charnel
Mulligan and other Lane county men walked home in twenty-four days, and
in three weeks Hulin was off again to California!

James Huddleston: Born Lafayette County, Va., in 1823. With A. P.
Ankeny started to California but decided upon Oregon. Arrived 1850, located
land claim south of Eugene Skinner, opened a tiny trading post under Skinner
porch roof, moved it in 1851 to landing place of Skinner's ferry, where
Ferry street bridge crosses. A. P. Ankeny, co-owner. Mr. Huddleston was
prominent in early settlement of Eugene. Married Samantha Davis, the little
girl who had tended the Skinner baby.

Richard B. Hayes: Came to Fern Ridge from Tennessee 1852. He
farmed there, was in the legislature four terms.

M. H. Harlow: Born in Barren County, Ky., 1811. Met Mormon troubles
when crossing through their "promised land." Fined, imprisoned on a charge
trumped up by them, he declared he had "reason to believe they broke a
portion of the 10th commandment and coveted some of my oxen." First
stopped in Yamhill County, came in 1851 to Willamette Forks, where he
took a land claim and farmed. This is just north of Eugene. Elected first
county clerk of Lane county 1852. Baptist church organized in his home in
1852 as "Willamette Forks Baptist Church of Jesus Christ." Mr. Harlow was
one of the stockholders in the McKenzie Company, to build road into Eastern
Oregon stock land. It was a toll road, collections made at McKenzie Bridge.

James Madison Hendricks (Matt): Born Cloverdale, Pleasant Hill country,
the first white child in the immediate community. Younger brother of Thomas
G. Hendricks. Early worked in Bristow-Hendricks store; later ran implement
store on corner where J. C. Penney's now stands; Broadway and Willamette.
Built his own implement business at Broadway and Oak, lived on present
site of Medical Center Building.

W. T. Osburn: Born in 1823 in Iowa, and crossed the plains in 1845
landing at Oregon City. He proceeded to California, and from there went

back across the plains in 1851. Made a third trek in '53 and the following year he started on his fourth trip across the prairies. Following his return, he came to Eugene, in 1861, and established a flour and sawmill business. Member of the first city council of Eugene.

C. C. Croner: Born on the Atlantic ocean during the journey of his parents from Germany to the United States. Parents settled in Ohio, and when twenty-one, the young Croner set out across the plains, which was in 1852. Going first to California, he came north to Albany in '53 and entered the grocery business with his brother. The following year he came to Eugene to live, established a similar business, and lived here the remainder of his life.

F. B. Dunn: Born in Illinois in 1833, and when barely twenty years old was seized with "western fever". After the trip across the plains he reached Albany entirely penniless and began clerking in a store as a means of living. He decided on Eugene as his home, again began clerking in a small store and by careful economy he saved enough money to open a little business of his own. This was the forerunner of the pioneer Dunn store. And 'way back in those days, "Grandma" Dunn used to beckon "Grandpa" home for lunch by stepping to the front porch and waving a white dish towel—plainly visible, in the sparse little town, from south Oak street to Penney's corner!

Dr. F. W. Prentice: Born 1844 in Essex, England. Came to America in 1870, to Eugene in 1887. Educated in public schools; graduated from College of Physicians and Surgeons, Cincinnati, Ohio, in 1878. Practiced and instructed in Illinois; graduated from University of Pennsylvania medical school with advanced degree, 1887. Came to Eugene in that fall, and practiced here continuously until his death. Interested in civic matters; a man of broad culture and professional skill. Republican; Moose, Mason.

E. J. McClanahan: Born Missouri 1844. No schooling, taught himself the three R's and many other things. Started out in the world when sixteen, first driving four-horse stage in middle west. Crossed plains in 1859 with mother and two brothers, hitting the Sierras in deep winter. First western job a six-horse stage from Folsom, Cal., to Carson City, Nev. Came to Eugene 1864; bought real estate, built houses, draying business, sawmilling. Later in commission business selling farmers' produce. In 1901 introduced first chicken incubator into Oregon. In California days, worked at staging for Jim Comstock of Comstock Lode fame, when the outfit numbered eight hundred head of horses and four hundred stagecoaches. Drove the main line (Sacramento to Portland), taking five days in four- or six-horse coach at ten cents a mile fare, carrying fourteen to twenty-two passengers daily. Stage drivers were men of importance in those days—McClanahan's friends were among San Francisco's big names: Flood, O'Brien, Mackie, Fair. Horace Greeley and Mark Twain were often passengers. Drove old coaches in Oregon; resembled Santa Claus more than anyone but himself; one of picturesque early day figures.

Clemens Hodes: Born Germany 1839, came to America at the age of seventeen. Reached Eugene about the early 70's. Elks, Mason. Died 1918.

A. C. Woodcock: Native son, born in Clackamas county in 1859. Parents crossed plains in 1845. Father engaged in blacksmith trade. Son was educated in public schools and graduated from the University in 1885. Admitted to bar in 1888 and practiced law in Eugene continuously for many years. Republican, Elks, Knights of Pythias, Mason.

Carey Thompson: Native son, born in Benton county in 1856. Father crossed plains in '52, mother came around the Horn in '55, and up the Columbia to Portland. Father spent nine years in gold fields, then moved up the McKenzie when Carey was fourteen. Latter educated in district schools; was a farmer and roadbuilder. Built Thompson's Resort in 1902.

Eli Bangs: Born in Michigan in 1851. Bound out to Michigan farmer at hard labor. Started out to make own way at the age of eleven years; freighted on plains, drove mule teams, broke prairie and teamed. Open livery stable in fall of '84 in small barn. Later built own large stable. Was the finest, largest and best equipped stable between Portland and San Francisco, having over one hundred and twenty fine horses and twenty hands helping. Owned stage route to the Bohemia mines; sale stables also; opened Bang's park, and a five-eighths mile race track. Livery stable finally motorized in 1911. Served on city council. Republican, Elks, Mason.

James Scott McMurry: Born in Illinois in 1848. Came to Oregon in '51 with parents (Fieldin McMurrys from Kentucky). Educated county schools and Monmouth college. Came to Eugene in 1879, and took up donation land claim near present Masonic cemetery. Republican.

A. G. Hovey: Came to Oregon in 1850 after searching for gold. Taught school, farmed, clerked, and in 1879 established Hovey and Humphrey bank which later became the Lane County bank. Served as Mayor and as state senator. Had many business interests in Eugene.

J. H. McClung: Born in Ohio in 1837, came to Oregon in 1856 across the Isthmus of Panama. Purchased one hundred and sixty acres of land west of town and farmed until 1859 when he and an uncle established the first drug store in Eugene. Later sold the store and became a surveyor. In 1883 he bought the old Grange store, known from that time on as McClung and Johnson. Built extensively; interested in local affairs. Served as school director, city council for ten years, mayor, senator from Lane county for two terms. Republican. I.O.O.F. Methodist.

George Melvin Miller: Native son, born in May 1853; parents crossed plains in 1852. Father was a Quaker, and an early day justice of the peace. The son was educated in public schools, then taught one year. Came to Eugene in '82 and entered law practice. In the 90's he tampered with a small model flying machine; spent years promoting the "New York to Florence Highway." In 1901 participated in final decision on boundary line between Canada and the United States. Brother of Joaquin Miller. Promoted the Fairmount district where his old home still stands. Was said of him that: "no man did more to present the advantages of Lane county and Eugene to prospective settlers than he." Republican.

J. S. Luckey: Born in Iowa, and came across the plains in 1850, making his way to Eugene four years later. He attended the schools here, and later established a small watch-making business which he developed into a pioneer jewelry store of Eugene. Served as county treasurer. Republican.

Elijah Bristow: Born in Virginia in 1788, first to build cabin in Lane County, at a place he called at once Pleasant Hill, 1846. Pictures show him with hair roached high above piercing eyes, and a silk stock knotted over a high white collar. Look is that of a particularly forceful, vigilant and determined man, for the gleam in his eye outshines the silk of his vest, and his lips are more set than his starched collar. These qualities are said to have made him the leader of a wagon train in 1845 which brought Wesley Shannon and Eugene F. Skinner to the west. It wintered at Fort Sutter, and "Uncle Bristow", Shannon and Skinner left it there to come by Indian pony to the Willamette Valley. At Dallas, Polk county, they remained a few months, grew restless and came up valley to find homes. At Pleasant Hill, Mr. Bristow gave land for a church and school, brought his wife, Susannah, and their family out in 1848. Died at his home, Sept. 19th, 1872. A "man of manners and integrity", history notes him.

John Cogswell: Born in Whitehall County, N. Y., in 1814. Came alone to California at age of fourteen in 1845, and a year later continued to Oregon. For years he jaunted. Back to "states" 1848 via the Isthmus, then to Oregon 1851, driving band of cattle by plains trail. Settled on Mohawk river 1853, then on McKenzie, then to Portland, and back to McKenzie. Remembered as kindly, white-haired grandfather of rather notable family.

George H. Armitage: Born in Queen's County, New York, in 1834. In 1846 first planned to come to Willamette Valley but heard that it was covered with water! Sailed for Astoria 1848, only passenger on steamer San Francisco. Took on six hundred at Valparaiso and one hundred and sixty at Panama, all bound for gold of California. Ship's captain ordered to cancel Oregon trip, put passengers off at San Francisco. Mr. Armitage tried mining, gave it up to come to Oregon City, Dec. 1, 1848, and on to vicinity of Eugene 1850. Built ferry across the McKenzie, turned it over to Jacob Spores. Had ranch on river bottom land, Coburg road.

Jesse Applegate: Born in Kentucky, came to Missouri with parents. When thirty-three years old he crossed to Oregon with brothers Lindsey and Charles. Coming by raft down Columbia River one son was drowned. Brothers settled in Polk county where Dallas now is. In 1849 Jesse and Charles went to Yoncalla. 1846 met and escorted an emigrant train through by southern or "Applegate Trail." Never lived in Eugene, but aided in forming Provisional Government for Oregon Country in 1845, prominent member first Union Republican Convention ever held in Oregon, at courthouse in Eugene, 1862. A great pioneer who left a great heritage and an honored name.

Mitchell Wilkins: Born in 1818, in Orange County, North Carolina. Went to Weston, Mo., and was there married to Permelia Ann Allen on

Christmas Day, 1844. In May, 1847, they started across the plains with the train of ninety-five wagons headed by Capt. Billy Vaughn. Landed near Silverton in October, and the following spring took up their donation land claim in the foothills north of what is now Coburg. Ultimately developed this into a ranch of 3,000 acres which became one of the best stock farms in Oregon, raising imported Devonshire and Hereford cattle, and blooded sheep. Becoming interested in politics, he was once nominated for governor on an independent ticket, but lost the election to his Democratic opponent. He served in the state legislature in 1862. Managed the State Fair and for many years was the president and moving spirit of the Oregon State Agricultural Association. Commissioner from Oregon to the Philadelphia Centennial Exposition of 1876, to that in New Orleans in 1884 and to the Chicago World's Fair in 1893. Died Jan. 31, 1904, at the age of 85. Republican.

George S. Washburne: Born in Lane County, 1855, youngest member of first University of Oregon graduating class of 1878. Read law with George B. Dorris, entered practice of law, 1879. Married Minnie Lockwood, 1881.

William Wilshire Bristow: Taught first school in county at Pleasant Hill; justice of the peace, member of state convention which framed the state constitution. Served three terms as senator. In 1865 came to Eugene as partner in Bristow mercantile business.

Jacob Gillespie: Born in Tennessee, 1809, came to Oregon, 1852, purchased the Abraham Peek donation land claim north of the Willamette River by the hill called Gillespie's Butte. On board of county commissioners, and a representative in territorial assembly.

Charles Walker Young: Born in Missouri, 1830, married Mary Gillespie, came to Oregon with wagon train captained by Jacob Gillespie. The two men took that land north of the river now the farm home of Cal Young. "Walker Young's spring", now on our Country Club course, was a picnic spot for mid-year Eugene.

"Uncle Ben", B. F. Dorris, was born in Tennessee, 1829, came by way of the Isthmus to Josephine County mines; to Eugene in 1868.

E. N. Calef: Born in Vermont, 1834, came to Oregon in 1858. Married Sarah N. Harlow, daughter of his neighbor, M. H. Harlow.

E. P. Coleman: Born in Illinois, 1842, came to Lane County in 1853. Took land north of Coburg where he farmed. Married Mary Walton, 1864.

Prior F. Blair: Born in Kentucky, came to Oregon in 1847. Married Ellen Mulligan. The Blair farm was an early landmark.

J. D. Matlock: Born in Tennessee, 1839. Came to Oregon in 1862. Teacher, school superintendent, mayor.

INDEX